The Institutional Imperative

D1808442

The Institutional Imperative

The Interface of Institutions and Networks

Anton C. Zijderveld

Amsterdam University Press

ISBN 90 5356 4306 (gebonden)
ISBN 90 5356 432 2 (paperback)

Cover design: Neno
Lay-out: Adriaan de Jonge

© Anton C. Zijderveld, Rotterdam / Amsterdam University Press, Amsterdam 2000

All rights reserved. Without limiting the rights under copyright reserved above, no part of this book may be reproduced, stored in or introduced into a retrieval system, or transmitted, in any form or by any means (electronic, mechanical, photocopying, recording, or otherwise), without the written permission of both the copyright owner and the author of this book.

To Peter and Brigitte Berger

Content

Preface

We live, it is often argued these days, not only in a post-industrial society, but also in a post-institutional society. Individuals, it is claimed, no longer act, think and feel in the context of traditional institutions. Instead they operate within flexible networks which are set up and maintained in accordance with their private interests. According to this opinion, we no longer live in a world of structures and systems, but in a fragmented world of permanent flows and transformations. Information and communication technologies enable us to communicate globally, and to transcend traditional borders such as those of the nation-state, but also those of traditional morality and cognition. In short, reality has allegedly become 'virtual' to such an extent that it actually makes little sense to think in terms of institutions any longer. However, in contrast to this position, often loosely labelled as 'post-modernism', there is currently also a renewed interest in institutions, particularly in the fields of economics and political science. It is called 'neo-institutionalism'. Yet, a sound theoretical foundation is missing here. This book sets out to rethink institutions and to construct a theory which links the network idea of post-modernism and the institution idea of neo-institutionalism. It ends with a plea for a movement dedicated to institutional conservation, comparable to the environmental movement.

The present arguments are embedded in, and refer often to an extensive literature. They are in particular the result of a very critical reading of Arnold Gehlen's seminal theory of institutions and institutionalization, with which I have been dealing intellectually for more than thirty years now. Gehlen viewed institutions as the necessary, humanly constructed, maintained and altered substitutes for a basic biological lack of so-called instincts. This interpretation of institutions as the historical and cultural transcendence of man's biological constitution will have to be discussed in some detail, as it pertains forcefully to the main arguments of this book. It will also have to be augmented and amended in the light of contemporary sociobiology and genetics.

In many respects, these thoughts touch on the theories of Emile

Durkheim, who viewed and defined institutions as traditional and collective patterns of thinking, feeling, and acting. It also, somewhat surprisingly perhaps, comes rather close to the ideas of George Herbert Mead, who founded these patterns of behavior in the meaningful interactions of people. That again is remarkably similar to Max Weber's focus on social interactions within the framework of meaning structures (*Sinngebilde*), which is another word for institutions. These thoughts and theories fall within a field of intellectual reflection referred to in Europe as *philosophical anthropology*. It is, as we shall see, closely tied to sociology and social psychology. Interestingly, its central focus on human action is similar to the main focus of American Pragmatism. Gehlen was, incidentally, one of the first to notice this resemblance in the 1930s.

Philosophical anthropology has been marginal in philosophy during the past decades. Maybe this neglect was caused by the rapid succession of various philosophical schools, or rather fashions such as behaviorism, existentialism, structuralism, Marxism, Freudianism, critical theory, deconstructionism, poststructuralism, and post-modernism. It is my contention that all these -isms did more to stimulate the political heart and its emotions than to enlighten the intellectual mind. In contrast, philosophical anthropology did not evolve into an ideological -ism, which is a sign of its political weakness but also its intellectual strength. In any case, reflections upon the condition of man, his position in the cosmos, his interaction with history and tradition, and the institutional framework within which people conduct their lives, is still pertinent and much needed. This kind of philosophical-anthropological reflection which is not, as we shall see, metaphysical but based on empirical facts, offers the social (behavioral) sciences, in particular a sound theoretical infrastructure.

This book is an attempt to rediscover the theoretical foundations needed to study the nature of institutions and their complex relations to the human individual. But it also tackles the post-modernist contention, that in this age of information and communication technologies human behavior occurs, rather, in the flexible context of networks. I shall argue, in chapter four in particular, that there is no opposition or contradiction between institutions and networks, although the two phenomena do need a coherent theory.

Preparations for this book occurred intermittently at Boston University's 'Institute for the Study of Economic Culture' (ISEC) of which Peter L. Berger is the founder and director. Financially, the project was made possible by a generous grant of the Bradley Foundation. Writing a book requires time without interruptions. Erasmus University Rotterdam offered me a time of almost monastic seclusion in the form of a sabbatical year. I am grateful to

René Foqué of the Catholic University at Louvain and the Erasmus University Rotterdam, for his critical yet sympathetic reading of an early draft of this book. Law is his field of expertise, which, of course, ensures a sound view on institutions. After all, institutions is what law is all about. The manuscript was also read and commented upon by Arjo Klamer, professor of economics at Erasmus University Rotterdam. Unlike the majority of the economists at our university, he adheres to an institutional approach and is aware of the moral ramifications of the social sciences.

I dedicate this book to Peter and Brigitte Berger who share my ongoing interest in institutions and my intellectual admiration and political rejection of Arnold Gehlen's philosophical anthropology and sociology. When I arrived in New York way back in the summer of 1963, in order to take up a teaching assistantship with Peter Berger, he met me at the boat of the Holland-America Line and took me out for lunch at an Italian restaurant. There we shared a recent discovery we both had made independently of each other: Gehlen's theory of institutions. Peter and Brigitte also introduced me to the seminal ideas of Helmuth Plessner, who is the other towering figure in twentieth century philosophical anthropology. His role theory, in particular, is of great importance to a theory of institutions, and will be discussed in chapter four. In 1963-64 I attended Peter's seminar on the sociology of knowledge, where *The Social Construction of Reality* (later co-authored by Thomas Luckmann and published in 1966) in a sense was born. It has been an influential treatise in which institutionalization occupies a central position. In my Dutch Ph.D.-dissertation, defended at the University of Leiden in March 1966, I elaborated the methodological dilemma one runs into when dealing with institutions as traditional and collective behavior patterns of individuals. In short, without the Bergers, their intellectual stimuli, and their friendship my dissertation on the methodological dilemma of institutionlization and this book on the nature and functions of institutions could not have been written.

Rotterdam, August 1999.

Rethinking Institutions

The anti-institutional mood

There is a very basic distrust vis-à-vis institutions such as the state, the family and marriage, the church, school, the business corporation, the union, the political party, etc. People these days are inclined to view institutions not only as impediments to privacy and individual liberty, but also as sources of alienation which endanger their authenticity and subjective identity. Many of us are in search of our personal Self, often with the assistance of psychologically trained counsellors or therapists. The Self, it is believed, resides in the alleged depths of the psyche or the soul. There, if anywhere, the sources of true authenticity are believed to be located. In other words, many of us are not just individualists, but subjectivists as well. This anti-institutional subjectivism is undergirded theoretically and philosophically. Various psychological and philosophical schools or currents have forged a penetrative ideology of subjectivism. Psychoanalysis (Freud), depth psychology (Jung), and existentialism (Heidegger) spring to the mind. In the past decades various so-called post-modernist philosophies have also contributed to this anti-institutional mood. In addition, non-Western philosophies and meditation techniques have fed this deeply ingrained anti-institutional subjectivism. *Ex Oriente lux* – the light comes from the East – is an old dictum which has regained meaning recently. Many Westerners have travelled to India, Nepal, Tibet and China in search of the light-Eastern countries and their philosophies are supposed to shed on their so-called Inner Being. Books on Eastern philosophies, often consumed in bits and pieces, and thus understood poorly, satisfy a large market, competing with publications on astrology and occultism. Gurus, who claim to be experts on these issues, lecture in halls and seminar rooms throughout the Western world, and sell thousands of copies of their books. Indeed, contemporary subjectivism is big business.

The recurrent theme is that the traditional institutions of the Western world – the state, the church, marriage and the family, the university, the union, the political party, the voluntary association, etc. – are being castigated as objectified, alienating structures that inhibit individual liberty, creativity, and authenticity. It is a kind of non-rational mood that has a deep, often unconscious, influence on many individuals in the affluent Western world. Naturally, seminars, meditation exercises, therapy sessions, journeys to far away regions, etc., are quite laborious and demand some sort of commitment and the deployment of mental and physical energies. The consumption of drugs is much easier. Drugs are the main access to one's 'inner being', to the pure Self stripped of all traces of objectivity as embodied in institutions, other human beings, and even one's own body. The *Nirwana* of intoxifications – allegedly, the truly authentic reality in which one floats about freely as in thin air, not bothered by values, norms, and the multiple controls of the world, uninhibited by the memories of the past and the anxieties of the future. The Self becomes the Cosmos. It is usually discovered too late that not only the body, but also the mind and the Self must eventually die in this radicalized subjectivism.

Affluence is an important variable here. In fact, this anti-institutional mood is one of the expressions – and probably the most fateful one – of rather spoiled generations of Western men and women. When people are powerless and poor, reigning institutions such as the state and the church, can be, and often will be, accused of being the sources of misery and destitution. The situation can cause resignation on the part of the poor and powerless. Drugs and alcohol may be consumed because they soothe the pains of poverty and powerlessness. This is not, of course, a search for authenticity and liberty, but a tragic longing for consolation and relief. But the lack of power and affluence may also stimulate rebellion and revolt, as in the recurrent peasant rebellions in the pre-modern world, and in political upheavals such as the communist revolutions in Russia, China and Cuba. Here too, there is usually little opportunity and readiness to focus on the soul, to indulge in exercises of self-fulfillment and personal growth under the supervision of professional counselors and therapists. Lecturing gurus will not travel through these regions of poverty and misery. Religious experiences, as found in pentacostal movements, triggered by charismatic prophets and preachers may be similar to anti-institutional subjectivism but they are in fact quite different. To begin with, they are collective experiences, group experiences, and are thus not couched in the hardcore individualism of the anti-institutional mood of Western affluence. Moreover, they lack the sophistication of the subjectivistic philosophies and therapeutic theories which are so typical of the latter.

The philosophies and theories of Western subjectivism have some sort of anti-rationalism in common. They often proclaim an ideological war on the Enlightenment and its rationalism, which, it is claimed, impoverish the human being, alienating him form his true Self. But there is a strange paradox at work here. Take the corporate world, for instance. It is remarkable that people, who in their daily activities are driven relentlessly by rational choices and procedures, often engage in courses and training seminars, organized and paid for by the company, in which they presumably discover their 'true selves', strengthen their consciousness and awareness, explore their authenticity, and, thereby, grow as a person. Indeed, it is a strange sight to observe businessmen, who in their daily activities are rationally inhibited and mentally constrained, throw themselves at the mercy of an organizational guru, who relentlessly strips them of their individual and personal dignity, treats them as a collectivity, and confronts them in front of the group with their emotions, sensitivities and irrationalities. This de-individualization, which bears an uncanny resemblance to religious or political (communist) confession sessions, is supposed to strengthen personal individuality. As a matter of fact, there is a para-business in the corporate world, called *wellness*. The paradox can be explained simply: the whole wellness business is a rational business firmly based on rational techniques of psychological manipulation, and on equally rational economic considerations of making profits.[1]

The anti-institutional mood is very complex and composed of multiple ambiguities and contradictions. Yet the basic notion prevails that man's 'true self', his inalienable authenticity and liberty, his source of creativity and originality, remains and becomes fully operable after he has turned his back on the institutions into which he has been encultured ever since his birth and early youth. In fact, there is a double strategy at work here. First, institutions such as the family and marriage, the school, the university, the state, the army, etc. are defined as *organizations* with rational functions ruled and are measured by efficiency and effectiveness. Therefore, it is easy to view them as alienating strictures which impose abstract forms of authority and control which, in their turn, again inspire people to protest and rebel. The abstract society, as I argued in another monograph[2], triggers the spirit of protest, as was demonstrated clearly by the so-called cultural revolution of 1968. However, the abstract society as a well-organized (bureaucratized) system was not at all endangered by the anti-institutional spirit of protest of 1968. On the contrary, it developed further under the aegis of a comprehensive welfare state,[3] in the direction of an informational society in which we are all bombarded by heaps of fragmented information, yet generally fail to mold them into meaningful and useful knowledge, let alone wisdom. Meanwhile, the spirit of protest of the 1960s evaporated and spread out over society as a kind of general, emotional discontent.[4]

Nowadays, many of us have become organizational men and women, operating in the market of global competition and rational choices. This is not just the case in the private business sector, but also in the public sector of governmental services. We are supposed to produce in an efficient and effective manner, to compete in quality, and to satisfy our customers; that is, we are supposed to operate in a highly rational manner. But at the same time, many of us are plagued by the perennial, typically human yearning for *meaning*. To phrase it differently, we want somehow to feel at home in the world, particularly when this world is complex, rapidly changing, hard to grasp, and difficult to understand. That is, the better organized we are, the stronger the desire for what in German existentialism has been called *Existenzerhellung*, i.e. the enlightening of our existence in this world. What is the meaning of it all, what are the basic values and norms that should give direction and coherence to our lives? For most of us, traditional institutions such as the church, the family, the school and the university seem to have lost their capacity to perform this existential task. They are on the whole well organized, but seem to have lost their institutional goal and substance. Many of us fill this institutional void with an anti-institutionalist subjectivism, i.e. with a search for meaning and authenticity in the presumed inner abodes of soul, psyche or consciousness.

As understandable, and maybe enticing as this anti-institutionalist subjectivism may be, it is a dangerous mood. In accordance with some basic tenets of philosophical anthropology (chapter two), we must realize that, unlike animals, human beings are dependent on well-functioning institutions for their survival as a species. As Gehlen in particular has convincingly argued, interaction or social behavior is essential for the survival of human beings, while institutions – as traditional patterns of behavior – ensure, by being taken for granted, the order and security needed for actions to be successful. An anti-institutional mood floating about in subjectivism must affect man's capacity to act and interact, and eventually reduce man to resignation and passive, esthetic quietism. Some of us can afford to be estheticists or mystics as long as the majority goes on with the production of food, housing, clothing, ideas, plans, etc. This can be compared with language: as boring as this may be, we do need ordinary speech in our daily lives. If we all turned into poets and next demanded that our daily speech be poetic, we would be unable to communicate and eventually perish as a species.

The anti-institutional mood would be dangerous, should it spread out massively and develop into a dominant anti-culture. I hasten to add that this is not yet the case. On the whole, anti-institutionalism and subjectivism are admittedly quite penetrating moods. However, they can only be indulged in by well-off people who are blind to the inherent dangers. The anti-institutional mood is, in a sense, a decadent phenomenon. Decadence is not an allegedly effeminate, moral weakness but a 'deliberate neglect of the essentials of self-preservation' (Robert M. Adams).[5] Institutions, as we shall see in this book, are indeed essentials of the self-preservation of the human species. However, as of yet most Western societies are not predominantly decadent, as is testified by the fact that they are still ruled in a civilized manner by democratic political systems, borne materially by relatively well-functioning economies, and guided by institutions such as the constitutional state, marriage and the family, the church, the union, etc. Institutions, however, have been transformed in the past decades and are still in a process of deep transformation. They are no longer, I shall argue in chapter four, 'thick' institutions but network-like 'thin' institutions. Yet, institutions they remain. Subjectivists of sorts do wise to recognize this fact and to mitigate their anti-institutional bent.

Yet, the anti-institutional mood fed by a pervasive subjectivism is definitely observable among intellectuals (academics, journalists and artists in particular), among many businessmen in the private sector, and among many politicians and bureaucrats in the public sector. It has even gained some sociological respectability in the post-modernist notion of a 'post-institutional network society', which will be discussed and dealt with in chapter four. In view of all this, a rethinking of institutions, their nature and functions, seems to be in order. Obviously, as traditional as institutions are and should be (after all, they are handed over from generation to generation), they cannot be the same as they were a hundred, fifty, or even fifteen years ago. Also in the twenty-first century we will not be able to survive without institutions, but they will be quite different from what they were in the nineteenth and have been for most of the twentieth century. They have acquired, as I shall argue in chapter four, network-like qualities. They are, and must be, far less rigid and authoritarian, without, however, losing their capacity to both control and stimulate human behavior. This requires a fundamental rethinking of the nature and functions of institutions, which is the main objective of this book. However, there is still another element in this anti-institutional complex which deserves our full attention: the predilection of many Western intellectuals to think, write and speak in terms of doom. In my view, this apocalyptic tendency is inherently part of the anti-institutional mood.

The apocalyptic mood

Among many intellectuals of the Western world, there is a remarkable preference for eschatological and even apocalyptic tidings. Gloomy messages were in former days the proper task of religious prophets and preachers. Today they are predominantly secular and issued by social scientists, philosophers and journalists. They are heeded and usually embraced without much critical reflection by politicians. We are being told that we are in the process of destroying the environment, that holes in the ozone layer around the globe spell irreparable doom for nature and the human species. The destruction of rain forests allegedly exacerbates this apocalyptic doom. The greying and de-greening of the populations of Western nations is also a favorite topic in this gloomy picture of a gradual decline of the West, and of the rest of the world in its wake. Although the populations of the Western world live healthier and longer lives than any other people anywhere and at any time, there is an almost apocalyptic anxiety about health. In fact, health is an essential component of the modern lifestyle, and concerns about diets, drink, passive smoking and environmentally induced allergies have sometimes reached the level of panic.[6] Lately, the international revival of Islam has been singled out as the initiator of a worldwide cultural war in which *islamism* is pointed out as the prime enemy of Western democracy and civilization.

There is seemingly no end to the series of books and pamphlets predicting or emphatically stating in a hardly concealed apocalyptic vein the end of various things: history, the state, the church, the family, democracy, and sometimes even mankind.

Eschatology – i.e. the preaching of the end of time – and apocalyptic thought – i.e. the belief in an impending cosmic doom – have succeeded the intellectually often dreary functionalism of technocrats and bureaucrats who firmly believed in rational planning and control. They contributed, we should not forget, to the reconstruction of the economy and society after two disastrous world wars. In this technocratic and bureaucratic functionalism, the state played a dominant role. After 1945 the world was partitioned into three parts: the democratic and capitalistic Anglo-American and Western-European First World; the totalitarian and communist Eastern European and Central-Asian Second World; and the ideologically neutral, sometimes democratic, sometimes totalitarian nations of Africa, South America and Asia, collectively labeled the Third World. In all three worlds the state was viewed as the dominant actor in economic and socio-cultural affairs. Rational planning and control was its main objective. More or less comprehensive, and more or less successful, the state acted in these three worlds as the main agent for the reconstruction of the economy and society, and it did so in most cases as a welfare state.

Post-war reconstruction was actually accomplished in the First World by the 1970s, and it was in this decade that the first cracks became visible in the welfare state. It became obvious in Western Europe in particular, that the comprehensive welfare state could not be maintained economically as public spending far exceeded public earning.[7] It also became obvious to many that the welfare state had an inverse effect on the vitality of the market, civil society and even moral culture, as it spread a stifling blanket of bureaucratic rules and regulations over them. In addition, the 1980s witnessed the spectacular collapse of the Soviet empire and its centralized control of the market and civil society. Remarkably, both events – the demise of the comprehensive welfare state in the First World and the collapse of the communist state in the Second World – did not stimulate an utopian spirit of global optimism, but rather paved the road for eschatological and apocalyptic ideas. The favorite theme of critical theorists and observers was and still is the end of this or that institution. Even if their observations often lack empirical evidence, their tidings of doom are gullibly absorbed by journalists, politicians and various citizens.

The end of the second millennium has been proposed as a cause. Indeed, eschatology and apocalyptic visions emerged abundantly at the end of the first millennium. But that was a time in which metaphysical and religious thoughts and emotions were deeply entrenched in the minds and moods of people. Secularism was almost absent in those days. Today the opposite is true. Technology, the sciences and formal bureaucracy have spun a web of functional rationality around us. Unlike our predecessors at the end of the first millennium, we live in a disenchanted world. Certainly, there are scores of re-enchantments, such as the virtual realities of computers, the periodic resurgences of religious movements, and the re-emergence of nationalism and ethnic hatred after the collapse of Soviet imperialism. However, they present notable exceptions vis-à-vis the predominant rationality of the sciences, technology and bureaucracy. In short, the end of the second millennium might have contributed to the present spread of eschatological and apocalyptic forms of thought and feeling, but in view of modernity's predominant rationality, one should not attribute too much importance to this fact. Behind all the talking and writing about the end of this and the end of that there is a very basic anti-institutionalism at work. It is my conviction that the eschatological and apocalyptic mood just described briefly is in essence the upshot of the anti-institutional mood. In other words, contemporary tidings of doom are essentially witnesses to the fact that there is little or no faith in traditional institutions. They are symptoms of a deep *institutional crisis* in the Western world. Post-modernist sociologists and philosophers proclaim the so-called flexible networks as the appropriate framework for a post-modern world. These networks are then introduced as the post-modern answer to traditional institutions, which, according to the post-modernist, are not in crisis, but simply have run their course. By now institutions have allegedly become obsolete.

This book is in basic disagreement with the main drift of this argument, although some basic tenets of post-modernism are acknowledged and integrated into the *institutional theory* that will be developed in the following pages. The book sets out to rethink institutions and institutionalization, and to integrate the 'network society' into the indispensable context of institutions. The nature and functions of contemporary institutions cannot be understood properly outside the context of networks. Admittedly, institutions can no longer be the 'thick' – i.e. heavily traditional, often tabooed and greedy – structures, they were in former days. Of course, there is neither conceptually nor politically or morally any need to defend traditionalism and formalistic institutionalism. I shall argue in chapter four that the days of 'thick' institutions are definitely over. Institutions have to be rethought today within a frame of reference that fully takes into account the fundamental transformations of our world, not least of which are those caused by information and communication technologies of the past decades. Postmodernists are wrong when they disregard institutions and proclaim the advent of a post-institutional society. But they are right when they put primary emphasis on the fact that we live in a world that is fragmented and highly flexible. The 'thin' institutions of today exist and function in a world that is decentered and without fixed boundaries and limits. This important point which is the core of chapter four, has to be considered here briefly first because it is crucial to a rethinking of institutions.

The decentered and borderless world

Classical social theorists have often emphasized that the socio-cultural evolution of the human species consists of a highly complex set of transformations, which in essence is a progressive structural differentiation. The various functions and roles that have to be performed in order for the human species to survive, are gradually couched in specialized social structures. Until recently this differentiation which increased in intensity in the Industrial Revolution, was kept together, and in this sense integrated, by rather fixed, solidly institutionalized centers: God and the church, the absolute monarch and the court, the socio-cultural elite and high society, the democratic state and parliament, the nation and its nation-state, scientific research and the university. Even in the case of a plurality of centers they were kept in mutual balance, as in the democratic nation-state and the university. In most European countries these two powerful centers were linked by material as well as immaterial bonds. The state subsidized the universities, the universities trained and delivered the required civil servants, politicians, managers and businessmen. Often the church, or at least religion, played an important role in all this as well.

These interrelated centers usually demarcated their borders and limits: political borders of the nation-states; sociological borders of class and status, the elite and the masses; physical borders of the sexes; psychological borders of gender differences; moral borders of traditional, usually religiously based values and norms. It was hard, often impossible, to transgress these borders and limits.

Due to increased prosperity, a globalized economy, improved and relatively inexpensive means of transportation, electronically revolutionized channels of communication and mass information, and the improvement and spread of formal education, we have recently entered a world which is not just polycentric but in fact ever more decentered and virtually borderless. Many of us live without authoritative centers that can provide our acting, thinking and feeling with a kind of pre-structured and taken-for-granted order and stability. If there are still authorities these days, these are personalized, flexible and provisional. Their powers are conditional, dependent on negotiations rather than on top-down directives. Moreover, borders or limits too have become individualized, particularized, and rather porous. In terms of morality, the dictum 'Anything Goes', the post-modernist variant of Nietzsche's *Jenseits von Gut und Böse* – beyond good and evil – is characteristic of this life without fixed borders.

Rethinking institutions cannot be successful these days without thoroughly taking into account this decentering and delimiting of the world we live in, which is a difficult task. There are two easy, but in my view fruitless, ways of dealing with this task. We could, against all odds, defend the traditional institutions, retreating, as it were, into a reactionary defense of the 'thick' institutions of the past. Arnold Gehlen opted for this solution, and, as we shall see in chapter two, had to proclaim the repressive state as the primary institution that maintains order and stability in the midst of the de-institutionalizing forces of modernity. This is not, of course, an attractive or very realistic option. The other easy way is the post-modern option, where flexible *networks* are pronounced to be the successors of traditional institutions. But it is questionable whether this is a satisfactory route to take. Even the biological constitution of the human species is such that it needs long-term, generation-transcending patterns of behavior in order to survive. If such networks do not fit into existing institutions, or if they do not themselves develop into semi-objective, durable institutions, they will fail to bring their proponents what the latter hope to receive from them: relationships with fellow human beings that are cognitively and emotionally satisfying, and effective in practice.

Basic misconceptions

Discussions about institutions are usually plagued with some basic misconceptions. This book will discuss and hopefully clarify them but it might be helpful to list them briefly from the ouset. The first misconception is that institutions are collectivities. They are not. Institutions are patterns of behavior, traditional ways of acting, thinking and feeling. Unlike habits which are individual patterns of behavior, institutions are collectively shared and enacted modes of acting, thinking and feeling which are passed on through education and emulation. But, once moe, they are not collectivities in the sense of groups and members. One can join collectivities, whereas institutions are internalized and enacted. One cannot join an institution the way one joins a club.

Secondly, the concept of institution is not equivalent to that of organization. It is useful to distinguish them analytically. As I shall argue in the first chapter, the concept of organization refers to functional rationality, to differentiations of power, to formal structures. Bureaucracy comes immediately to mind when the concept of organization is used. The concept of institution refers rather to substantial rationality, to authority, and to ideological values and norms. The notion of culture, as in 'corporate culture', comes to mind when one applies the concept of institution. This distinction of organizations and institutions which will be explained in more detail in chapter one, is not an ontological but an analytical distinction. It may at first seem rather abstract and formalistic, but, as I hope to demonstrate, it is crucial for an appropriate rethinking of institutions.

Thirdly, institutions as traditional patterns of behavior are often held to be structures that curb creativity and stifle individual freedom. In a sense they do, but apart from being unavoidable (not just socially and culturally, but even, as we shall see, biologically) institutions can and usually do create a space in which creative ideas, feelings and actions emerge, while they stipulate the appropriate contexts – the limits as well as the potentialities – of liberty. As Arnold Gehlen has pointed out, institutions set creative energies free precisely because they liberate us from the time and energy consumed in tasks to plan and design our actions, thoughts and feelings each time we set out to act in and upon the world. Institutions provide us, Gehlen has claimed, with a *bienfaisante certitude,* a benign certainty, because they are traditional and, if internalized solidly enough, taken for granted. Naturally, and this point will also return in our ensuing arguments, institutions can be, and in history very often have been, too strong and overbearing, as in the case of most religiously and magically undergirded institutions. They then suffer from *traditionalism* which puts a magical taboo on them, preventing them from changing and developing according to the needs of the times. Traditionalist institutions, needless to say, stifle creativity, promote a general moral complacency and cultural dreariness, and they most certainly curb liberty. Yet, the anti-institutional mood of modernity, or, if you want, of post-modernity, is inclined to view all institutions – even the weak ones of today which are no longer firmly couched in tradition – as inhibitors of creativity and liberty. This, I shall argue, is a fatal misconception. Unlike animals, human beings simply need institutions and their inherent traditions for their survival as a species. That is the anthropological bottom line.

1. Cf. Hansfried Kellner, Frank W. Heuberger (eds.), *Hidden Technocrats. The New Class and New Capitalism*, (New Brunswick, NJ: Transaction Publishers, 1992). In particular: Hansfried Kellner, Peter L. Berger, 'Life-Style Engineering: Some Theoretical Reflections', *o.c.*, pp. 1-22. Cf. also Frank W. Heuberger, Laura L. Nash (eds.), *The Fatal Embrace? Assessing Holistic Trends in Human Resources Programs*, (New Brunswick, NJ: Transaction Publishers, 1994).
2. *The Abstract Society*, (Garden City, NY: Doubleday, 1970).
3. See my *The Waning of the Welfare State. The End of Comprehensive State Succor*, (New Brunswick, NJ: Transaction Publishers, 1999).
4. See in particular César Graña, *Modernity and its Discontents*, 1964, (New York: Harper Torchbooks, 1967).
5. Robert M. Adams, *Decadent Societies*, (San Francisco: North Point Press, 1983), p. 36.
6. Cf. Peter L. Berger (ed.), *Health, Lifestyle & Environment. Countering the Panic*, (New York: Manhattan Institute, 1991).
7. Cf. my *The Waning of the Welfare State*.

CHAPTER ONE

Concepts and Premises

Neo-Kantian predilections

This book aims to present a theory of institutions as the indispensable context for our acts, thoughts and feelings. This context, it is claimed, is not static but dynamic. The institutions of our society came to us from the past, and are thus embodiments of tradition. But they change their nature and functions in the ongoing process of history, and they do so rapidly and radically in the process of modernization. In modernity institutions are closely related to networks. In fact, it will be argued in chapter four that today's institutions need to be 'thin' and networks need to be 'thick' in order to function as effective and sustainable structures. Such a theoretical endeavor demands a methodological explanation, albeit a brief and incomplete one since substantial theory, not formal methodology is the aim of this book. Readers who are not interested in such a rather academic exercise, can easily skip this chapter and move on to chapter two. It may be, however, that while reading, or after having read, the succeeding chapters, readers may become curious about the author's methodological premises. They may also wonder why such a fuss is being made about conceptual distinctions such as those between organization and institution, institute and institution, or functional and substantial rationality.

I must start with the confession that I am an amateur methodologically. Methodology is a branch of philosophy which tries to understand the nature and functions of scientific concepts and theories, their relations with empirical reality, with experience and common sense. When are theories true, when are they false? What actually is a theory? As a true amateur I have read the various methodological debates eclectically without making a definitive choice for one or the other position. Popper, Kuhn, and Lakatos were for many years the towering figures in these debates. Popper, in particular his stance on falsification as the benchmark of science, was my philosophical favorite. But his critical rationalism and empiricism seemed to me too restraining, and he had, I found, a rather poor understanding of the social sciences. Phenomenology, in particular the lucid essays of Alfred Schutz, has exerted a strong influence on my sociological mind, as it reveals to the sociologist that so-called empirical reality is not the reality laid bare by preferably quantitative methods and techniques of sociological research. Sociocultural reality is rather a *Lebenswelt,* i.e. a pre-reflective, usually taken-for-granted lifeworld. But phenomenology did not become my main methodological frame of reference, particularly as it deviated into so-called Ethnomethodology which I have always seen as an unfortunate derailment. Instead, Symbolic Interactionism, particularly the seminal thoughts of its philosophical founder George Herbert Mead, exerted a lasting influence on my way of looking at reality sociologically. Lately Richard Rorty's unconventional ideas have attracted my methodologically wandering mind. The surprising methodological role he adjudicates to irony, and his lucid style of thinking and writing which stands in distinct contrast to most philosophers, have won me over. But his post-modern relativism (a label he will probably reject) with its emphasis on aesthetics rather than formal logic, exhibits a basic weakness, not just methodologically but morally as well.

My amateurish eclecticism did not preclude a methodological preference to which I have adhered with a stubbornness that perhaps can also be attributed to my philosophical dilettantism. In philosophy, I admit, it was not Hegel and the neo-Hegelians but Kant and the neo-Kantians whom I felt most comfortable with intellectually. I probably have the prejudicial view that there is a watershed between Hegelians and Kantians, the former being fond of obscure thoughts and complex sentences, the latter being keen on lucidity and linguistic clarity. Hegelians are fascinated by Being, engage in ontology, and often beyond that into metaphysics. Kantians are fascinated by Knowledge, engage in epistemology, and are usually inhibited when it comes to matters of metaphysics. Hegelians, I find, are generally humorless and stern, Kantians often have a good sense of humor and delight in irony. My main critique of Jürgen Habermas, for instance, is that he is so relentlessly serious. It is impossible to detect a single *Witz* in his voluminous body of writing. In that respect, but in other respects as well, he represents to me Hegelianism rather than Kantianism. As to the often celebrated Theodor Adorno, even my dog Eliot has a greater sense of humor than he had.

I have always been fascinated by Kant and cherished a preference for the neo-Kantians of the so-called Southern German School. The epistemology of neo-Kantianism as it was designed by Wilhelm Windelband, Heinrich Rickert and in their wake applied to sociology by Max Weber somehow agreed with my mind. It is a sort of elective affinity that is hard to resist. Starting from Kant's thesis that *das Ding-an-sich*, i.e. objective reality outside subjective consciousness does of course exist but cannot be known, they strongly opposed the correspondence theory in epistemology which claims that concepts and theories are true when they depict reality. In particular Weber's *Wissenschaftslehre* has been influential, as it designed a methodology in which concepts and theories do not constitute more or less precise pictures or mirror images of empirical reality. To Weber socio-scientific concepts are rather artificial (analytical) constructions. They constitute a virtual and contingent reality consisting of possibilities and probabilities. This runs counter to the empiricism of Anglo-Saxon philosophy and sociology. In fact, neo-Kantian epistemology in general and Weber's *ideal types* in particular are usually misunderstood by Anglo-Saxon empiricists. *Ideal types* (in German *reine Typen*) are not normatively ideal (as in 'an ideal son-in-law'), but analytical and rather artificial. They are rationally constructed concepts which indicate what empirical reality would look like if it were a strictly (functional) rational reality – which, fortunately, it is not. There is in this epistemology a rarely observed irony at work. (Humor as well: in his *Wissenschaftslehre* Max Weber can suddenly interrupt his often labyrinthine German sentences with some light-footed verses by the popular poet Wilhelm Busch which has a hilarious effect.)

Until recently, this kind of neo-Kantian epistemology was not very popular in Europe. After World War II many European philosophers and social scientists were strongly influenced by French or German existentialism which does not excel in kantian lucidity, let alone irony. A close reading of a few pages of *Être et le Néant* or *Sein und Zeit* will prove my point. Or they followed uncritically the philosophical and socio-scientific pundits of Anglo-Saxon empiricism. If the latter was rejected (it was often pejoratively labelled neo-positivism), most European sociologists were, if they let themselves be guided by philosophers and theorists at all, more influenced by Hegel and Marx (cf. the so-called Critical Theory of the *Frankfurter Schule*) than by Kant and Weber. The latter's emphasis on the necessity to refrain from normative valuejudgments while doing sociological research and teaching sociology in the lecture hall or classroom, in particular was rejected. Because the basic premises of neo-Kantianism were usually barely understood, Weber's stance on value-judgments was misinterpreted as a plea for a 'value-free sociology'. This despite the fact that Weber time and again emphasized the (sociological) fact that human beings, and thus social scientists too, are *wertverbunden*, i.e. value-related.[1]

This neglect of Kant and kantianism has been reversed recently. In so-called deconstructionism there is a renewed interest in the philosophy of Kant.[2] It stands to reason that the neo-Kantian (Weberian) notion of ideal types as virtual realities will be rediscovered as components of an epistemology that fits the *episteme* of the new information and communication technology remarkably well. In the world of ICT – as in Max Weber's world of 'ideal types' and 'elective affinities' – possibilities, probabilities, and contingencies are more relevant and of greater interest than empirical realities and unilinear causalities. Both worlds also have in common that in them humor and irony occupy strategic positions. Weber of course could not yet speak of 'virtual reality', but his idea that 'ideal types' constituted *utopias* (i.e. realities that exist nowhere) comes close to it.

Ideal types and contingencies

The most fundamental function of theories is to get reality into focus. They are not just food for thought and reflection, but above all instruments that can help us to look at, to behold empirical reality – i.e. the lifeworld which we experience (usually pe-reflectively) by means of the senses. Theories are at times microscopic, enabling the beholder to look at reality in a minute manner; at times macroscopic, surveying things in a generalized manner; at times telescopic, comparing the here-and-now with the there-and-then. If theories are likened metaphorically to optical instruments, concepts can be viewed as the various lenses which help us to bring the world into focus.

The optical nature of theories and concepts ought to be heeded. There is within and outside the world of sciences and humanities the persistent opinion that a theory and its concepts in order to be 'true' ought to reflect reality in a naturalistic way. They are viewed as pictures of reality and the more realistic or naturalistic these pictures are, the more 'true' they are believed to be. This correspondence between theory and reality is, of course, a rather problematic position to take. Reality, whether 'nature' or 'culture', is essentially extremely complex, and in perpetual change. If we were able to give an exact picture or mirror image of this complexity and perpetual change, if we could construct, say with the help of a computer, a theoretical model that would contain all the variables, factors and change agents that make up reality, we would not come any closer to what we want to achieve in the first place which is, after all, *understanding, grasping reality.* We would merely duplicate reality in a model, and then undoubtedly experience the urge to understand this duplicated reality.

Thus, theories, models and concepts are not (and cannot be) pictures of reality. After all, the reduction of complexity is the first and most basic rule of science. Theories, models and concepts are actually rational, methodically and logically guided distortions of reality. Let us for the sake of argument focus on concepts which, of course, are the stuff theories are made of. In everyday speech we employ scores of words which refer to empirical realities but do not depict or portray them. Latemedieval nominalists have already pointed out that a concept such as 'horse' is a construction for the sake of communication. There are in reality many different specimens of horses which we have given names, which in their turn refer to innumerable different individual horses who in time come and go. The concept of 'horse' is just a name which in a crude way covers an ever changing and moving complexity. In short, nominalism emphasizes the analytical, constructed, anti-naturalistic character of words and concepts. If this is the state of affairs in everyday language, it is even more so in scientific language.

Nominalist epistemology was revived in Germany's neo-Kantian philosophy which never tired of rejecting the conceptual realism or naturalism of the correspondence theory. It found its way in sociology through the seminal methodological writings of Max Weber. In particular his 'ideal types' (*reine Typen, Idealtypen*), mentioned above, gave testimony to his nominalism, as did, by the way, his habit of defining components of socio-cultural reality in terms of *chances*. His often quoted, elegant definition of power is a good example of this nominalistic and probabilistic brand of methodology. Power is, Weber argued, the chance one has to realize one's own will, if necessary against the will of others. Moreover, he never grew tired of emphasizing the fact that institutions such as the state, the family, the church, etc. did not exist empirically. They happened to be abbreviated, short-hand 'names' for scores of incredibly complex actions and interactions of individual human beings. The institution of marriage does not exist ontologically. It is but a shorthand name for many different, changing actions, interactions, thoughts and feelings of married individuals. If one wants to study this institution empirically, one has to investigate the actions, interactions, thoughts and feelings of married people. In other words, he would have taken strong exception to Emile Durkheim's methodological rule to treat institutions – called by him 'social facts' – *comme des choses,* or 'like things'.

Sociological concepts, Weber argued in his *Wissenschaftslehre*, do not reflect or mirror reality. On the contrary, sociological concepts are in a sense conscious distortions of reality. They are not realistic or naturalistic but analytic and *ideal* in the sense of being artificial, constructed, analytical. Weber also often called *Idealtypen reine Typen*, i.e. 'pure' types, indicating that they are rationally constructed and in this sense artificial. They do refer to an experienced reality, however, since they are empirical, not metaphysical. Yet, the reality they refer to is rationally distorted since the ideal types consciously overemphasize certain aspects or dimensions of experiential reality (particularly their functional rationality) and consciously underemphasize others (in particular non-rationality and irrationality). He even referred to the ideal types metaphorically as 'utopias' which was his way of saying that they constituted a virtual reality. Weber, incidentally, emphasized the virtual, constructed nature of his ideal types by putting them between inverted commas. By comparing and contrasting the virtual reality of these constructed concepts with empirical, experiential, and in that sense 'real' reality, it was hoped the latter's infinite and therefore irrational complexity could be understood in a rational manner.

These analytic concepts are imposed on reality in terms of value-relatedness (*Wertverbundenheit*). It is from a set of particular values that some dimensions of reality under scrutiny are overemphasized or underemphasized, and this is done in order to eventually arrive at a rational understanding (*Verstehen*) of reality. Thus, understanding in Weber's epistemology is not a method. The method is the construction of ideal types from a value-related position, as well as the subsequent comparison of empirical reality with these artificial types. *Verstehen* is hopefully the result of the comparison of these conceptual constructs with experiential reality. The aim of the juxtaposition of reality and the constructed types is not 'truth' but 'understanding', and it is never certain, whether this heuristic goal will in fact be reached. Therefore, *plausibility*, or if you want heuristic usefulness – not verification or falsification – is all the neo-Kantian sociologist can hope for. Most of Weber's ideal types, incidentally, have proven their heuristic mettle since many of them are still employed, such as the three ideal types of legitimacy (charisma, tradition, and legal-procedural rationality), the two types of ethic (the ethic of ultimate ends and of responsibility), and the type of modern bureaucracy.

The basic concepts of this essay are also ideal types: institutions and organizations, institutional culture and organizational society, institutions and networks, organizational power and institutional authority, and functional and substantial rationality. For the sake of contrast, ideal types are often placed on the two extreme ends of a continuum: *Gemeinschaft* and *Gesellschaft* (Toennies), mechanical and organic solidarity (Durkheim), functional and substantial rationality (Mannheim) aristocracy and democracy (Tocqueville), status and contract (Maine). The idea is that reality in all its complexity 'moves' between these extremes, sometimes closer to the one, sometimes closer to the other. This, admittedly, is a rather crude method but at the same time it seems to have proven its heuristic mettle, as most of them are still being used. Somehow the constructed types at both ends of the artificial continuum managed to produce heuristic results. They apparently help to receive a better rational understanding of the predominantly irrational lifeworld. In this book, the constructed extremes of 'organization' and 'institution' play a particularly crucial role.

What then are the basic concepts of the institutional theory that I shall develop in the next chapters? In this first chapter I limit myself to institutionalization and the institutional perspective, and to the, at first sight, somewhat curious distinction between institution and organization on the one hand, and between institution and institute on the other. The concepts modernization, modernity and network also play an important role but it is better to discuss them in a broader theoretical frame of reference, respectively in chapter three and chapter four.

Institutionalization

We must begin with a brief discussion of institutionalization as the process which as it were 'produces' the institutions. This concept is rather vague. Therefore we must try to formulate a more or less succinct definition. Moreover, the focus on institutionalization and institutions contains, it should be stressed, a specific perspective, a particular approach to socio-cultural reality. This perspective, *institutionalism* – or, as it has recently been called, *neo-institutionalism* – can be reconstructed after the basic elements of the process of institutionalization have been discussed.

To begin with, the intriguing thing about institutions is that they are traditional and collective patterns of behavior (of acting, thinking and feeling) which 'existed' before we were born, and in all probability will continue to 'exist' after we have died. We, living in this day and age, did not invent the state, family, marriage, church, school, voluntary association, and all other institutions, but grew up in them, and we help to pass them on to next generations. Yet, we do somehow contribute to the perpetual change of institutions. Some of us leave a heavy imprint on the institutions, while the traces of most people in the world of institutions remains minute. But during the passage of successive generations, and under the impact of changing socio-economic, political and physical circumstances, institutions change. Their transformation is sometimes slow and gradual, sometimes rapid and revolutionary.

There is another intriguing aspect of institutions. At some point in our cultural evolution individuals must have started them but it is impossible to trace back these historical origins. When and why did *homo sapiens* decide to live in stable relationships resembling our institution marriage, when and how did the institution school, or the institution state originate? These are relatively slow evolutionary processes but, as in the case of an epidemic disease, there must have been a beginning which was enacted by one or more individuals. At the end of this chapter and in the next chapter I shall discuss the question of to what extent instututions are biologically (genetically) grounded. Yet, since they are only observable and experienced as historical and cultural phenomena one wonders when, where and by whom institutions were started. As in the case of an epidemic such as AIDS, the question about the precise historical origin of an institution such as marriage is unanswerable and therefore rather pointless. One can, however, try to construct an historically plausible, hypothetical theory of the origins of institutions.[3]

However, for the sake of the present argument one can also engage in a little thought experiment. It is admittedly not a very sophisticated method but it may be helpful for heuristic purposes. The emergence of an institution thus is comparable to the formation of an informal, unofficial path in a lawn. On college campuses one often sees around squares of grass 'official' paths to walk on, usually covered by concrete. But since there is the drive in all of us to cut corners, one often also sees 'unofficial', uncovered paths in the grass cutting the edges of the square. There must have been a 'number one' who was the first to tread outside the 'official' paths. He or she probably did so on the same day the 'official' sidewalk had been finished. Many individuals then followed in these first footsteps, and very soon an 'unofficial' path became visible, 'inviting' people in ever greater numbers to follow its course, cutting the edges of the grass square. After all imitation is often the response to an outside, 'objective' stimulus. Maintenance officials of the college may have then decided to cover the 'unofficial' path with concrete also, rendering it 'official'. They may have also decided to post a sign next to it, saying: 'It is forbidden to walk on the grass'. Indeed, in most cases an institution has reached a definitive stage when it is legally approved. Law is the final legitimation of an institution. The institution of marriage must have started and developed this way. Some individuals in the mythological past – say Adam and Eve – started it, others followed in their footsteps. Gradually the institution became ever more 'objective' and 'natural' , inviting and stimulating succeding generations to imitate this marital behavior. In the course of its evolution legal signs were set up, in addition to the moral sign not to tread outside this traditionally established, and officially accepted 'path'. Naturally, outside the marital institution 'unofficial' paths have emerged, the latest one being the claim of homosexuals to have the right to a legally grounded marriage. Apparently the urge to be married, to live one's life in the context of this institution, is irresistible.

These considerations suggest the following definition of institutionalization:

Institutionalization is the historical process in which initially individual and subjective behavior (such as the unity of acting, thinking and feeling) is imitated, and then repeated in time to such an extent that it devel-

*ops into a collective and objective pattern of behavior, which in its turn
exerts a stimulating and controlling influence on subsequent individual
and subjective actions, thoughts and feelings. This creates taken-for-
granted routines that may clear the way for the design of new actions,
thoughts and feelings, if, that is, these routines do not fossilize into stifling expressions of traditionalism.*

A few points in the definition deserve our special attention. To begin with,
institutionalization is a historical process in which individual and subjec-
tively experienced behavior is objectified into behavior patterns which are
detached as it were from the individuals concerned. In fact, we are born in a
world of institutions, socialized and encultured into them, and we die eventually out of them, while they are passed on to subsequent generations. Even
our individuality is not a private attainment but has been taught and learned
in and through institutions like the family, the school and the club. Secondly, institutions as the upshot of institutionalization are not deliberately
planned but grow and develop over a period of time. In other words, we are
not the inventors of our institutions. They were there when we were born,
and they develop slowly and piecemeal. As J. O. Hertzler aptly formulated
it: 'Historically institutions have grown piecemeal by minor adjustments
and innumerable small accretions.'[4] They remind the sociological observer
of glacier formations. Thirdly, when objectively in existence and functioning well, institutions tend to exert a strong control over individuals forcing
them to perform social roles. Imitation is essential to human behavior. Imi-
tative behavior is to a large extent institutional role behavior. Fourthly, institutional control may restrict our freedom but it ensures a social stability
and integration which sets energies free that can be deployed creatively and
inventively. It is one of the institutional ambiguities that will be discussed at
the end of the next chapter.

   Neo-liberal individualism usually overlooks the fact that over a period of
time institutions have the tendency to become autonomous vis-à-vis the individuals who act, think and feel within their context. Arnold Gehlen, as we
shall see in the next chapter, emphasized this point strongly. Well functioning institutions, he argued, are objective and collective patterns of behavior
that have their own regularities (*Eigengesetzlichkeit*) and even their own
value (*Selbstwert*). They do not have to be justified and legitimated. The
mere fact of existing, and having existed for such a long time, are the justifications and legitimations of their controlling function. Gehlen defined institutions as 'empty forms' (*Leerformen*) which can and indeed will be filled in
the transition of time by motives and aims that were not theirs to begin with.
The Swiss Guard of the Vatican seems on the surface (medieval uniforms,

helmets and weapons) to have remained unaltered since the days it was set up as a private papal guard manned by trustworthy young men of noble descent from Switzerland. Today it is not a real guard anymore but a symbolic embellishment of the papal institution. New motives and a new aim were gradually 'put into' this empty form of behavior.

All this illustrates the fallacy of the functionalist idea that the ultimate aim of institutions is the satisfaction of human needs.[5] This functionalist theory is rather simple and runs as follows: there are basic biological and social needs which are satisfied through actions. These actions are permanently needed for the satisfaction of the needs, and will in time become schematic. That is, they gradually grow into collective habits and paterns of behavior. There is, for example, the biological need for sexual intercourse. The behavior that satisfies this need, grows into a regular pattern – the institution of marriage. This is, of course, a rather ahistorical and instrumental explanation of the origin of institutions. The original motive of this institution may have been the societal regulation of sexual intercourse, but when the institution exists as an objective and autonomous structure, it will trigger and then regulate other, possibly quite different needs – such as, for instance, the need to stabilize emotions of love and affection, and the need to dispose of a stable parenting facility. Solidly objectified and autonomous institutions may even liberate individuals from their primary needs, set them free to design motives and aims which in their turn may create or trigger new needs. For instance, the goal of a formal dinner party is usually not the satisfaction of the need for food. It certainly is not meant to appease one's hunger. It is, in a sense, a *Leerform,* an empty form which is filled with other motives and aims, such as networking, flirting, gossiping, forging political compromises, and making maffia deals.

The institutional perspective

As this definition indicates institutionalization entails a rather specific view of human behavior – an institutional perspective which emphasizes the historically grown patterns into which human behavior is, as it were, molded. The perspective is also called *institutionalism*, or *neo-institutionalism*.[6] The concept of behavior is taken here in a broad sense, covering not just externally visible action but also internal processes such as thinking and feeling. Emile Durkheim circumscribed these patterns of behavior aptly as 'ways of acting, thinking and feeling'. It is important to emphasize that these patterns of behavior are passed on from generation to generation, causing a chain of tradition into which individual human beings are born, into which they are socialized and encultured, and out of which they will eventually die. Consequently, institutions constitute the historical components of a tradition which connects present generations with their predecessors in time. Sociologically, the chain of being is a chain of institutions. In any case the institutional perspective in the social sciences and the humanities is in essence a historical one. Institutional economics, sociology, psychology, etc. is historical economics, sociology, psychology, etc.

In sociology the institutional perspective has admittedly been strongly functionalist, since it has always emphasized the coercion and control on the part of the institutions for the sake of structural or systemic order and stability. It led to a rather fruitless debate in the 1960s and 1970s in which conflict and change on the part of individuals and their concerted actions (social movements) were juxtaposed to institutional coercion, control and order on the part of structures and systems. The debate was fruitless, since it was carried out by people who were obviously driven by political and ideological prejudices. The conflict-and-change party labeled itself politically left-of-center or even radical, while they denounced the harmony-and-order party as politically right-of-center and conservative. Conservatism needless to add was an objectionable position to take. The debate was political, ideological and emotional rather than intellectual, academic and scientific.

The issue of change is a crucial one in the institutional perspective. Modernity, as we shall see in chapter three, is the cultural upshot of revolutionary technological developments which began with the Industrial Revolution and continue today with the electronic revolution. Some even believe we have entered a new phase in this evolution which they call post-modernism or post-modernity. Structural differentiation, societal and cultural fragmentation and incessant changes and developments are the essence of this post-modern, or better, late-modern state of affairs. At first sight, this does not square with the institutions which produce duration, permanence, objectivism and order instead of change, development, subjectivism and contingency. As we shall see, in most post-modernist philosophies the emphasis is no longer on institutions but on networks which are, according to their proponents, flexible and alterable to the needs and desires of participating individuals. The institutionalist, however, is rather inclined to believe that even the most flexible and alterable of networks will eventually institutionalize, if they are to be effective and influential. Moreover, it should also be borne in mind that institutions have network-like origins. The issue will be discussed in more detail in chapter four where the institutional perspective will be confronted with the network perspective.

Institution and organization

Usually, the concepts of institution and organization are not distinguished but employed alternatively. Yet, sociologically it does make a difference whether one views the family, the church, the army, the university, the corporation, the union, or the state as organizations, or as institutions. Both concepts should be distinguished, albeit in an ideal-typical and not in an ontological manner.

To begin with, these concepts refer to two quite *dimensions* of socio-cultural reality, not to two components or sectors of reality. Of course, society is not divided into organizations on the one hand and institutions on the other. The family, the church, the army, the university, the corporation, the union, the state, etc. are examples of organizations *and* institutions. They have, so to say, organizational and institutional dimensions. In other words, the concepts of organization and institution refer to certain sociological facets of socio-cultural reality, not to components or sectors of it. They are analytical not ontological concepts.

If, for example, I were to look at society in terms of the concept of organization, I would be interested first and foremost in formal structures of command, in hierarchies of power and decision making, and in the divisions of staff and line functions. The structure of say the army or the university as an organization can be drawn on a map or chart. As organizations the university or the army contain a specific type of rationality. It is the functional rationality which consists of the careful matching of means, methods or procedures on the one hand, and the goals that have been set by the organization on the other. Irrespective of the contents of the ends, functionally, rational 'organization men' (managers) will search for the most efficient and effectual means to realize the ends. Weber called this organizational type of rationality *Zweckrationalität*, goal-rationality. This is not helpful since this type of rationality is more concerned with means than with goals. In fact, it is more a means-rationality, or procedural rationality than a goal-rationality.

Functional rationality is not totally value-free, since it espouses efficiency (the persistent search for the lowest costs) and effectiveness (the persistent focus upon the goals that have been set and must be effectuated). Both efficiency and effectivity are typically modern values, as we shall see later. But in terms of morality they are, of course, rather 'thin' values. Morally 'thick' values, such as loyalty, trust, honesty and humaneness, do not belong to the domain of functional rationality. Indeed, this type of rationality which is at the core of organizations, is functional, not moral.

If, in contrast, one were to focus on society in terms of the concept of institution one would see a rather different kind of reality. For instance, when approached sociologically as an institution, the university presents itself, to begin with, as a historical entity which has been passed on by former generations and therefore carries an idiosyncratic tradition. This tradition is not only debated, in modernity most of the time rather critically, but also celebrated in ceremonies, commemorations, legends, and myths. As an institution, the university espouses rather 'thick' values and norms such as academic freedom (no ideological constraints), academic honesty (no scientific misconduct such as plagiarism), higher education of the young, the relentless pursuit of truth through research, the perpetual substitution of prejudice by knowledge, etc. These values and norms are 'forged' in patterns of behavior, into traditional and established ways of acting, thinking and feeling which are characteristic of the university. They make up a corporate culture which yields a special brand of people: academic men and women with an academic mind and mentality, and academic ways of acting, thinking and feeling. Indeed, as an institution the university is a 'piece' of culture.

Certainly, the rationality of an institution is not merely functional but due to the values and norms involved rather substantial. Institutional rationality is substantial rationality. Weber fittingly called it *Wertrationalität*, value-rationality. In this type of rationality, the concern is not with the careful matching of ends and means, but rather with the definition of the ends to be realized. One needs a substantial value-rationality in order to formulate and set out the goals one wants to realize in an institution. However, there is more to this.

Karl Mannheim who broadened Weber's typology of *Zweckrationalität* and *Wertrationalität*, reformulating it in terms of functional and substantial rationality, defined the latter as man's capacity to view and experience reality, which in and of itself is irrationally chaotic and complex, as a coherent and understandable reality, as a meaningful *Gestalt*.[7] The substantially rational individual is able to discern coherent lines and structures in reality which is chaotic and irrational. He is only able to do so because he is related to values and norms. It is in terms of values and norms that we can separate the relevant from the irrelevant, the valuable from the invaluable, the important from the unimportant, the significant from the insignificant. Someone who is incapable of making such distinctions, based on values and norms, is substantially irrational, or *irre*, mentally and emotionally disturbed.

Again, if we approach socio-cultural reality in terms of the concept of institution, we focus first and foremost on values and norms, and beyond that on substantial rationality. This is important, since there is the persistent prejudice that the institutional focus on values and norms was an irrational one. It is a typically modern prejudice stemming from the fact that in modernity, functional rationality is believed to be the only possible rationality.

36

Everything that is not functionally rational is simply defined as being irrational. In economics for instance *homo economicus* is an individual driven by *rational choice*. His rationality, however, is exclusively functional and instrumental.[8] The ironic thing is that this one-sided focus on means, methods and procedures entails a persistent disregard of ends and goals. That, of course, turns out to be rather irrational. Not before long, means, methods and procedures are declared to be ends, aims, and goals. This inversion reaps sheer irrationality. It is the irrationality of what has aptly been called goal displacement. It is as irrational as the fixation on ends without much consideration for means and procedures.[9]

Institution and institute

Institutionalization is a universal process. Whenever and wherever people set out together to realize certain goals, their actions and interactions almost immediately form patterns of behavior to which values and norms are related. Even anarchists who yearn for a return to a non-institutionalized way of life, called 'nature', and consequently decide to turn their back on the institutional patterns of behavior of bourgeois society, find in due time that patterns of behavior, even patterns of command and authority, are being formed, into which newcomers, that is people from outside the commune or infants born into the commune, have to be inaugurated – or, sociologically speaking, socialized and encultured. Institutional patterns emerge which incidentally often bear an uncanny resemblance to the institutions they had left behind, when turning their backs on civilization.

As we shall see in the next chapter, Gehlen provided a feasible explanation for the universality of institutions. At this point, it suffices to point out that basic human actions and interactions – those of love relations and procreation, of economic production and consumption, of political power and authority, of religious rites and ceremonies, of work and leisure, etc. – are somehow forged in traditional, institutional patterns into which individuals socialize and enculturate, and out of which they eventually die. As cultural anthropologists have demonstrated this fact is universal.

When people live together in groups and set out to divide the labor needed in order to survive, basic institutions will emerge eventually, resembling what we usually call 'family', 'marriage', 'market', 'state', 'church', etc. There are more or less fixed and standard roles which adhere to these institutions, such as 'spouses', 'children', 'producers', 'consumers', 'priests', 'prophets', 'believers', etc. Yet, as anthropologists are quick to point out, these are Western concepts which pertain to Western civilization. Therefore they are ethnocentric, unless one uses them metaphorically, as with the anthropological concept 'tribe' which is sometimes used metaphorically in a Western context, when referring to 'staff' and 'line' as two distinct 'tribes' within the same organization. But it is quite hazardous to employ concepts such as 'the law', 'the family', 'marriage', 'state' etc. as metaphors when describing and analyzing pre-industrial, non-Western societies and cultures.

However, there is more at play here than an exchange of metaphors. Apparently, throughout the ages the human species has molded its most basic activities, such as the ones mentioned above, on institutional patterns which were passed on from generation to generation thereby acquiring an objective and coercive momentum. Thus, what is universal is not the monogamic, heterosexual marriage and the nuclear family based upon it which are still typical of our own culture, but *the fact that* people somehow mold their intersexual and procreative activities and relations in an institutional pattern . Likewise, it is not the church and the nation-state we have been accustomed to what is universal, but *the fact that* people somehow organize and institutionalize their religious and political activities. Religious beliefs and rites are universal, the Roman Catholic Church or the Russian Orthodox Church are not. Economic exchanges are universal, the capitalist market is not.

It is, therefore, heuristically helpful to distinguish the universal patterns of behavior from their particular, historically and culturally specific, empirical realizations. The former could be called *institutions*, the latter *institutes*. Thus, *the fact that* people throughout the ages and all over the world enact their intersexual and procreative relations within traditional patterns refers to institutions like 'marriage' and 'family'; yet polygamic or monogamic marriages, matrilineal or patrilineal families are historically and culturally specific institutes. The fact that people distribute power unequally and then set up structures of authority and command is a universal institution; the Western constitutional state however is a historically specific institute.

I strongly favor this conceptual distinction mainly for two reasons. First, it helps us to grasp adequately the phenomenon of cultural change. Certainly in modernity, rapid cultural changes can be observed which affect almost all institutions: marriage, the family, the church, the university, the army, etc. Yet, one should remember that these changes (or revolutions, if one wants to use this robust concept) occur on the 'superficial' level of the historical institutes, not on the 'deeper' level of the universal institutions. Institutions are, in structuralist terms, anthropologically basic and probably biologically (genetically) determined competence structures. They are comparable to the linguistic roots which are limited in number, out of which a multiplicity of different words can be formed. Indeed, institutions come close to what Vilfredo Pareto called 'residues', while institutes are the 'derivations' that emerge in great historical diversity from the 'residues'. Pareto's conceptual distinction between 'residues' and 'derivations' is essential for a sociologically correct understanding of change: 'derivations', in our case institutes, are, as Pareto phrased it, usually flexible like rubber bands that can be stretched to any length required, but 'residues', in our case institutions, change very slowly, if at all.

It is helpful to conceive of institutions in terms of verbs rather than nouns. The church as an empirical institute is a historical and culturally specific realization of religion as an institution. Religion as an institution is then best conceived of as 'being religious', 'believing in supernatural, or metaphysical forces' which is a universal component of the human condition. Throughout the centuries and in most societies covering the globe people have organized themselves for their defense. In fact, engaging in warfare and defense is a universal kind of human behavior. It is the institution which the Western army (with its admittedly complex history and evolution) exemplifies. Schools and universities are historical specifications and realizations of the institution education in the sense of schooling and educating people, in particular children and adolescents. As hazardous as such comparisons may be, one could liken the distinction between institutions and institutes to that of genus and species in evolutionary theory, or to that of genotype and phenotype in genetic theory.

Second, this conceptual distinction also helps us to avoid a superficial kind of cultural pessimism, or, for that matter, cultural optimism. Various theories purport the end of institutions. Some of these are conservative and pessimistic, as in Gehlen's case who laments the allegedly devastating impact of de-institutionalization and subjectivism on the human species. Other theories are, on the contrary, more progressively inclined and optimistic, as in the case of many post-modernist treatises which laud the diversifications, fragmentations, and flexibilities of the postindustrial world. It would serve us to be reminded of the fact that the real end of institutions would entail the end of human civilization. Institutions as universal behavior patterns cannot disappear since they are the very foundations of the human species. One would have to believe in some sort of metaphysical and apocalyptic *Götterdämmerung* to seriously predict the end of institutions. The end of the *Third Reich,* or of the 'Empire of the Rising Sun', or of the 'Soviet Imperium' might to the people concerned have had apocalyptic dimensions, but it was historically developed institutes not universal institutions that went down. Moreover, even historically and culturally specific institutes will rarely come to their end. Rather they will change their structure, their meaning and maybe even their composition but continue to be fed by their institutional roots. Tocqueville realized this when he pointed out that revolutions are rarely the convulsive, uprooting events they are often held to be. Revolutions usually have relatively long incubation periods, while the regime emerging after a revolution usually resembles its pre-revolutionary predecessor in a remarkable and often uncanny manner. The difference is often that post-revolutionary regimes are more repressive, more intolerant, more paranoid, and more eager to amass power than the toppled regimes.

Western monogamic and heterosexual marriage as the core of the bourgeois nuclear family has been under seige in the past two or three decades. Its traditional male domination in particular has been castigated. The institute has definitely been subjected to various changes, yet the underlying institution – the fact that people forge their sexual relations and bonds in fixed patterns – hardly has. From this institution, alternative institutes have emerged. For example, in the 1950s living together without being married was considered as a deviation from the standard institute, and therefore socially frowned upon. Being born out of wedlock and labelled a 'bastard', was socially shameful. But this deviant pattern institutionalized in the succeeding decades, and has by now become an institute. Young couples often decide to live together for several years without being formaly married, and then decide to 'enter' marriage for various reasons. (Interestingly enough, I observed several cases in which divorce occurred shortly after the formal marriage, which spelled the end of a bond that had lasted for many years before the marriage. Institutes have a curious influence on people.) Another alternative institute is the so-called LAT-relationship: living apart together. In the gay community the homosexual marriage is in discussion. One could ask the question, however, whether the desire to model fixed homosexual relationships after a typically Western, heterosexual institute does not in fact testify to a rather unemancipated mentality which is solidly bourgeois to boot. Monogamic, heterosexual marriage is unconsciously and erroneously elevated to the status of an institution which it obviously is not. Truly emancipated homosexuals should instead maintain their own type of living arrangements, their own specific institute. Likewise, in the past decades the so-called single parent family has developed into a sociologically determinable institute which is much in debate these days, in particular since it presents quite a burden to the social welfare budget of most Western nations.

The same kind of argument can be put forward in view of secularization. Secularization is not and cannot be seen as the gradual decline of religion under the impact of modernization. Organized religion is in fact a universal institution which has become and continues to become empirical in scores of particular, historically and culturally specific institutes, of which the Roman-Catholic Church and the various Protestant churches are obvious examples. The institute of the church as a historically and culturally specific sociological phenomenon has been changing all the time, as a quick glance at church history can demonstrate. In modernity these changes on the institute level are profound. Yet, the institutional roots of the various religious institutes are not subjected to such transformations. Atheists who throughout modernity have been proclaiming the end of religion, have usually satisfied their wishful thinking more than uncovered the secrets of social and cultural change.

Certainly one could maintain the same kind of distinction with regard to the concept of organization. Like cultural institutes, *social organs* are the historically and socially distinctive, empirical realizations of universal and ahistorical roots or structures, called *organizations*. However, since we are here primarily interested in institutions, institutes and institutionalization, we will not pursue this conceptual exercise in the direction of organizations and organs further.

Finally, it is admittedly awkward to maintain the distinction between institution and institute, particularly since sociology is an empirical discipline and thus primarily interested in the empirical and historical realizations on the institute level. In fact, if taken strictly, sociologists ought to speak and write almost exclusively in terms of institutes, and skip the concept of institution. This does not work, and is not really necessary either. To begin with, institutes are the empirical and historical realizations of institutions. There is, therefore, nothing wrong in calling the Western, monogamic and heterosexual marriage an institution, as long as one realizes at all times that it is, strictly taken, 'only' an empirical and historical realization and specification of a universal institution. Thus, after one has taken the distinction between universal residues (institutions) on the one hand, and historical and empirical derivations (institutes) on the other into account, after one has engraved it into one's sociological mind, it is not entirely necessary to avoid the concept institution all the time. One knows that in speaking about institutions one is actually referring to their historical realizations and empirical enactments.

1. The classic text that illustrates this misunderstanding is Alvin Gouldner's presidential address delivered at the annual meetings of the Society for the Study of Social Problems, August 28, 1961: 'Anti-Minotaur: The Myth of a Value-Free Sociology', in: Jack D. Douglas (ed.), *The Relevance of Sociology*, (New York: Appleton-Century-Crofts, Educational Division of the Meredith Corporation, 1970), pp. 64-84.
2. Cf. Jacques Derrida, *Raising the Tone of Philosophy. Late Essays by Immanuel*

Kant, Transformative Critique, (Baltimore: Johns Hopkins University Press, 1998).

3. Arnold Gehlen whose theory of institutions will be discussed in the next chapter made an attempt to reconstruct the origins of institutions in his book *Urmensch und Spätkultur,* (Bonn: Athenäum Verlag, 1956). Using a Kantian concept he called this reconstruction an anthroplogical search for basic human categories (*Kategorienforschung*).

4. J. O. Hertzler, *American Institutions,* (Boston: Allyn and Bacon, 1961), p. 86.

5. This was the position Bronislav Malinowski took in his treatise *The Scientific Theory of Culture,* 1944, (New York: Oxford University Press. A Galaxy book, 1964).

6. I find these concepts somewhat awkward since nouns ending with -ism usually indicate philosophical, political or religious ideologies or ideological movements. Examples are positivism, Marxism, and Puritanism. I prefer the more neutral concept 'institutional perspective' to 'institutionalism' or 'neo-institutionalism', although it is not always possible to avoid them.

7. Mannheim's theory of rationality and irrationality in modernity is remarkable. See in particular Part I of his *Man and Society in an Age of Reconstruction,* 1940, (London: Routledge & Kegan Paul, 1960, 10th ed.), pp. 39-78. On the concepts of substantial and functional rationality: pp. 51-57.

8. Cf. James S. Coleman, Thomas J. Ferraro (eds.), *Rational Choice Theory. Advocacy and Critique,* (London: Sage Publications, 1992).

9. The classic text on this inversion of means and aims is Jacques Ellul, *The Technological Society,* 1954, translated by J. Wilkinson, (New York: Vintage Books, 1964).

CHAPTER TWO

Institutions and the Transcendence of Biology

Philosophical anthropology

As I said in the Preface, European philosophy after World War II went through successive stages in which various -isms struggled for intellectual and often political hegemony. Because this is the very nature of -isms, these currents of philosophical thought and their schools of adepts and followers were predominantly ideological. Existentialism, Marxism, Freudianism, structuralism, poststructuralism or deconstructionism, and post-modernism with their unavoidable sages such as Sartre, Jaspers and Heidegger, Lukacs, Bloch and Marcuse, Lévi-Strauss, Foucault and Chomsky, Derrida, Lyotard and Baudrillard, filled and still fill the pages of philosophical journals, dissertations and textbooks. There were also and still are various cross-fertilizations which, of course, did not contribute to the clarity of philosophical thought and discourse. To be sure, the philosophical layman, interested in basic philosophical issues, has had a hard time in the past decades in understanding what is actually going on in this field, let alone in discovering what the most relevant ideas and theories are. Not being well trained in theory and logic, sociologists in particular – it is my experience – have great difficulties in separating the philosophical charlatans from the sincere and honest thinkers.

In particular Paris has been the seedbed of alternate philosophical -isms (except logical positivism which has largely been an Anglo-Saxon and Scandinavian prerogative). These French -isms often remind one of religious sects trying to overthrow anything that smacks of orthodoxy and traditional, institutional thought. As is the nature of sects, they either wither away rapidly, or are successful, attract believers and then develop into a church which cherishes and defends its very own orthodoxy. Needless to add that these -isms guard their fixed ideas and commonplaces as the corner stones of correct speech and thought. The next sect will then emerge and repeat the process. It is, indeed, questionable whether this is progress.

In the first half of the 20th century, however, there were two philosophical schools of thought which did not develop into ideological -isms and which, probably for that very reason, were not able to maintain their place in the center of the philosophical discourse of the past few decades: *phenomenology* and *philosophical anthropology*. Both claimed 'scientific' status and tried, not always successfully, to shield their philosophical methodology from metaphysics and ideology. Edmund Husserl, usually seen as the founder of phenomenology, claimed for instance that his approach was a rigorous and scientific one, while Arnold Gehlen, a prominent representative of philosophical anthropology, stated emphatically that his theory of human action (*Handlungslehre*) which was also a theory of institutions (*Institutionslehre*), should be seen as a brand of 'empirical philosophy'. By that he distanced himself from German Idealism (Hegel, Kant) and came close to American Pragmatism (Dewey and Mead). Although both schools did not really succeed in avoiding ideological and metaphysical notions, they did not position themselves as distinct ideological, let alone metaphysical -isms. They thus did not satisfy the ideological and either covert or overt metaphysical needs of students and academics. However, both of them have been seminal for the sociology of knowledge and the related school of sociological thought, known as *Kultursoziologie*, cultural sociology. Here institutions and institutionalization play a crucial role.[1]

This book is inspired in particular by European philosophical anthropology as it has been developed by Helmuth Plessner (1892-1985) and Arnold Gehlen (1904-1976). The present chapter focuses on those elements of their theoretical legacy that are pertinent to the institutional perspective. Their biologically founded anthropology, however, needs to be supplemented and amended by recent developments in biology, in genetics and so-called sociobiology in particular. The contributions of Edward Wilson and Richard Dawkins will be briefly discussed at the end of this chapter, since their ideas bear in particular on the theory of institutions presented here.

It is not my intention to discuss the history of philosophical anthropology which according to some goes back to the philosophy of Fichte, but began according to others with philosopher-sociologist Max Scheler. Nor will biologists such as Hans Driesch, Adolf Portmann and Konrad Lorenz be covered, despite their decisive influence on philosophical anthropology.[2] The focus is rather on portions of Plessner's and Gehlen's philosophical-anthropological systems which are relevant to the presently reconstructed institutional approach, and they will be complemented and also rectified by some basic ideas of Wilson and Dawkins. This completion and rectification strengthens the conceptualization of this book, in particular the conceptual distinction between 'institutions' as universal and 'institutes' as historical patterns of behavior.

Plessner on social roles

Plessner completed his Ph.D.degree at the University of Leipzig under the supervision of the biologist Hans Driesch with a thesis on the starfish.[3] But from early on he was more than just a biologist. Upon the completion of his dissertation he pursued further studies in history, sociology and philosophy. Despite his rather Germanic style of thinking and writing, he had a keen sense of political issues and processes. He was one of the first to warn others of the rise of German fascism. Although he was intellectually strongly assimilated into the rich tradition of German culture, he left his native country when the Nazi's rose to power, since he was Jewish by descent. Through his Dutch friend and colleague, the biologist and psychologist F.J.J. Buytendijk,[4] he acquired a professorship at the University of Groningen, the Netherlands. The story goes that Buytendijk used a budget meant for the acquisition of a chimpanzee for his laboratory to cover the costs of Plessner's appointment. He taught at Groningen from 1934 till 1952 but went into hiding during the war. He taught at the University of Göttingen from 1952 till his retirement in 1963. Plessner was a prolific writer which is testified by his posthumously published collective writings of ten volumes.

Of all his publications his book on the successive stages in the organic world has been the most influential.[5] It is an evolutionist philosophy based on biological premises. He begins with the simple question of the essential difference between the inorganic and the organic world. The answer is *positionality*. An inorganic object is simply located in time and space, is simply here and now, or there and then. In contrast, a living being – plant, animal, man – occupies a position in time and space. Plants, animals and human beings emerge in time and space, are dependent on time and space, often also resist time and space. Moreover, unlike dead objects which are simply where they are and end when they end, organic beings have limits that are part of their being. They are especially limited vis-à-vis their environment and limited in terms of time, since they can and eventually will wither away and die. A rock can be crushed and pulverized, but cannot die. The crushing is not part of its existence, as death is in the case of living 'beings'.

The positionality of life forms (plants, animals, human beings) is an ongoing process. A living 'being' is something that grows and lives in close contact with reality. It grows inwardly and outwardly. Dead things may be moved, but they do not grow, evolve. They can change. Rocks, for instance, can become weather-beaten. But that is not the sort of change organic forms go through. Unlike dead things, organic 'beings' grow according to some sort of plan. There are, we shall see instantly, three basic stages (*Stufen* says Plessner) in this evolution. But first we should register one other characteristic of organic forms. Unlike inorganic forms, they possess a nucleus with periferal characteristics that provides them with some sort of subjectivity. However, Plessner hastens to add that this should be taken in an abstract way, not in terms of 'mind' or 'consciousness'. Unlike stones which are merely there and do not relate to their environment, plants have a nucleus which is somehow related to their surroundings – light, air, water, earth. Plessner speaks of a positional field.

He then distinguishes three basic types of positionality and views them in an evolutionary perspective. *Plants*, to begin with, have an open organizational form and allow themselves to be merged into their natural milieu. This happens without mediation, directly and without a 'self' that gives directions. Plants suck up water and carbon dioxide and secrete oxygen. Their development is in unison with their environment.

Animals are a next step in organic life. Theirs is a closed organizational form: a distance exists between them and their environment to which they relate from an inner center. In the higher primates this center is the central nervous system. Animals are not just bodies, but live in bodies. However, they do not have an 'ego', or a 'self', or 'subjectivity'. Yet, unlike plants animals act, they occupy space, and they confront, if necessary, the outer world. Plessner speaks of the animal's frontality. It does not just occupy a place in the world, but it takes a stand. Their relation to reality is indirect, and although they occupy, unlike plants, a 'centric position', they are themselves unaware of this fact.

Human beings also occupy a natural position in the world, and do so from a center, i.e. from the central nervous system. However, they realize their position consciously; they can identify with or distance themselves from themselves, from others, from objects, plants and animals, from the here-and-now and from the then-and-there. In other words, unlike plants and animals, man occupies an *eccentric position*. This, it should be emphasized, is not a moral feature but a structural characteristic of their biological constitution. Man is a body, has a body, and is aware of it. He is the subject of his experiences, perceptions and actions. He has a distinct will and acts in a motivated manner.

These structural characteristics of man's biological constitution entail that he lives in three worlds: the natural outer world (*Aussenwelt*), the subjective inner world (*Innenwelt*) and the shared social world (*Mitwelt*). As a body man is part of the outer world. But living simultaneously in a body he is also part of the inner world where he has experiences, sensations and thoughts. The human being can, however, also distance himself from both realities. He is able to perceive that he *is* not only a body but also *has* a body, that he *is* a psyche or soul and *has* a psyche or soul. He can think and he can think about his thinking; he can feel and he can reflect about his feelings. In fact, he is able to feel his feelings. Finally, together with others, man is part of the shared social world where his self merges with the others, forming a collective 'we', a community. In this shared world man develops culture through labor. That is, he creates artefacts, houses, clothes, symbols, values, norms, rituals, ceremonies, and institutions.

Plessner's institutional perspective is highlighted by his theory of man as the ambiguous player of social roles. In an essay 'Limits of Community. A Critique of Social Radicalism' (1924),[6] he takes the position of a cultural critic, and attacks the typically modern attempts to strip oneself of social roles, to reject formalities, and to lay bare publicly one's mind and soul. Such a social striptease, he believes, renders a person ridiculous. Social roles are like masks which we wear in our daily social interactions. They create, as it were, a twilight zone somewhere between subjectivity and objectivity: 'Man generalizes and objectifies himself through a mask, behind which he becomes invisible to a certain degree, without however disappearing completely as a Person.' But the social roles we play, provide much more than that: they give our actions a *Nimbus*, an aura which gives meaning to the actions.

This is Plessner's anti-existentialism: it is not authenticity, allegedly fostered by psychological nudism and social expressionism, but the public playing of social roles, the wearing of masks, the respecting of formalities and ceremonies which are the very foundations of civilization. This should not be interpreted as a Germanic lack of a sense of humor, nor as a petit-bourgeois withdrawl behind social screens. On the contrary, Plessner finds the public exposure of inner experiences and feelings repulsive because they are in most cases grim, serious, humorless and not at all playful. Indeed, the playful person is not the prototypical human being in existentialism.

In contrast, the playing impulse is crucial in Plessner's anthropology. Like Johan Huizinga, he sees the human being as in essence a *homo ludens*. This playful impulse becomes evident in the urge to dress up, to don social roles, to wear masks in public. Radical and eternally serious moralists abhor masks and roles, Plessner observes, as did incidentally Oscar Wilde long before him. He uses the concept *Wertrigorismus* – value rigorism. It is an attitude which without any sense of humor looks for direct relations between man and man. It is an attitude of relentlessness in which liberty cannot be experienced, because liberty needs distance – distance from others, distance also from oneself. In this early essay, Plessner defends the playfulness and superficiality of formalities and ceremonies as the foundations of civility and civilization against the humorless, self-appointed moral censors who adhere to 'a morality of inexorable Authenticity and of harming oneself and others on principle'.

In later publications Plessner emphasized the importance of a balance between the individual and the society, between interiority and exteriority, subjectivity and objectivity, the private and the public. He designed a theory of man as a double, a *Doppelgänger*, a *homo duplex*. This idea is coupled to another notion which is fundamental to his anthropology: the idea that unlike other living beings – plants and animals – man occupies an *eccentric position* in the cosmos. Plants are tied directly, without intermediary, to a fixed milieu. They suck up water and carbon dioxide and give off oxygen. Animals relate to their environment through a 'center', occupying a 'centric position'. In the lower species this center consists of the senses, in the higher species of the central nervous system. But the human being occupies an 'eccentric position' because unlike the animal, man can reflect upon himself, upon his place in the world. He, the role player and the wearer of masks, has an *indirect* bond with his environment and with himself.

Naturally, Plessner was fascinated by actors in the theater. In an insightful essay on 'The Anthropology of the Actor' (1948)[7] he focuses on the duplication that takes place when an actor performs a theater role. The playwright and the director design the role and thereby impose limits on the actor. But the latter's individuality and artistic creativity do not submerge in this pre-designed role. On the contrary, the great actor can express his artistic individuality precisely by performing this role. In pre-war Germany Gustaf Gründgens was often identified with Goethe's Faust, as for a long time Brecht's Galilei was identified in America with Charles Laughton.

But, Plessner continues, there is also the audience which beholds the performance of the role, identifies with it, or with portions of it. Members of the audience thus in a sense duplicate themselves as well. It is as in real life where we all play roles, social roles, which we did not design or invent but which were handed down to us by former generations through the chain of tradition. We play these predesigned roles like the actors on the stage, namely as individuals. In performing these roles some of us are greater virtuosos than others, but very few are like puppets on a string.

Modern individuals, Plessner warns, complain of alienation believing that their inner world, their subjectivity and authenticity are violated by the roles they have to play. They adhere to subjectivism and expressionism, and fail to see that it is precisely these roles and masks which provide them with an opportunity to experience and express their individuality and authenticity in an objective, albeit indirect manner. He viewed Heidegger's existentialist lamentations about the supposed alienation of man's authenticity – *das Man* – as a philosophical expression of this typically modern subjectivism.

Plessner believed that by his theorem of anthropological duplicity he had grasped the essence of human society in general. But he also believed that the double nature of man as the player of social roles had become particularly evident, and problematic, in the modern, industrialized and rationalized world, characterized as it is by labor and the division of labor. In this society people play scores of rather different, often fragmented roles that belong to their specific societal position and its related social functions. More than ever before, these functions and their related roles, and thus not one or the other private, individual and subjective 'nature', tell us and the others who and what we are. In a sense, the individual has become unimportant and even irrelevant in this intricate system of functions and roles. Today he would probably emphasize the fact that this situation has been exacerbated by the advent of the post-industrial, informational society which we will discuss in chapter four.

Plessner's role theory, of course, comes close to sociological Functionalism. But he is aware of this trap, and takes refuge again in man's constitutional ambiguity. Even in industrialized and bureaucratized society, the human being is not the sum of his roles and functions. But he realizes immediately that this conclusion brings us close to vague and murky ideas about 'authenticity'. He warns of such a conclusion: 'Heidegger *ante portas*!' Functions and roles do not at all destroy man's authenticity, intimicy and privacy. On the contrary, they enable him to exist and prosper, just as the actor can exhibit his artistic creativity and individuality by playing the theater role on the stage. Man needs indirectness, mediation, and the alienation of roles and masks in order to experience and express his individuality and authenticity. I can only be myself by being at the same time someone else. The American reader is, of course, reminded of George Herbert Mead's theorem of the I and the Me in the Social Self. Plessner was apparently unfamiliar with this idea, unlike Gehlen, whom we shall discuss shortly, who emphasized the fact that human freedom can only emerge through the alienation of institutions. Indeed, what Plessner called roles, was called institutions by Gehlen.

Plessner addressed the Marxist notion of alineation in his academic lecture held at the University of Göttingen: 'The Problem of the Public Realm and the Idea of Alienation' (1960).[8] All that remains of Marxism as a source of inspiration, Plessner argues, is the notion of alienation. But this notion has completely changed meaning. In the days of Marx the idea of alienation still had a concrete, existential content. In the nineteenth century the industrial worker as wage slave experienced the humiliation of being reduced to an object of exploitation. Now this abasement has become a rather marginal phenomenon. Alienation has been disengaged from the industrial worker, and became attached to the over-rationalized, bureaucratized society as a system that is expected to function as smoothly as possible. There is no room for either creativity or liberty. Man plays a predestined role in this system. He is a bearer of functions, a *Funktionsträger*.

The transformation of the meaning of alienation – it is a transformation, one could say, from Marx to Kafka – runs parallel to a basic transformation of the public realm. It is in Plessner's own words '*ein Wandel der Öffentlichkeit*', a change of the public realm. The public realm has become an order, a system which is able to manipulate people and to establish a 'totality of the anonymous'. In Plessner's view this abstract anonymity has caused the re-emergence of romanticism, with Heidegger's existentialism as a late fruit of this romantic turn. But again, Heidegger's subjectivist search for anti-social authenticity is ultimately a rather dangerous illusion: 'The search for freedom and authenticity in inner subjectivity – the appeal of existentialism – promotes the reification of man in the public realm as much as the eschatology of Marxism which places man in a waiting position, in view of the end of history. Only a concept of the public realm which is liberated from the seductions of the alienation concept and which is radically demythologized ensures the leeway of responsibility which will enable our societal freedom.' This is a laborious way of saying that one must maintain and accept the fundamental tension of a *homo duplex*, extended between subjective authenticity and objective alienation, in order to experience and realize one's freedom, irrepeatable individuality, and creativity.

In chapter four I shall introduce the distinction between traditional 'thick' and modern 'thin' institutions. Plessner, like Gehlen, is still thinking in terms of rather strongly 'objective' and 'thick' institutions, while modernization has meanwhile progressed towards a post-industrial, informational society which to many is a post-institutional, 'network society'.[9] It is, as I shall argue in chapter four, a society with 'thin' institutions and a heightened form of subjectivism. Plessner's warning phrased as 'Heidegger *ante portas*' can be re-phrased: despite his fascist type of gnosticism and his blatant flirtations with National Socialism[10] Heidegger has been drawn into the gates of philosophy by the post-modernists, who also love to embrace the idea of a post-institutional society, based exclusively on flexible networks and institutional 'flows'. The days of 'thick' institutions are over and very few of us yearn for their return, as Gehlen did. Yet, it is, as I shall argue, anthropologically, sociologically and politically dangerous to reject institutions and take refuge in the slippery abodes of emotional subjectivism and network flexibilities.

But we must first complete our conceptualization of philosophical anthropology. Plessner's anthropology in which the idea of man as the player of social roles occupies a central position stands in need of an addition.

Gehlen's theory of institutions, which in many respects is very similar to Plessner's role theory, offers this much needed addition. His ideas are particularly pertinent since he founded his theory of institutions on a theory of action. Moreover, he designed an impressive, albeit philosophically and politically objectionable theory of institutional conservatism. His reactionary defense of objective, very 'thick' institutions is in fact the radical opposite of post-modernist relativism and its vision of a post-institutional society of flexible networks and 'flows'.

Gehlen on institutions

Like Plessner, Gehlen completed his graduate studies at the University of Leipzig with a Ph.D.dissertation supervised by Driesch.[11] Like Plessner, he left behind many publications dealing with anthropological and sociological issues, but his style of writing and thinking was quite different. At times he wrote stately, if not pompously, at other times also frivolously and sarcastically. He commanded over an enormous erudition which he loved to show off and which he put to use in his writings eclectically and sometimes rather loosely. Particularly when he was commenting on modernity and on what he saw as decadent fads and fashions, his style could be sardonic and often quite witty too. His membership in the National Socialist party in the 1930s and during the war, and his unrelenting conservatism after 1945, often bordering on a reactionary resentment, remained a blot on his intellectual reputation until after his death.

Without defending his political stance, it should be said in all honesty that the position he adopted in his anthropology was alien to the platitudinous biologism of the Nazis, as will be demonstrated shortly. He was also, unlike his National Socialist colleagues, a fierce opponent of the German tradition of Idealism, and exposed himself to Anglo-Saxon empiricism, in particular to Pragmatism (John Dewey) and Social Behaviorism (George Herbert Mead). He tried to design an anthropology that could claim to be empirical. He had a great interest in biology and zoology (Portmann, Lorenz) and in ethnology (Margaret Mead, Ruth Benedict). In addition, Gehlen saw his brand of philosophical anthropology as a specimen of sociology. He was fond of Max Weber, Vilfredo Pareto, Joseph Schumpeter, but ignored contemporary sociologists with a hardly concealed contempt, with some exceptions such as David Riesman and Helmuth Schelsky. In his later publications he demonstrated a remarkable preference for the thoughts and writings of Hannah Arendt.

Gehlen's anthropology took human action (*Handeln*), and not the mind

(*Geist*) as its point of departure. In the 1930's he designed an impressive theory of human behavior in a book entitled *Der Mensch*. It came out in 1940 and was re-written and reprinted several times in the decades following the war. Several ideas in this seminal book are similar to those developed by Plessner who, as a result, accused Gehlen of plagiarism. This was, however, hard to prove. It is more likely that their common intellectual ancestry in Driesch's biological school functioned as a shared heritage.

In order to understand himself man, Gehlen claimed, distances himself from himself by comparing himself with non-human life forms. Comparisons with animals in particular have served this goal. In the history of Western culture there has been an ongoing search for features or characteristics that human beings have and animals lack: 'soul' and 'mind' or 'consciousness' were the most favorite assets. This search, Gehlen argued, has been unsatisfactory, since it has only yielded useless, metaphysical speculations. If we compare humans and animals scientifically, especially biologically, we must conclude that in evolutionary terms we, the humans, are rather faulty creatures. Gehlen was fond of quoting the philosopher Herder who branded the human being as a *Mängelwesen* – a defective creature.

Animals are biologically equipped with specialized organs which are adjusted to their natural surroundings. That is, animals possess specialized reaction patterns ('instincts') which enable them to react to changes in their environments adequately and smoothly, that is, without much reflection and quite efficiently. In contrast, the human being is at birth biologically ill-equipped for survival, lacks specialized instincts, and is born with only unspecialized and uncoordinated instinctive residues. In fact, the newborn baby is still a foetus, a biological bundle of helplessness, and as such not very fit for evolutionary survival. The zoologist Adolf Portmann coined the phrase that newborn babies actually experience an 'extra-uterine spring'.[12]

The animal, however, is biologically tied to a specific natural environment or milieu. It is actually imprisoned by its natural surroundings. Outside of this milieu, the animal would succumb: the polar bear can not survive in the desert, on shore the fish will suffocate. In contrast, man the biologically undetermined, non-specialized being, is not bound by any natural milieu. He is, as Max Scheler has aptly formulated, *welt-offen*, 'world-open'. People can be found all over the globe, on the North Pole and the South Pole, in the desert, under water and in the air. The absolute prerequisite is, however, coordinated action, by which a 'second nature' is created. This 'second nature' is called 'culture' and it is adjusted to us. The animal merely lives and survives, caught in the strictures of its natural surroundings. Man, on the contrary, leads his life, acts in and upon it, and is biologically free, 'world-open'. His life is run in a human world of artefacts, clothes, houses, means of transportation, means of production; a world also of values, norms and meanings, language and institutions. In short, his world is not a biologically conditioned and predetermined milieu, but a historical culture. For that reason, man is not just a faulty creature unfit for survival but a true Prometheus who creates his own environment and his own destiny. (Incidentally, it stands to reason that Nazi philosophers who were caught in semi-Darwinian biologism were fierce opponents of Gehlen's brand of anthropology.)

Philosophical Idealism claims man commands that 'mind', or 'intelligence', or 'consciousness' which enables him to act and to create culture. According to Gehlen, it is the other way around. Even a superficial observation of a baby in a crib demonstrates the fact that the human being is a 'senso-motorial' unity: movements of the body accompany listening with the ears, looking with the eyes, smelling with the nose, and tasting with the mouth. It is a system whose components determine and influence each other. In addition, movements and sounds from the outside world are registered and processed by this senso-motorial system: babies watch the mobile hanging in their crib, try to touch or grab it with their hands; they search for the voice that comes out of the mouths of the adults bending over their cribs. Very soon they will react to these vocal gestures by using their own voices. It is at this point that Gehlen refers to Mead's theory of gestures and meaningful interactions. This is all very similar, of course, to Plessner's concept of the 'eccentric position' of man.

There is, it should be stressed, no inborn system of specialized organs and instincts which register and process the incoming stimuli. Man is, after all, as Nietzsche phrased it, 'the unfixed animal' (*das nicht festgestellte Tier*).[13] Not just the newborn, but all human beings are constantly exposed to an abundance of exterior stimuli, while from the inside scores of undifferentiated impulses push to be realized and processed into actions. Both – the stimuli and the impulses – put human beings under extreme pressure. Therefore, it is essential that for a balanced, healthy development of the human individual he is relieved of this pressure. As we shall see, Gehlen claimed that *institutions* perform this relief function. But before we discuss his institutional theory, we must still discuss somewhat further his behavioral theory.

The animal's movements and actions are biologically fixed and closely tied to its natural milieu. In contrast, human movements and actions are not at all biologically tied to exterior stimuli and interior impulses. They can distance themselves from them, deny and suppress them. There is, Gehlen argued, a gap, a *hiatus*, between man's actions and the stimuli and impulses. It is a kind of free and empty space which is filled with dreams, fantasies and plans. It enables man to do what the animal, caught as it is in its body and natural environment, can never accomplish: to transfer oneself into the future or into the past, to take on the role of the other while interacting with the other, to write poems and novels, compose sonata's and symphonies, prepare lectures, design buildings, etc.

At this point, Gehlen introduced the idea of the behavior circle (*Handlungskreis*). Human behavior is a systemic unity of acting, thinking and feeling, in which an 'inner world' of experiences, thoughts and feelings, and an 'outer world' of facts and events relate to each other and constantly influence each other. This is at first hard to understand since we have been brainwashed by the Cartesian dualism of subjectivity versus objectivity. A simple example may illustrate what Gehlen meant with the behavior circle. Someone trying to unlock a door in the dark experiences this circle in mind and body: the lock is invisible, the hand makes searching movements with the key, the search is accompanied by an irritated or frustrated moaning and a tense staring (the senso-motorial unity is fully at work!), the hand and the key experience the resistance of the objective reality of the lock and the door. But then, after a couple of feedbacks, there is this sudden click and the door is unlocked. Gehlen, of course, described the cybernetic principle of feedback, and he did so as early as the 1930s, when he wrote *Der Mensch*.

Thus, human behavior is in Gehlen's anthropology much more than an automatic process of stimulus and response. It is a senso-motorial unity of feeling, thinking and acting, and at the same time a social, meaningful interaction with fellow human beings – indeed a symbolic interaction. It stands to reason that he dedicated special attention to language, taken in the sense of speech (*parole*). On this point also his theory comes close to that of Mead. The newly born baby registers and processes the vocal gestures from the outside and sends out vocal gestures in response. These are still sheer baby noises which are accompanied by facial and bodily gestures. But the feedback mechanism of the behavior circle causes the gradual emergence of meaningful vocal sounds, words and eventually sentences.

As did Mead, Gehlen located mind or cognition in the same feedback mechanism: thinking is a silent speaking with oneself. Both thought and speech are thus not the preconditions of actions and interactions, but it is the other way around: behavior is subjected to the feedback process of the behavioral circle causing the gradual emergence of meaning, meaningful speech and meaningful (inter)action. In the beginning was the act, then emerged the mind. Gehlen founded this idea upon his hiatus theorem: the gap between behavior on the one hand and the stimuli and impulses on the other created in his view the appropriate space in which the interaction between mind and body, between subjectivity and objectivity could be possible.

After this intricate analysis of human behavior Gehlen continued his explorations of man's nature by focusing on *institutions*. Human behavior, from the vocal and bodily gestures of babies to the speech and the symbolic interactions of adults, will unavoidably develop habits, patterns, and stereotypes. This process of habit formation and stereotyping sets in with the division of labor. In order to survive in nature to which he is not at all biologically adjusted, as we saw before, man has to act. That is, he has to produce a second nature – culture – which is adjusted to him. In order to be productive these actions have to be organized efficiently. As has been observed by philosophers from Plato to Hobbes, Smith and Marx, the division of labor has been the ultimate organization of man's productive activities.

There is, of course, no limit to a process in which an ever more differentiated structure of specialized functions emerge which – and this is crucial – will be passed on from generation to generation. Specializations of production are not being invented from scratch by each successive generation but handed over to next generations – handing over *tradere*, tradition! These specialized functions are objective in the sense that individuals are trained to perform them. They are, Plessner would say, objective social roles. Gehlen sees them rather as behavioral patterns, as action models, as institutions which are passed on to and learned by subsequent generations.

Institutions can be small scale patterns, like the marriage bond between two individuals, or the steady exchange of letters between friends over an extended period of time. But there are also the large scale institutions, such as the state, the church, the army, the university – albeit in various gradations of size and comprehensiveness. However, they all have in common that they possess a degree of objectivity and acquire a kind of taken-for-granted autonomy vis-à-vis the individuals who act within their context. In fact, institutions tend to disengage from the primary needs and motives which originally caused their emergence. They acquire their own, autonomous regularity, their own taken-for-granted value independent of their utility value. They are important, relevant and legitimate for the simple reason that they exist. In a traditional, rural society questions about the meaning and utility of institutions like the church or marriage are never raised. They are taken for granted, they are relevant, useful, valuable and meaningful simply because they are enacted and therefore exist. In fact, they are held to be 'natural'.

This is characteristic of institutions that have a firm base in society: they are taken for granted and the original motives for their emergence are superseded by goals which are quite different and often also quite ceremonial and formalistic. Gehlen called this goal displacement 'separation of motive and goal'. But he goes one step further. If institutions function well, they will exert a distinct influence on the impulses which we discussed earlier. Traditional institutions, which are taken for granted, turn the direction of the impulses around from an inner-directed to an outer-directed thrust, and they will rouse them, stir them up, and stimulate them. A religious ritual in a church service will stir up religious feelings and may even cause an ecstasy which carries people along and gives them the feeling of being an inseparable part of a larger whole.

However, the most important function of institutions is their relief function. Inner impulses and needs, as we saw earlier, press upon the individual who is at the same time being subjected to multiple stimuli from the outer world. Institutions mold the inner impulses and needs according to their own goals, and they organize the outer stimuli as they are molded into stereotypical patterns. Moreover, the division of labor liberates the individual from the innumerable options of behavior that confront him. For instance, while some clan members go off hunting, satisfying the primary need for food, others stay home as the specialists who produce and improve the necessary weapons, thereby satisfying the hunters' primary need for adequate and efficient means of production. As a result, the institutions emerging from the division of labor function as a kind of background fulfillment of needs, and thereby establish a beneficial security (*bienfaisante certitude*), a taken-for-grantedness that is no longer in need of reflection and deliberation. Culture has thereby evolved into (second) nature.

From this point on Gehlen's analysis turns into cultural criticism and becomes expressedly normative, if not metaphysical. He embraces, as we shall see, a conservative, even at times reactionary stance, when it comes to an assessment of contemporary, fully modernized society. His style of writing and argumentation is by turns ironic, often even sarcastic.

Being biologically insufficiently equipped to survive in nature, man should stick to the institutions of his culture. In fact, Gehlen even claimed that man ought to let himself be consumed by his culture's institutions. Meanwhile, he singled out the state as the institution which is most crucial of all, when it comes to guaranteeing and defending the existing institutional order. It stands to reason that the army and the military were in this vision the major institutional instruments. The state ought to employ them in its task to maintain order, stability and safety. It is at this point that we may understand his intellectual collaboration with the Nazis, and although he despised communism as a political system, he did appreciate its emphasis upon a strong and centralized state. He used every opportunity to ridicule the liberal democracy of the post-war German Federal Republic, and was particulary fond of directing his sharp arrows of contempt at liberal and left-wing intellectuals. But he was quite ambiguous here, although many attributed it to his opportunism. In any case, he was always fond of disputes and critical debates, and seemed to have little use for people who agreed with him.

It was not freedom or liberty, nor creativity or self-expression – in his view feminine and weak values – but service, self-sacrifice and duty – in his view the highest, 'manly' values – which constituted the foundations of vital institutions. When institutions lose their grip over people, when people continuously reflect and deliberate about their institutions, a society will be subjected to institutional decline. Gehlen calls it *Institutionsabbau*, or an institutional phase-out. The call for a voice, for giving people a democratic say in the process of policy making, is wisked away by Gehlen as endless tosh.

When institutions lose their control over individuals, people will be thrown back upon their inner subjectivity, where they are exposed to a continuous clash of unstructured and chaotic inner impulses and needs on the one hand, and chaotic and unstructured, massive stimuli from the outer world on the other hand. Without institutional control, impulses and stimuli are no longer canalized. Chaos and gradual degeneration of a man's psyche and of society's structures at large will be the result. Without the objectivity of strong, traditional institutions subjected to the supervision of a strong and demanding state, man and society will be thrown back on a pervasive subjectivism which thrives on emotions, sensations, and endless and fruitless reflections. Culture, Gehlen claimed, thus degenerates into a late-culture (*Spätkultur*)[14], history into late-history (*post-histoire*). This, Gehlen added, has been the situation of Western societies ever since the Industrial Revolution. He it as a progressive degeneration, a process which he believed intensified after World War II.

Institutions can degenerate due to crises – revolts and revolutions, invasions by aggressive alien cultures, natural mega-disasters such as massive earthquakes and floods, and the more gradual decline of the socio-economic and cultural order. But Western civilization has been, according to Gehlen, for some time now subjected to a gradual decline of its institutions due to a pervasive, still progressing process of industrialization. The process is, Gehlen argues, a historical-cultural threshold.

Gehlen sees in the evolutionary history of mankind two such cultural thresholds which he called absolute to boot. The first absolute threshold that man transgressed occurred in the neolithic era. It was the transition from a dynamic hunting culture to a more static and domesticated agricultural society. In this transition, monotheism pushed aside animism and polytheism, and traditional institutions took a firm grip on sedentary human beings. The second absolute threshold took place in modernity when agrarian culture yielded to industrial culture. This transition, Gehlen claimed while writing in the 1940s and 1950s, is still not completed. He would probably view today's revolutionary developments in the information and communication technology not as post-industrialism but rather as a further radicalization of industrialism. Meanwhile, the monotheism of the first threshold gave way to a pervasive desacralization, disenchantment and secularization of the world which paved the way for the spectacular advance of the (natural) sciences and allied rational technologies. Naturally, rational bureaucracy as the dominant principle of organization also contributed to the penetration of rationality in all corners and compartments of modern life. Not one sector in society, not a nerve in man's body and soul is exempt from the influence of this rationalization. The process started two centuries ago and will continue its advance in maybe another two centuries. Meanwhile, it is impossible, Gehlen adds in a rare apocalyptic reflection, to determine what will perish in this fire, what will be melted down, and what will be able to resist successfully.

One thing is certain, however: while we cross this second absolute threshold institutions, formerly taken for granted, are being reduced to phrases, hollow conventions, idle formulas. Insecurity is the unavoidable result. The taken-for-granted aspect diminishes, while permanent reflections and deliberations with others and with oneself increase. As a result, a common and quite general indeterminacy gets hold of society as a whole. Moreover, since man's firm connection with institutions is gradually being severed, he is thrown back upon himself – upon his subjectivity, the abodes of his inner world. The impressions and stimuli which in an industrial society continue to grow in number and in intensity, pour in incessantly and massively, and impinge on the impulses and desires which, left to their own devices, are chaotic and unstructured. This, of course, contributes to insecurity, mental confusion and psychological stress and instability. The institutions are no longer able to drain these tensions and confusions away. All one can do with them, is to reflect upon them and to experience them in narcissistic, if not masochistic sensations. In this context Gehlen has some pertinent and sarcastic things to say about psychotherapies and the theories of Freud and Jung, the supreme ideologues of our *Spätkultur*.

This de-institutionalization and its upshot, subjectivism, affect the very anthropological foundation of humanity: behavior. Being biologically ill equipped to survive in nature, we saw before, man needs to act, needs to produce in order to compensate for this evolutionary weakness. Subjectivism, however, shies away from action and production, and is much more contemplative and keen on consumption. Gehlen calls it the 'quietism of the wish to consume'. He regards it as a new form of passivity which should be seen, he claims, as a historical variant of 'femininization'. In a sense, he continues, subjectivism entails a pervasive form of 'primitivization' as well, because being subjected to complex and abstract societal structures and thrown back upon one's own chaotic impulses and needs, man searches for the security of simple, concrete, useful, easy to handle ideas, notions, theorems and theories. Modern media deliver precisely that: images, sounds and simple language.

But there is a paradox at work here, because this primitivization is paired with a growing 'intellectualization' or, as Gehlen dubs it, 'conceptualization' (*Verbegrifflichung*). Science, technology and bureaucracy – the Big Three of Modernity, so to say – promote a steady rationalization and an equivalent weakening of the sensory dimensions of human perception. It is a strange paradox: on the one hand, modern man revels in emotional, irrational, passive consumption, while on the other hand, he lives with and thinks in abstract concepts which are the instruments of his permanent reflections. The paradox can be explained rather easily: when thoughts are no longer formed and directed by institutions, they will grow abstract and float around freely, while simultaneously emotions and impulses are set free to thrive and prosper. Gehlen finds multiple examples in the world of politics and in particular in the world of modern art. One of his finest books, incidentally, is a perceptive historical-sociological analysis of modern art.[15]

Intellectuals – academics, students, journalists, writers, artists – are singled out by Gehlen as the producers of the abstract ideas, notions, theorems and theories which are then drained away and delivered to permanent subjectivistic reflections on the part of these producers and their customers. Gehlen is fond of quoting Schumpeter on this point who once described intellectuals as people who possess and guard the power of (written and spoken) words (and, we should add, of images and pictures too), but who unlike other people do not have any direct responsibility over practical matters. They constitute a class which is privileged since they are practically and legally exempt from insoluble ethical conflicts and problems. In a sense, within the context of a democratic society they are in the comfortable position of being able to say and do what they want, and they are most of the time eager to make abundant use of this prerogative. In doing so they are not plagued by the ethic of responsibility, which stands to reason because responsibility is a concept that only makes sense, if there are concrete consequences to be settled in public. There are no consequences in the case of the words and actions of intellectuals. The moral consequences of this fact, Gehlen concludes wryly, are disastrous.

We arrive here at the heart of Gehlen's theory of institutions – his moral philosophy.[16] There are two central ideas which draw attention here. First, his belief that subjectivism will not lead to immoralism or amoralism, but on the contrary to a hypertrophied morality. Secondly, that the state is the only institution which could successfully curb subjectivism, if, that is, the state demonstrates in practice an ethos of strength and stern will, and not an ethos of weak, familistic humanitarianism.

To begin with the first point, when institutions are no longer able to guide the actions of individuals, and when people, as a result, whirl around in permanent reflections, fed by abstract concepts and irrational impulses, morality will grow abstract, vague, general and thereby rather pervasive and penetrative. In a sense, morality will grow neutral but, Gehlen warns, that does not mean that it will also be more tolerant than the traditional and firmly institutionalized morality of agrarian society. Modern morality presents a kind of nihilism which allows and validates everything, except one thing: the defense and maintenance of a traditional, allegedly conservative ethos based upon clear values and norms, tied to clear distinctions of class and status. Such an alleged conservatism, Gehlen claims, encounters a fanatic defense of freedom which in fact is a non-committal liberty, and a defense of equality which in fact is rather egalitarian. This fanatic libertarianism and egalitarianism, spread about in particular by the intellectual elite composed of left-of-center academics, journalists and artists, constitutes an inflated hyper-morality.

Under the disguise of a benign humanitarianism this hyper-morality is usually quite aggressive. Only very few people have the will and the courage to stand up to it. Being inclined to adjust to the passive ethos of subjectivism, most people accept the aggressiveness of these pundits of hyper-morality. This adjustment is facilitated because hyper-morality is kind, humane, and gentle. That is, as long as one does not oppose it. The choice in favor of hyper-morality is, of course, expedited by the absence of vital institutions as objective points of orientation.

Remarkably and also somewhat surprisingly in view of his previously discussed theory of the 'second threshold', Gehlen believes that this hyper-morality is not that modern at all, but rather a survival of an ancient, premodern clannish morality. It is a survival of the ethos of the extended family whose members were benign towards each other and vicious towards outsiders and strangers. Morally the members of the clan or the extended family were subjected to an ethos of solidarity, equality and fraternity. In Weber's well-known typology this was a rather irrational (and Gehlen would add, weak and feminine) ethic of ultimate ends. It stood in sharp contrast to the warrior morality of princes, rulers and states which, again in Weber's typology, presented a stern and strong ethos of responsibility. The former is oceanic, vague and soft; the latter practical, concrete and harsh. Gehlen compares them to Nietzsche's well known morality types *Sklavenmoral* and

Herrenmoral. Indeed, in his view, modern hyper-morality is typically an oceanic slave morality that feeds on submissive, allegedly democratic egalitarianism and libertarianism. It is also an abstract familism which spreads a soft blanket of humanitarianism over insecure, directionless individuals who are made to believe that the whole world constitutes a Family of Man.

Gehlen confronts this hyper-morality head-on with a call for a stern and, if necessary, harsh and uncompromising morality of responsibility. It is in effect a plea for a true *Herrenmoral* which can ultimately only be enacted and promoted by the state. Speaking of the German Federal Republic he pleads for a political morality which will not ideologically gloss over the defeat of the German nation (he means 1945, of course), or sweep it under the carpet of affluence and consumption. In line with such a morality the German state must admit without cheap confessions that the murder of countless innocent people should never have happened, but it should also act without hesitation and false humanitarian pretenses when law and order, security and safety, have to be restored. Above all, the state has in this respect a moral and pedagogical task to perform.

Yet Gehlen realizes that this state is a thing of the past. The modern affluent society gave birth to a welfare state which has spread a blanket of comprehensive care over its citizens. Referring to the abundant subsidies dispensed by this caring state, he jibes that Leviathan has turned into a milk cow. It engenders in people an ethos of easy consumption and happiness, which ousted the ethos appropriate to the state – an ethos of service and duty. At this point he is fond of ridiculing the allegedly increasing gender confusion and the rise of what he called femininization. When beginning their military service, recruits of the *Bundeswehr*, he jibes, stand in front of the barracks nowadays wearing earrings under long curls, carrying babies on their arms, accompanied by their wives or partners. As young fathers they probably push prams caringly through the shopping malls. Where the army was the model institution in the Preussian past, nowadays the family is the model institution for society and scores of societal organizations including the army. Virtues such as loyalty, fidelity and duty have become alien components of a bygone morality. Instead, modern subjectivists search for self-expression, self-fulfillment, emotional satisfaction, and, of course, authenticity.

It stands to reason that Gehlen's defense of a state ethos over a familial ethos is at odds with Christianity which, as witnessed by the Sermon on the Mount, propagates a morality of brotherly love and sacrifice. Christian ethic is also at odds with any kind of divinization of the state and abhors an allegedly strong and honorable *Herrenmoral*. Gehlen is fully aware of this and goes to some length to criticize Protestant theology. In a sense he repeats the debate between the 'German Christians' (*Deutsche Christen*) who collaborated with the nazi regime and the 'Confessing Church' (*Bekennende Kirche*) that opposed it. He sympathizes clearly with the former. His arrows of contempt are directed in particular at Karl Barth, who was, along with the pacifist Martin Niemöller, the most influential theologian of the 'Confessing Church'.

Meanwhile, it should be noted that in this theory of morality and hypermorality the Industrial Revolution no longer figures as an absolute cultural threshold which Gehlen had singled out before as the objective cause and origin of the decline of institutions. Now it is modern man, in particular the modern intellectual, who is portrayed as the originator of the apocalyptic *Spätkultur*. Moreover, Gehlen hardly conceals the fact that for him the 'defeat of 1945' is still a part of undigested history. Although he did abhor the holocaust (and has never been anti-semitic), he joined the Nazi party and remained a member until the end of the Third Reich. Particularly in his moral philosophy it becomes painfully clear that as a German he could not come to terms with the enormous gap between Nazi Germany's totalitarian regime of 1933-45 and the democracy which after 1945 was restored in the German Federal Republic. Ironically, in a subjectivistic and permanent reflection, he airs his political frustration and moral resentment in statements which in their vulgarity stand in contrast to the remainder of his intellectual legacy which excels in creative thoughtfulness and intellectual pizzazz and creativity.

There is, moreover, a contradiction in the reactionary political stance he took. Are not fascism and Nazism the pre-eminent products of resentful subjectivism caused by the dramatic decline of democratic institutions after the demise of Bismarck's unified empire and during the chaos of the Weimar Republic? The totalitarian state which the Nazis, or for that matter the Bolsheviks, erected and maintained with the use of brutal force, was of course in no way the strong moral state which Gehlen envisaged as the possible dam against the degeneration of society and culture allegedly brought about by subjectivism.

There is still another riddle in Gehlen's collaboration with the Nazis. Their philosophy was a concoction for simplistic biologism and platitudinous Social Darwinism, serving as legitimations of their murderous racism. Their platitudinously romantic notion of *das Volk* as the ultimate Germanic *Gemeinschaft* did fit Heidegger's subjectivistic and Germanic brand of existentialism but not at all Gehlen's anti-biologistic, anti-metaphysical theory of behavior and behavioral institutions. Also, unlike Heidegger's murky philosophy, it left no room for racism. In fact, during the war he was taken to task severely by Nazi 'philosophers' about these points. Gehlen, moreover, demonstrated time and again that he was not at all a 'Germanic' thinker. He was in search of an empirical, anti-idealistic philosophy, inspired by Anglo-Saxon pragmatism and behaviorism and he was also clearly influenced by French philosophers such as Bergson and Sorel who are often quoted and praised by him. Later, in the 1960s and 1970s he was intellectually taken with by the writings of Hannah Arendt. He would not even bother to mention Heidegger or similar Germanic theorists and thinkers. He preferred to debate with philosophical and sociological opponents such as Adorno and Habermas whose ideas he appreciated intellectually but, needless to say, rejected politically.

Finally, an important source of Gehlen's moral and political faults is a methodological one. He systematically absolutizes and reifies institutions, and neglects their historical and thus alterable nature. As we saw in the first chapter, it is important to distinguish analytically and methodologically between universal, ahistorical institutions and concrete, historical institutes. Marriage as a sustainable and durable partnership between two individuals is an institution which can be found all over the world and far back in history. Yet, monogamic, heterosexual marriage is a specifically Western institute. When this institute changes over time – when for example homosexual couples plea for the legal confirmation of their durable bond – one could lament this change, but it is not a decline of the institution, called marriage. In fact, institutions are, as Gehlen himself argued, fundamental anthropological structures. He preferred the Kantian concept 'categories' and that renders them *a priori*. There cannot therefore be any *Institutionsabbau*, the decline or destruction of institutions. Existing, empirical, historical institutes, however, can decline or change radically. Institutes come and go, or what is more probable, as we will see in the next chapter, they *transform*. In a fully modernized society this transformation of institutes occurs more rapidly than in traditional, agrarian societies but this difference in speed and kind is still not substantial enough to conclude that modern societies are on the brink of institutional degeneration and collapse.

Wilson on *culturgens*, Dawkins on *memes*

Inspired by their teacher Driesch, Plessner and Gehlen tried to design a philosophical anthropology within the context of Darwinian evolutionary biology. Gehlen was also much inspired by zoologists such as Adolf Portmann and ethologists like Konrad Lorenz, and by cultural anthropologists like Ruth Benedict and Margaret Mead as well. But despite their biological training Plessner and Gehlen managed to avoid the pitfalls of a platitudinous biologism which certainly in Germany in the 1930s was notoriously popular. They emphasized, each in their own idiosyncratic ways, the fact that it is the specific nature of human beings as a species to transcend biology. Gehlen in particular focussed on the biological weaknesses of the human species which are apparent, if one compares man with the animal. In strictly biological terms, man's constitution is not in itself very fit for survival. He needs a compensation which is offered by the cultural institutions as traditional patterns of behavior. Institutions, as we saw in chapter one, are objectified and collective forms of action and interaction. They constitute in a sense a 'second nature', i.e. culture, which is adapted to man's need for stability. An adaptation which 'first nature' fails to offer. Or phrased differently, during the evolutionary process the human species had to liberate itself from the confinements of its biological condition in order to survive. Institutions constitute a 'second nature' of semi-instinctive, yet learned adaptive reflexes. These reflexes, this learned institutional behavior is, of course, historical, not biological. They enable the human species to survive as a lifeform.

These biological considerations, mainly put to writing in the 1930s, are now outdated. Particularly in view of *sociobiology* and modern *genetics* these theories should be revised and amended. But I hasten to add that Edward Wilson's seminal sociobiological thoughts and Richard Dawkins's ideas about the interplay of genes and 'memes', which I shall discuss briefly in the present section, suffer from a double fault.[17] First, their main focus is rather one-sidedly psychological because their unit of analysis is the individual. Much like rational-choice economists they fail to focus on collectivities: on groups, generations, tribes, societies, nations. These collectivities are, of course, made up of individuals but since Emile Durkheim, sociologists know that a social and cultural whole is always more than and different from the sum of its constituent components. To Wilson and Dawkins the essence of culture is the individual mind, not the collective mind of groups, generations, tribes, societies, and nations. The tribal culture of a pre-industrial, so-called 'primitive' society, or for that matter the corporate culture of a modern, industrial firm cannot be understood adequately, if one only focuses psychologically on the mind and behavior of isolated individuals. It is a collective culture which is passed on to newcomers and new generations who in a sense are coerced by them to act, think and feel in predetermined ways. Wilson and Dawkins lack a basic sociological understanding of collective behavior, let alone of Durkheim's focus on institutional patterns of behavior as a 'collective consciousness'.

Secondly, Wilson and Dawkins seem to ignore the fact that man is an acting and interacting animal, that it is not the mind and psyche as such, but *behavior* (taken as the unity of acting, thinking and feeling) which is the core of man's nature. Mind in the human brain, as demonstrated for instance by George Herbert Mead, is not the cause and origin of culture but should instead be seen as an emergent property, arising from man's ongoing actions and interactions. Wilson and Dawkins c.s. adhere to the Cartesian dictum 'I think, therefore I am'. This was re-phrased in Mead's 'social behaviorism': we interact, therefore we are able to think.

With this double warning in mind, I shall now briefly discuss the contributions of Wilson's sociobiology and Dawkins's genetics to the reformulation of European philosophical anthropology. As will become apparent, their contributions are particularly relevant to the conceptual distinction between 'institutions' and 'institutes' developed in chapter one.

A weak spot in European ethology and philosophical anthropology has been the introduction of 'instincts' as the biological determinants of animal conduct. It is actually a black box concept, as it is hard to determine what instincts precisely are and where in the body they can be located. Consequently, it is of little help to define next man's special position in the cosmos in terms of lack of instincts. What are precisely, to quote a concept of Gehlen, 'residual instincts'? The intentions were clear: like Plessner, Gehlen, who was, as we have seen, averse to metaphysics and philosophical Idealism, tried to found anthropology on biology, and both of them argued in terms of Darwinian evolutionary theory. Both of them also tried to avoid a primitive and platitudinous kind of biologism and made an attempt to somehow connect the realm of 'nature' with that of 'nurture' without giving causal primacy to either one. But certainly in view of modern genetics and sociobiology their views of 'nature' are rather outdated.

Genes, located in chromosomes and the 'double helix', and not alleged instincts are the basic components of what life is made up of. In answer to the critics who saw in his brand of sociobiology a crude form of biological determinism, Wilson emphasized that culture cannot be reduced to physiology and biology, and that cultures differ greatly in time and in space. But despite this often bewildering variety of cultures, human beings are potentially able to understand one another and to somehow communicate with one another. This must be attributed to the simple fact that they all inherited human genes from their ancestors. This is a remarkable fact. As Wilson pointed out, a Manhattan resident and a tribesman in New Guinea, separated from each other not just by thousands of kilometers but also by thousands of years of history and different cultural developments, are somehow able to communicate with each other. They share a set of genes that make such meaningful encounters possible. All human beings inherit from former generations the competence and inclination to adopt certain forms of behavior and certain social structures which in fact justify the concept of 'human nature'. Typical elements of this human nature are, according to Wilson, the division of labor between the sexes, the bond between parents and children, the heightened altruism towards the next of kin, the avoidance of incest, suspicion regarding strangers, a sense of tribal community, hierarchies of dominance, male dominance, territorial aggression with regard to scarce resources, etc.

Social scientists have always attributed these human chracteristics to culture and thus to learned behavior. The sociobiologist rather attributes these apparently universal components of human nature to the fund of human genes. But Wilson hastens to add that they are enacted and historically realized in a vast variety of cultural settings. This then poses the problem of genetic versus cultural determinism (usually rather crudely formulated as the nature-nurture debate): to what extent is human behavior genetically determined, to what extent is it culturally learned and adopted? Or is there perhaps some sort of interaction between the genetic and the cultural factors in the evolution of the human species?

Everybody knows, Wilson begins, that human behavior is culturally transmitted, but culture is a product of the brain which is again a product of genetic evolution. The brain contains large amounts of perceptions which were imputed through the sense organs. Moreover, it is the brain which determines what is and what is not to be learned. These elementary components of the brain – the perceptions and the learned material – exert an as yet unknown influence upon the cultural environment. However, this very process of genetic evolution took place within a culture-dominated environment, with the result that cultural changes in their turn may have affected the brain and its further development. The question then arises what kind of interplay between the genetic and the cultural evolution created the human mind?

Wilson and his fellow researchers formulated a controversial hypothesis which they dubbed the *gen-culture co-evolution*. Man's very complex biological evolution in which genes occupy a strategic position, was accompanied by an equally complex cultural evolution in which *culturgens* play the crucial role. These are bits of information, value judgments, modes of behavior, thought patterns, etc. which are available within a particular cultural context. Individuals choose from the available 'culturgens' during the course of their lives. That is, human beings adopt certain marriage ceremonies, religious rituals, creation myths, scientific theorems, ethical prescripts, patterns of thought, etc. from a great amount of available alternatives. As an equivalent of natural selection some of these choices reap better survival and reproduction chances than others. There are, Wilson claims, certain physiologically based preferences which he calls 'epigenetic rules': the rules which during genetic evolution fostered the choice of successful 'culturgens' and developed gradually during the evolution of many generations into so-called human nature.

But this is not the place to discuss Wilson's theory critically in detail. Naturally, the idea of a gen-culture co-evolution has been criticized by biologists. I am unable to assess this debate for lack of proper biological knowledge. However, there was also, as could have been expected, quite a row in the ranks of cultural anthropologists, when in the 1970s Wilson published his sociobiological theory for the first time. They decried his approach as deterministic. Much of this critique can be attributed to a rather tenacious humanistic stance which usually rejects – ironically as in a Pavlov-reaction – any attempt to somehow bridge the natural sciences and the humanities. This reaction is a bit short-sighted. Even the staunchest defender of the humanities would admit that there are universal 'institutions', universal 'structures' (Lévi-Strauss), universal 'competences' (Chomsky), instinct-like 'residues' (Pareto). It is then but a small step to define these 'structures', 'competences', 'residues' – i.e. *institutions* – as being ultimately grounded in man's biological constitution. They are limited in number, are not or very little subject to change, and somehow constitute a discernible universal human nature. And then there are the historical and alterable *institutes*, 'culturgens' (Wilson), 'memes' (Dawson), spread all-over the globe in great numbers and in a bewildering variety.

It is logical to view institutions as the biological, genetic foundation of institutes. A comparison with language is helpful. Languages consist of a restricted number of linguistic roots from which many words can be produced. The roots do not change much, but the words and their composition in sentences enter into an infinite number of variations. They alter continuously over time. Language is perpetually changing and developing. Furthermore, as linguistic structuralism has pointed out, the many languages which exist (and have existed) all over the globe must somehow have (had) a common source or foundation which can be best defined in terms of a limited amount of linguistic *competences*. Sociobiologists will be inclined to view these competences in biological, i.e. genetic terms.

Like Wilson, Dawkins thinks Darwinians can no longer afford to disregard the spectacular phenomena of culture, cultural evolution and cultural variability. He begins by emphasizing a basic similarity between 'nature' and 'culture': nature is subjected to and for its survival dependent on *replication* and the genes are the replicators; culture, on the other hand, depends for its survival and continuity on *imitation* which is a different kind of replication.

Dawkins abbreviated the Greek noun for imitation, – *to mimema* – and constructed the neologism *meme* as the cultural equivalent of the biological gene. 'Memes' are what Wilson has called 'culturgens'.

As examples of memes Dawkins mentions ideas, musical tunes, catchphrases, in short bits and pieces of culture. But he also adds techniques of making pots or building arches, which, in view of our definition of institutions as patterns of behavior, is quite significant. Culture consists indeed of material goods (books, houses, chairs, cars, etc.), immaterial goods (art, music, science, ideas, emotions, etc.), services (healthcare, public policies, banking, etc.) and above all, of ways of acting, thinking and feeling (institutions). Dawkins seems to restrict his notion of memes to immaterial goods and institutions, although he does not elaborate on the latter. He seems to lump them together with the immaterial goods, treating them as mental things, pieces of the mind, products of the (individual) brain. This is an unfortunate restriction.

Just as genes reproduce and propagate themselves in the gene pool by being transmitted from body to body through sperm or eggs, memes are passed on in the meme pool (i.e. culture) from person to person, from brain to brain, and this happens through imitation. In a discussion with someone else I may pick up an interesting idea – a meme – which I then take with me, brood upon, and eventually pass on (amended or maybe distorted) to a third person. The idea becomes popular, and is passed on from brain to brain through written and spoken words, just as genes replicate themselves via sperm and cells.

Dawkins considers the idea of God as a very prominent and forceful meme. It is unknown how it emerged in the meme pool, probably a very long time ago. But how does it replicate itself? Via written and spoken words, via ceremonies and rituals, embellished by music and art. Why does it have such an apparent and almost everlasting survival value – survival, of course, in the context of the meme pool? Its value lies, Dawkins believes, in its great psychological appeal, in its capacity to provide answers to grave existential questions and problems regarding life and death, injustice and inadequacies, etc. 'God exists, if only in the form of a meme with high survival value, or infective power, in the environment provided by human culture.'[18]

Just as some genes are more successful in their replication and propagation within the gene pool than other genes, some memes last longer in the meme pool than others. Cultural success is thus analogous to natural selection. The replication of memes goes, in the first place, from brain to brain: the tune, or the idea catches on, sticks in one's mind and is passed on to other brains. But Dawkins also puts emphasis on the material reproduction in books and sheet music that can be passed on from generation to generation.

Sociologists prefer to emphasize the imitation processes that occur in human actions and interactions. If Dawkins claims that Jewish laws were able to propagate themselves so successfully over thousands of years because of the permanence of written records, he forgets that prior to the diaspora they were passed on orally for many centuries from generation to generation. Jewish tradition memes were first replicated and propagated in the *shul*. Purposeful actions and meaningful interactions within the context of organizations and institutions are the indispensable carriers of cultural memes. In short, it is not brains but actions and interactions (behavior) which are the carriers of Dawkins's memes. It is not just individuals who think, but institutions as well, as Mary Douglas has argued.[19]

Returning once again to the distinction between universal institutions and historical institutes the suggestive idea emerges that the former are biological (genetic) structures and the latter historical (cultural) 'memeplexes'. I must admit though that I am not competent to determine if, how, and to what extent genes and memes, institutions and institutes, are causally interdependent. Wilson came up with the idea of a parallel evolution ('culturgen co-evolution'). Susan Blackmore is even more radical in separating biological and cultural evolution. If I understand her correctly, her 'science of memetics' in which 'the meme's eye view' is taken, comes close to an almost 'idealist' position. There are, according to Blackmore, two different, independent types of replicators and correspondingly two different, independent Darwinian evolutions: the genes and the memes. The latter are replicated and transported from mind to mind through language. Imitation is the crucial process here.

A final remark: these sociobiological and genetic theories demonstrate the obsoleteness of C.P. Snow's 'two cultures'.[20] There is in fact a remarkable elective affinity these days between the natural and the cultural sciences. Sociologists should participate in and contribute to the debates about genes, memes, culturgens, memeplexes, co-evolution, etc. In these debates observations are being made which certainly bear on (cultural) sociology, although they are still too much focused on the individual brain and individual behavior. Emile Durkheim preluded some basic notions of 'meme co-evolution' when he remarked that *individual* consciousness somehow emerges from the physiological brain cells, next acquires a momentum of its own, and then through interaction and imitation develops into a *collective* consciousness. The notion of 'memeplexes' is also very similar to Durkheim's idea of institutions. Such a sociological framework is still lacking in the present sociobiological debates. A sociological theory of institutions, I am convinced, could be a much needed replenishment.[21]

Institutional ambiguities

We must now in conclusion briefly summarize the advantages of institutions and their endemic dangers.

To start with the latter, one does not have to be an existentialist to admit that institutions have a tendency to curb man's freedom and creativity. They are, after all, collective patterns of behavior, or as Durkheim aptly called them, collective ways of acting, thinking and feeling. These patterns have been passed on to us by previous generations, and as much as we may change and alter them, we do pass them on again to the next generations. Institutions thus are inherently traditional, and therefore more 'things' of the past than of the future. They have, as Gehlen in particular emphasized, the tendency to acquire a measure of autonomy and objectivity. It is admittedly a bit uncomfortable to reflect upon this, but it is an inescapable fact that we are born into an institutional context, and that we will sooner or later all die out of it. Meanwhile, the institutions will continue to do their work. Sociologically, Paul Tillich's 'chain of being' is in effect a chain of institutions.

Yet there is more than just a curtailment of freedom and creativity. As Durkheim argued convincingly, institutions are coercive structures that mold our acting, thinking and feeling. And they do so, as Gehlen once wrote, according to their own regularity (*Eigengesetzlichkeit*). This almost willfull coercion on the part of institutions imposes strong restrictions on individual behavior. To take a simple example, as a sociology teacher in a university I am supposed to teach sociology in the classroom and not to recite poems or sing songs. That is to say, like countless other university professors before me, with me and doubtlessly after me, I have the duty to perform a pre-designed role that is part of a rather ancient institution with, up untill recently, a quite venerable tradition. Of course, as Plessner emphasized, I have the liberty to perform the role creatively. After all , I do it my way! Yet, it cannot be denied that the institutional rules pertaining to this social role impose strict and rather coercive restrictions on my behavior in (and even outside) the classroom.

Being traditional and autonomous, institutions tend to grow abstract, formalistic, and ceremonial. That is, their initial sense and meaning, their original substantial rationality, and their original reason for existence tend to evaporate during the passage of time. They exist and they function for the simple reason that they exist and function. In due time these functions can differ considerably from the original motives that were laid at their foundation. To take up this example once more, the Swiss Guard at the Vatican is still composed of Swiss soldiers who are dressed and armed as they were dressed and armed centuries ago. The original motive behind this curious institution was to be the papal bodyguards, and it was believed in those days that the Swiss, as mercenaries in various European countries, were considered to be the most reliable recruits for the job. This original motive and function has meanwhile faded. The Swiss Guard today functions rather as a ceremonial embellishment of the papal dignity and authority. If the pope has bodyguards these days, they must be professionally trained policemen in plain clothes.[22]

Ceremonialism is usually harmless, but if it extends into formalism it may be harmful, since it will block developments and innovations. This is further exacerbated, when people believe their institutions were given by God or the gods. In traditional agrarian societies institutions often acquired such metaphysical and often also magical features: they were given by God, the gods or Nature, they were holy and sacred, and therefore taboo. Changes were then seen and experienced as sacrilegious blasphemies. Institutions, even the radically secularized ones, have indeed the tendency to stifle change and development.

Yet, the predesigned roles we play, and the traditional institutions we grow into and eventually will die out of, carry promises as well. Institutionalized roles, to begin with, help us to reduce the overwhelming complexity of behavioral alternatives. If we did not learn to perform roles on the stage called 'society', we would act erratically, do this, that and the other or, more probably, nothing at all. We would sooner or later – most probably very soon – be exposed to a severe clash of inner impulses and outer stimuli, and then perish in chaos and confusion. In traditional rural society roles were part of a rather strict and limited script to which people adhered collectively. In contrast, modern individuals have infinitely more room for improvisations and impromptus. There is, so to speak, a floating space within which they are able to improvise and experiment. However, as 'thin' as modern institutes may be (see chapter four) they do impose certain limits on modern behavior. As much as modern individuals may dream of and long for a life without limits (chapter five), they will have to cope with the biological bottom line that human existence is impossible without institutions. There is, in other words, an institutional imperative. Moreover, we should realize that these very institutional limits offer great opportunities for improvisations and experimentation. Indeed, many of man's experiments, innovations and improvisations consist of the ongoing exploration of his biological and cultural limits. This exploration begins with the refusal to take these limits for granted. In this respect Max Scheler's definition of man as a creature that is able to say 'No!' to reality, to deny even life itself, is profound.[23]

Moreover, the coercive autonomy of institutions, so much emphasized by Durkheim and Gehlen, should not be exaggerated. To begin with, the two of them, and related institutional theorists, tend to reify institutions, that is, to treat them as if they were concrete and empirical realities. In order to avoid this methodological fallacy one should heed Max Weber's rather nominalistic observation that institutions such as marriage, school or state consists in actual fact of countless actions and interactions between married people, students and politicians or bureaucrats. Marriage, school and state are but 'names', concepts which Weber – although this is a somewhat irritating habit – used to place inside quotation marks: 'marriage', 'school' and 'state'. Yet, Weber did not stick to this kind of individualism. He fully acknowledged the sociological fact that there are meaningful configurations which transcend individual actions and interactions, and even go beyond the generations. He called them 'meaning structures' (*Sinngebilde*). These are, of course, institutions.

If looked at in a more nominalistic vein, institutions are not just coercive strictures but also meaningful structures that render human behavior understandable. We understand the words 'two times two is four', when we realize that they were murmured in a shop, or in a classroom. In the shop they indicate that the price of a commodity is being calculated, in the classroom the very same formula relates to teaching and learning the tables of multiplication. Indeed, without institutions human behavior would be completely incomprehensible. Ethnologists begin to understand a pre-industrial tribe after they have become acquainted with its basic institutions. This was precisely Bronislaw Malinowski's point, when he told his contemporaries that fieldwork and participant observation, not the collection of tools and objects, are the main roads to an understanding of strange and foreign cultures. The first thing an anthropologist ought to do, is to learn the language of the people he sets out to study. Next, the focus of the true cultural anthropologist is on their idiosyncratic institutions, their traditional and collective ways of acting, thinking and feeling.

One need not embrace Gehlen's conservatism to acknowledge the basic fact that institutions or institutional roles also provide human beings with a taken-for-granted commonsense and a basic pre-reflective consensus. My role as a university professor is institutionalized to such an extent that I do not have to negotiate with my students how to conduct the lecture session each time I walk into the lecture hall or the classroom. Likewise, when driving my car through the traffic of my city – an intricate institution indeed! – I do, of course, pay attention to the movements of my fellow drivers but large portions of my behavior is pre-reflective, or under-reflective. It is an institutionalized routine. When the traffic light, for example, turns green I do not hesitate, I do not ask myself reflectively what the meaning of the red, yellow and green lights actually is or could possibly be. My foot presses the accelerator without further deliberations and therefore without any delay. In other words, institutions promote efficiency and help us to conduct our lives smoothly.

Finally, institutions provide us, as Gehlen puts it, with a beneficent security and above all with a meaningful order. Due to the fact that the behavior of others is institutionalized, we can depend and count on them in our interactions, and we can minimize our risks in dealing with them. Indeed, institutions are the cornerstones of our trust. In this sense, they function as the lubricants of our daily actions and interactions. Social life and economic transactions are impossible without institutions. This means, that the anarchist dream of a radically free and equal community in which there are no institutions like church, state, marriage, family and school is a sociological impossibility. In fact, it is a sociological utopia, a sociological 'nowhere' which easily turns into a nightmare. In a radically anarchistic, de-institutionalized community people would have to debate and to negotiate each step, each decision, each conclusion, and they would have to do so each day, each moment of the day. Social and economic life would stagnate, and then collapse into chaos. The historical experience has taught that anarchistic communes develop divisions of labor almost immediately, and someone soon takes up the role of leader. That is, liberty and equality are subjected to restrictions which over time show the tendency to aggravate.

Institutionalization is indeed inescapable, whenever and wherever people live, act, and interact together. This is also why societies after a radical upheaval such as a revolution seem to develop patterns of repression which not so much in ideological content as in institutional forms are very similar to the forms of repression people had rebelled against. Often the terror after the revolution is infinitely more inhuman and bloodthirsty, as was demonstrated by the regimes that took command after the bourgeois French Revolution in 1789, the Bolshevist Russian Revolution in 1917, and the islamic-shiite Iranian Revolution in 1979.

---

1. Peter L. Berger, Thomas Luckmann, *The Social Construction of Reality. A Treatise in the Sociology of Knowledge,* (Garden City, NY: Doubleday, 1966).
2. See Marjorie Grene, *Approaches to a Philosophical Biology,* 1965, (New York, London: Basic Books, 1968).The first three chapters discuss the ideas of Adolf Portmann, Helmuth Plessner and F.J.J. Buytendijk.
3. Cf. 'Helmuth Plessner', Grene, *o.c.,* pp. 55-118; Hans Redeker, *Helmuth Plessner oder Die verkörperte Philosophie,* (Berlin: Duncker & Humblot, 1993).
4. Cf. Grene, *o.c.,* pp. 119-182.
5. Helmuth Plessner, *Die Stufen des Organischen und der Mensch,* 1926, (Berlin: Walter de Gruyter, 1965)

6. Helmuth Plessner, 'Grenzen der Gemeinschaft. Eine Kritik des sozialen Radikalismus', 1924, in *Gesammelte Schriften V,* (Frankfurt am Main: Suhrkamp Verlag, 1981), pp. 7-134.

7. Helmuth Plessner, 'Zur Anthropologie des Schauspielers', 1948, in *Zwischen Philosophie und Gesellschaft* (Between Philosophy and Society), (Bern: Francke Verlag, 1953), pp. 180-192.

8. Helmuth Plessner, *Das Problem der Oeffentlichkeit und die Idee der Entfremdung,* Göttinger Universitätsreden, 28 (Göttingen, 1960).

9. Cf. Manuel Castells, *The Rise of the Network Society,* vol. I of *The Information Age. Economy, Society and Culture,* 1996, (Oxford, UK: Blackwell, 1997).

10. Cf. Victor Farías, *Heidegger and Nazism,* (Philadelphia: Temple University Press, 1989).

11. Cf. Peter L. Berger, Hansfried Kellner, 'Arnold Gehlen and the Theory of Institutions', in *Social Research,* 32:1,(1965), pp. 110ff. Two of Gehlen's books have been published in English translation: *Man: His Nature and Place in the World,* (New York: Columbia University Press, 1988) and *Man in the Age of Technolo gy,* 1980, *(New York: Columbia University Press,* 1989).

12. Cf. Grene, 'Adolf Portmann', *o.c.,* pp.3-54.

13. Friedrich Nietzsche, *Jenseits von Gut und Böse,* para 62, (*Werke in Drei Bände,* Band Zwei, Karl Schlechta, ed., (München: Carl Hanser Verlag, 1955), p. 623.

14. See his treatise *Urmensch und Spätkultur,* (Aboriginal Man and Late Culture), (Bonn: Athenäum Verlag, 1956).

15. Arnold Gehlen, *Zeit-Bilder. Zur Soziologie und Ästhetik der modernen Malerei,* (Towards a Sociology and Esthetic Theory of Modern Art), 1960, (Frankfurt am Main: Vittorio Klostermann, 1986).

16. Arnold Gehlen, *Moral und Hypermoral. Eine pluralistische Ethik*, (Morality and Hypermorality. A Pluralistic Ethic), (Frankfurt am Main: Athenäum Verlag, 1969).

17. The literature on sociobiology and modern genetics is massive. In this section I used Edward O. Wilson, *Naturalist,* (New York: Island Press/Shearwater Books, 1994), in particular chapters 16 and 17; Richard Dawkins, *The Selfish Gene,* 1976, (Oxford, New York: Oxford University Press, 1989); Richard Dawkins, *River Out of Eden,* 1995, (London: Phoenix, 1997); and Susan Blackmore, *The Meme Machine,* (Oxford: Oxford University Press, 1999).

18. Dawkins, *The Selfish Gene,* p. 193.

19. Mary Douglas, *How Institutions Think,* (Syracuse, NY: Syracuse University Press, 1986).

20. See Edward O. Wilson, *Consilience. The Unity of Knowledge,* (New York: Alfred A. Knopf, 1998).

21. In view of Blackmore's recurrent emphasis on imitation it may be interesting to reread again Gabriel Tarde, *The Laws of Imitation,* 1888, translated by Elsie C. Parsons, (New York: Henry Holt, 1903).

22. See M.J. Smucker and A.C. Zijderveld, 'Structure and Meaning: Implications for the Analysis of Social Change', *The British Journal of Sociology,* 21:4, (December 1970), pp. 375-389.

23. Max Scheler, *Die Stellung des Menschen im Kosmos,* (Man's Position in the Cosmos), 1928, (Bern: Francke Verlag, 1962), p. 55: "Compared to the animal that always says 'Yes' to reality (....), man is the 'Naysayer', the 'ascetic of life', the eternal Protestant against all mere reality." My translation, AZ.

CHAPTER THREE

Institutions and History

A strained relationship

The end of history does not exist outside ideology and mythology. Human beings come to an end, but history does not as long as the human species exists. Whatever people do, think and feel, time marches on relentlessly. It is a somewhat morbid reflection, but to my mind nothing illustrates the essence of history more clearly and convincingly than our death. I am in good company though, because this was precisely what Koheleth (Ecclesiastes) in the Bible also meant. In any case, our lives ending in death are but small particles of history, and that is why history expresses the relativity of our individual existences. History is hated for this by many people. Naturally tyrants are the first to hate and, of course, dread history with a passion. They always try to manipulate the present, mythologize the past, and dictate the future. They believe such a destruction or dissolution of history legitimizes and prolongs the power they possess and hold on to. But even the strongest and most violent tyrant is eventually done in by death and thereby removed from the stage of history. Their bodies may be buried in impressive mausoleums, and even displayed in an embalmed state, as in Lenin's case. Yet, sooner or later most tyrants will be remembered by next generations as the leading actors in a nightmare.

History consists, of course, of a complex set of processes which connect the present to the past and the future. The reason why tyrants hate and dread history so passionately and try desperately to destroy or dissolve it, is simply because it cannot be manipulated. Tyrannical destruction or dissolution of history is usually attempted by means of a radical and strongly mythological re-writing of the past, an equally radical and mythological fixation of the future, and a mythological suffocation of the present. Such attempts, history has proved time and again, are doomed to fail eventually. The Nazi Third Reich and the communist Realm of Freedom and Equality presented perfect examples of attempts to put an end to history by usingapocalyptic mythologies and practices. They and not history came to an end. And an ignominious end it was in both cases. One should realize that the End of History has its own history. It wis on the whole a history of violence, terror and dehumanization.

However, there is still another end of history. For different political and socio-economic reasons people can lose their sense of the past and the future, and be lulled into a dull acceptance of the present. With extreme poverty, for instance, life is completely occupied by the daily struggle for survival. The past that led to this poverty is better not remembered, the future has nothing in store to dream about. Ironically, the opposite situation in which people enjoy extreme wealth and affluence, often has the very same effect. *Carpe diem* is the device, while the past and the future evaporate in the ongoing struggle to ward off boredom by a perpetual consumption of gadgets, food, drinks, drugs, ideas, and relationships. As with poverty, time spent in decadence ticks away relentlessly without being structured into anything worthy of being called history.[1]

These are, of course, extreme cases. In general, the lives of most people are extended between a past remembered and a future envisioned and dreamed about. Unlike animals, human beings are thoroughly embedded in history. But then, what exactly is history? The ordinary notion of history which, incidentally, is also quite tenacious among professional historians, is rather simplified: it is allegedly everything connected with the past. But an equally simple reflection casts doubt on such a definition. What happened one second ago is, according to this simple definition, history. But what happened one second ago, is in our experience still the present. Moreover, if we then define the future as everything that happens in the next second, we annihilate the present, because if the past began a second ago and the future sets in in the next second, the present is Point Zero. This might at first strike one as a profound idea (which has been elaborated phenomenologically by Edmund Husserl). But on second thought, certainly if looked at sociologically, this annihilation of the present is quite senseless, if not ridiculous. In fact, history starts with the present! The past is, to a considerable degree, a construction of the present, because we select from the myriad of past 'facts' (events, experiences, thoughts, feelings, memories, etc.) those that are deemed to be *presently* relevant to us. As the cliché goes, each generation writes its own history. There are scores of socio-economic, socio-cultural and political *interests* in the present that come into play, when people focus their attention on the past.[2] But the same holds true for the future. The present is inseparably linked to the future, since people have dreams, make plans, cherish utopian ideals, and they do so in terms of their individual and collective interests.

History, in short, is a chain that connects the past to the present and the present to the future. The present is the connecting link, the individual and collective interests are the triggers or the engines that put this chain in motion. In the present, scores of constructions and reconstructions of the past take place continuously. This happens above all in formal and informal, private and public, collective and individual memories. Memories, including individual and private memories, are framed in institutional structures.[3] Memories are attached to institutions such as the state, the family, the church, the school, the army, etc. Institutions are indeed the *cadres sociaux de la mémoire*. Leafing through family albums, for instance, gives a vivid impression of memories as social 'things'. These photographs give the beholder a distinct, often somewhat melancholic and almost existential sense of history.[4] Looking at the stilled faces of one's dead ancestors invites one unwittingly to reflect upon one's own inevitable death in the future. But the memories are often also more rational and systematic, i.e. scientific, as in the case of history as a humanities subject, taught and practiced within the institutional context of universities. Meanwhile, constructions of the future also occur in the present. Private or collective dreams and fantasies, philosophical and literary utopias, or, again, more rationally and systematically, planning procedures and scenario constructions, are attempts to grab hold of the future. Once more, such dreams and constructions usually take place in terms of the private and public, individual and collective interests of the present.

One thing is of special importance in this definition of history: it is not just 'the past', i.e. everything that has happened until this present moment. History is an ongoing process which places the present in the dynamic context of both the past and the future. The present, not the past is the axis of history. It is from the here-and-now that we look back and (re)construct the past and in doing so we are driven by individual and collective interests. It is likewise from the here-and-now and influenced by present interests that we look forward to and construct the future in dreams and in plans. Moreover, it is within the context of *institutions* that history develops and relentlessly marches on, as it is within institutional frames of reference that memories of the past and plans for the future are at all possible. Philosophy but also the social and cultural sciences, and certainly any theory of institutions, should incorporate these facts into their concepts, and into their visions of reality. That is, they should not be ontologically static, but historically dynamic.

Durkheim's lectures on James's Pragmatism are in this regard quite interesting.[5] In lucid expositions, he gave his students a fair summary of James's dynamic ideas, and then attacked them fiercely from a rationalist point of view, stressing the overwhelming importance of traditional, collective, and in that sense, objective institutions, since they guarantee order and security vis-à-vis the vicissitudes of individual actions, thoughts and emotions. I believe, incidentally, that Durkheim was directing his criticism beyond James and at his colleague Bergson, whose so-called Vitalism he abhorred as an irresponsible and unscientific (because irrational) anti-institutionalism. In any case, by emphasizing the 'cash value' of human behavior as the only and ultimate validation, Durkheim argued, James actually killed Truth and delivered us to the relativism of chance, contingency, uncertainty, perpetual change – and in the end to the terrors of chaos. Durkheim opposed this vision with a fierce *institutionalism*. Institutions, he advised sociologists, should be viewed and treated as objective 'things' which control individual behavior, guarantee order and stability, and thereby offer a firm context in which individuals can act and interact meaningfully and fruitfully. Or, to phrase it differently, the institutions we grew up in and eventually will die out of, ward off the terror of *anomie*, i.e. of meaningless chaos. Where anomie reigns, humanity will succumb.

Durkheim's stance suggests that there is an inherent tension between institutions and history. Since they are being passed on from generation to generation, institutions are part of history. They are even, if you want, products of history. Institutions, as we discussed them in the preceding chapters, are in a sense 'frozen' (glacier-like) actions, thoughts and feelings; traditional patterns of behavior; objectified socio-cultural roles coming to us from the past. As such they function as the molds in accordance with which people in the present have to conduct their actions and interactions. The very fact that institutions incorporate tradition ties them solidly to the past. Yet, they have an important function in molding the future. As Gehlen argued, the routine and taken-for-granted nature of institutions liberate us from the laborious task of designing and planning our actions each day anew, thus freeing energy which enables us to to design new ideas, make plans for tomorrow, and dream about utopian worlds. In other words, they open the road to the future. Moreover, as Gehlen also argued, institutions have the tendency to become *Leerformen* , i.e. empty forms, which may and will attract new motives and aims. They are, as it were, the casts in which the future is molded.

Yet, there is an innate tendency in institutions to neutralize, or even dissolve history. This is clearly observable when they objectify to such an extent that they become ritualistic systems. Deviations from the paths laid out by such fossilized institutions, are abhorred and severely punished. Innovations are shunned. Religious fundamentalism which puts sacred scripts and magically tabooed rituals on the pedestal of Absolute Truth is a good example. Tradition, in particular the institutions of the past, are absolutized. It is an *institutional traditionalism* which is generally eager to neutralize, or dissolve history.

In the present Western world such traditionalism is quite rare. It does occur but mostly on the fringes of our fully modernized society. From there it may spread electronically, as in the case of the protestant, fundamentalist television preachers in America. Up until now, however, traditionalism has remained rather marginal in most Western societies, certainly in Western Europe. To be sure, these societies exhibit the exact opposite of fundamentalism and institutional traditionalism. There is, as I argued in the Introduction, a penetrative *anti-institutional mood* at work in most of us. Unlike fundamentalism this mood is very liberal when it comes to doctrines and moral precepts. It is not fundamental Truth but a rather lackadaisical 'anything goes' which characterizes this anti-institutional mood. The paradox is that this *anti-institutionalism* is usually as eager to neutralize or dissolve history as traditionalism is. We should dwell on this for a moment.

Ironically anti-institutionalism has its own history. It even goes back several centuries. The anti-institutional mood usually emerges in times of rapid transition and radical transformation, as in the post-medieval, early-modern Renaissance, sixteenth-century Reformation, eighteenth-century Enlightenment, and late-modern Age of Information and Communication Technologies (ICT). These were and are times in which people oppose stale ideologies, and search for new contents in old, empty forms of life. Times also in which traditions and their established authorities have lost their taken-for-granted legitimacy. In such times of transition and transformation institutions are likely to be experienced as a burden, as alien and alienating 'things'. Actually three processes coalesce here. First there is the revolt against institutions, next there is the anti-institutional subjectivism, and finally there is the subjectivistic, anti-historical animus. It deserves further scrutiny.

Subjectivism versus history

A universal feature of the anti-institutional mood is an irrational subjectivism which revolts against the allegedly alienating objectivity and coercive autonomy of traditional institutions. It turns inward believing that the point of existential gravity is to be found in man's inner realms, in his 'psyche', 'soul', 'consciousness', and 'Self'. There and only there does the individual hope to find his inalienable authenticity, his true identity. This alleged authenticity, or true identity, is then expressed again – in the arts and sciences, in religious movements, in fashionable lifestyles, in political ideas and actions. All these expressions are eager to avoid, and at times even eager to attack, traditional institutions, such as the art museum, the university, the church, the club and the political party. Anti-institutional subjectivism is at the same time anti-institutional *expressionism*.

Gehlen, as we saw earlier, argued that this anti-institutional subjectivism and expressionism emerged during the rise of the Industrial Society which he defined as a 'cultural threshold' of human evolution. It is, however, a much older phenomenon, as is illustrated by *gnosticism* (or *manicheism*) which was a radically subjectivistic type of religiosity that originated in Iran. It re-emerged in the turmoil of Hellenism, took hold of various peasant revolts during the Middle Ages, and penetrated deeply into nineteenth century philosophy (cf. e.g. Hegel and Marx; *Entfremdung* is a typically gnostic ailment), and nineteenth-century Romanticism (cf. e.g. Hölderlin and Fichte; *Weltschmerz* is also a typically gnostic disease). Each time Western civilization was in turmoil, gnostic or manicheistic subjectivism emerged. It expressed itself in irrational revolts against the traditional, 'objective' institutions – the state, the family, the church, the university.[6] Institutions were demonized as they were believed to represent and embody a realm of alienation and inauthenticity.[7]

Ever since the Renaissance and the Reformation, Western civilization has suffered a broken relationship with institutions. In the Renaissance the bonds of feudalism, ideologically held together by the church of Rome, were broken like shackles. It opened the world up like a huge field of exploration and self-expression to individual men and women. The Reformation shattered the massive Roman Catholic mediations between the individual believer and God (the sacraments, the saints, the ecclesiastic hierarchy, etc.). In Calvinism, in particular, the individual was thrown back on his own, private relationship with a predestinating, remote and rather strange and abstract God. This individualism brought about by the Renaissance and Reformation altered the relationship between institutions and the individual radically and dramatically. Next the Enlightenment promoted a pervasive secularization and rationalization by teaching the modern individual to liberate himself from the irrational shackles of beliefs and superstitions, and to rely exclusively on his own reason and resolution. In a sense, the Enlightenment was the eighteenth-century successor of seventeenth-century Puritanism. After all, the thoroughly methodical and rational Puritan was thrown back upon his own individuality, confronted by an alien God of predestination, and called upon to work hard in the world and to conduct his life rationally and frugally. The bounderies between the Puritan and his God were very narrow indeed and could easily crack. Faith was then, of course, easily replaced by Reason, Predestination by Fate, History of Salvation by Progress. And indeed, the work ethic of relentless labor and rational thrift in honor of God was secularized and rationalized into the economic ethos of production, profit and investment in honor of Capital.

All this intensified in modernity. Institutions passed on from generation to generation (marriage, the family, the church, the state, the school, the university, etc.) are constantly being questioned by subjectivist and expressionist individuals. Not so much by ordinary people however, but by artists and intellectuals, by writers, philosophers, journalists and academics who now constitute a New Elite – indeed a Knowledge Class as they have also been named.[8] They in particular accuse institutions of being coercive and inhibiting structures, the very source of their sense of alienation. Institutions are especially taken to task for being strong impediments to the growth and development of individual emotions, sensations, thoughts and actions. Institutions, it is believed, curb man's authenticity and identity, his liberty, and his ability to express himself in a creative manner. Love, it is believed, should be free and vicarious, faith should be sectarian and emotional, art should be sensual and non-committal, thought should be free-floating, science should be existential and applicable.

This has been a development beyond individualism: modern man is taken away by a penetrating, almost taken-for-granted subjectivism and expressionism. Retreating to their inner realms, subjectivists search perpetually for 'experiences' and 'kicks' which, if necessary, are triggered artifically by various intoxicants, ranging from drugs and alcohol, to exciting philosophies and life styles, and giddy hypes and fashions in the arts and sciences. They next set out to express themselves in the world, where they then run into the traditional institutions with their inherent limits and controls. Incidentally, such intoxicants are indispensable, because man who is biologically an incomplete being depends on external impulses. The internal impulses are limited and finite, and will dry up, if they are not regularly revitalized from without. If institutions are prevented from doing this job, people need to take refuge to artificial stimulants.

The end effect of all this is a typically manicheistic dualism – the 'objective' world of the institutions as the realm of inauthenticity and alienation is placed in opposition to the 'subjective' world of sensations, emotions, and non-rational consciousness. These, and not the institutions, are inaugurated as the proper realms of authenticity, liberty and true identity. Gnostic anti-institutionalists believe that they are able to experience in the supposed deep levels of their consciousness and emotions, both reality and authenticity. Freud's 'psychoanalysis' with its focus on the allegedly 'deep' strata of the unconscious; Jung's 'depth psychology' which overtly presented itself as a gnostic philosophy; and a plethora of esoteric philosophies, usually concocted eclectically from Western and Eastern ideas, function as the appropriate ideologies for the satisfaction of modern man's subjectivism and expressionism. New Age, an insufficient label for scores of irrational ideas, esoteric notions, and expressive lifestyles, exemplifies today's gnostic anti-institutionalism. However, this manicheistic animus against institutions occurs under a more rational and philosophically respectable disguise. Many post-modernists, for instance, are clearly manicheistic in their ideologically inspired calls for, or apocalyptic proclamations of, the end of history, the end of democracy, the end of the nation-state, the end of the environment.[9]

However, time and again people have had to learn, often the hard way, that life cannot be lived without institutions passed on by previous generations. Institutions are not merely alienating instruments of coercion and control which in a sense they are and have to be. They are also indispensable components of an order that provides us with security, certainty, and above all, meaning. If they function well, institutions constitute what the ancient Greeks called a *nomos* that is, a meaningful infrastructure which provides people with a proper place in the world.[10] If that order, for whatever reason, collapses, we face the terror of *anomie*. Anomie is not lawlessness or norm-lessness but the reign of senseless, illegitimate, and inhuman laws and norms. It is above all, a state of general meaninglessness which deprives people of the possibility to orient and position themselves in the world, in society and in history, in a way that provides their lives with stability and direction. If subjectivists love to complain about the typical gnostic malady, called *alienation,* allegedly brought on by 'objective' and coercive institutions, it serves to point out that a radical decline or even collapse of traditional institutions would result in *anomie*. Without really embracing the socio-economic consequences of Marxism, many a romantic subjectivist has flirted in the past with Marxism and even with Lenin's and Stalin's brand of communism. As the impressive volume *The God That Failed* (1949) demonstrated several of them realized in time, and much to their regret and chagrin, that the communist 'realm of freedom and equality' had brought about a Kafkaesque world in which anomie was rampant. The laws and norms were repressive, and nobody was certain anymore about his or her fate during the next day or night.[11] The communist god had failed because it had not delivered what it had promised, namely liberty, equality and solidarity. Instead it had erected a reign of terror which spread an all-embracing and very penetrative anomie. I shall return to alienation and anomie in the Conclusion.

From cosmos to history and back[12]

Historicism as the metaphysical ideology which claims that there is a positive direction – a *telos* – in history has led, as Karl Popper argued convincingly, to the ideology and practice of a 'closed society'.[13] But Popper did not realize, or refused to acknowledge, that the neutralization of history in ideology and practice would sooner or later have the same effect. It will eventually yield a dreary functionalism as well as a technocratic, instrumentalist and static approach to the status quo and its institutions. Society and culture are then viewed, and in policy treated, as ahistorical 'closed systems' in which inputs and outputs play a sort of zero-sum game. In a sense such 'closed systems' constitute a 'closed cosmos'. A society in the grip of a comprehensive bureaucracy, like the former Soviet Union, comes to the mind, if one searches for a historical example, but the phenomenon is much older than that. In fact, the 'closed cosmos' constitutes a kind of historical trope. For instance, looked at ideal-typically the Medieval world and the world of Antiquity (Ancient Greece and Rome) demonstrate, apart from scores of differences, a basic similarity as to their visions and experiences of the structure of society and culture. Greek, Roman and medieval men all felt to be parts of an encompassing, more or less closed world. This world was experienced as a *syndesmos*, that is, as a system that binds people tightly together. In a small, by now almost forgotten essay entitled 'The End of the Modern Era' (1950)[14] the cultural philosopher Romano Guardini described the similarity of the medieval and the Greco-Roman world thus: 'Both saw and, what is even more important, experienced the world as a limited configuration, as a framed Gestalt – expressed in a plastic manner, as a sphere.'[15]

In this closed cosmos man is not viewed, and does not experience himself, as an actor, as a historical creature that molds himself into an individual and a personality, but rather as an inherent component of a surrounding, rather static reality, as a cog in a circularly moving system. His actions are therefore not essential features by which he positions himself in history and society. They rather constitute an accidental, yet fateful circumstance which can be explained totally from the cyclical and reasonable path the cosmos takes. Fate and tragedy are the crucial ingredients of this world view, not mind and action.[16]

Thus, the Greek citizen – if he was a free and propertied male, since paupers, women and slaves were excluded – knew himself to be an insoluble part of the *polis*, the city-state, in which he felt that, as long as he obeyed the laws, his liberty was safeguarded and in fact realized by it. The *polis* was experienced as a micro-cosmos, and so was, even more so, the extended family.[17] In addition, what he experienced as the essence of his being, the *logos* that is, the capability of reason and reasonableness was closely linked to the rational and reasonable order of the cosmos at large, the macro-cosmos. An authentic *historical* awareness in which man experiences himself as an open possibility in an open world exposed to an open future, could not emerge in such a closed world view. Things and nature (defined as cosmos) were the main themes of Greek philosophy, not history and events. The historiographies of Herodotus, Thucydides and Polybius were thoroughly conditioned by this static-cosmic world view. They focussed exclusively on the past. Greek historiography was in fact exercised as a kind of natural science. It described, one could say, things tied to the past, not events and processes directed towards the future. Karl Loewith summed it up aptly as follows: 'Greek philosophers and historians were convinced that whatever is to happen will be of the same pattern and character as past and present events; they never indulged in the prospective possibilities of the future.'[18]

This static-cosmic world view was severely shocked and shaken, when during the Peloponnesian Wars and after the fall of Athens the *polis* entered into a deep socio-cultural, economic and political crisis. Traditions lost their meaningfulness, taken-for-granted certainties tumbled, and doubts as to the reasonable order of the encompassing cosmos emerged. The ensuing fears and doubts were expressed and sublimated by the individualistic and relativistic philosophies of the Sophists, and voiced by the tragedians, Euripides in particular, whose heroes were pitiful individuals plagued by doubts and feelings of remorse. The individualism and relativism of the Sophists, and the aesthetic subjectivism of Euripides were in their turn confronted by a philosopher like Plato who in a conservative, or rather reactionary vein tried to restore the closed world view through his cosmic doctrine of metaphysical Ideas. If empirical reality seemed to be fragmented and torn apart by contradictions, the eternal Ideas came to the Platonic rescue. They restored the sense of cosmic order and harmony again. His metaphysical world of ideas as super-reality was, of course, but a virtual reality. It could not prevent the eventual political and socio-cultural desintegration of the Hellenic world.

With the assistance of the vast scope of Aristotle's comprehensive philosophy, which covered empirical, experiential as well as metaphysical, speculative reality, the idea of a cosmic and rational order was restored in the Middle Ages after a long period of confusion and disorientation due to the fall of Rome. The Platonic cosmos returned in a Christian-theological form. The *syndesmos* was now re-defined as the *Corpus Christianum* which was experienced as a *corpus mysticum*. Plato and Aristotle were incorporated elegantly and then theologically superseded by Thomas Aquinas, whose major intellectual contribution was characteristically entitled *Summa Theologiae*, which covered more than just theology; it was a philosophical, sociological and political treatise as well.

Naturally, a sense of history could not really emerge in this cosmic *corpus mysticum*. That occurred on the fringes of the Roman Catholic *syndesmos* in scores of reformatory and sectarian movements, albeit often in a mytho-logical vein as in the theory of the three stages of history, designed by the Franciscan monk Joachim of Fiore.[19] A modern conception of history as the bond between present, past and future emerged in the Renaissance and the Reformation. Yet the most radical vision of history remained buried in the Old Testament and was, so to speak, unearthed by the Reformation. In fact, the theology of history, seen as an eschatological history of salvation, as de-veloped in the prophetic tradition of Ancient Israel, had been distinctly anti-cosmic. Jahweh created the world, *bereshit*, i.e. in the beginning, as part of a plan with the world that was to be realized by His chosen people of Israel. This was a remarkable conception of history as a linear rather than circular process which contained a radical disenchantment with the world. Because it was not physical reality, such as large trees or huge rocks; societal institu-tions such as the monarchy; or biological forces such as fertility and sexuali-ty which were sacred or divine, and magically taboo (as the surrounding nations generally believed) but the *acts* of Jahweh with Israel and the sur-rounding nations, i.e. *history,* was believed to be sacred! And taboo was the *shem Jahwe,* that is the name, the identity of God. The deeds of Jahweh among his beloved people were historical events, and these events constitut-ed an eschatology, i.e. a chain of events with a beginning and an end. Escha-tological and linear history was the core of the Judaic prophetic world view, not the mythological and cyclical 'eternal return of the same'.[20]

Apart from St. Augustine's theology of history which remained a tribu-tary of neo-Platonism and the apocalyptic visions of Joachimism, which bore solidly gnostic notions, medieval theology and philosophy remained incapable of a historical vision. Even the Nominalists who in opposition to Platonic Realism focussed on the empirical reality of individual phenome-na, failed to grasp the historical nature of the world they were living in. In the medieval Corpus Christianum history was, so to speak, absorbed by the absolute will of a cosmic God who was believed to have been represented on earth by the Pope in Rome. R. G. Collingwood aptly phrased it: 'What has happened here is that the pendulum of thought has swung from an abstract and one-sided humanism in Greco-Roman historiography to an equally ab-stract and one-sided theocentric view in medieval. The work of providence in history is recognized, but recognized in a way that leaves nothing for man to do.'[21]

During the Middle Ages this cosmic and theocentric world view, institu-tionalized in Rome by the Catholic Church and the Pope, was constantly un-der fire politically: by German emperors (cf. Otto III and the ongoing in-vestiture conflict), by reform minded monastic orders, by rebellious peasant movements, and most fatally by the anti-papal Reformation. Particularly in the Reformation's Calvinist tradition the prophetic tradition of the Old Testament was taken up again, and a theology of history returned to Western civilization. The historical influence of Protestantism was fateful. Unintentionally, as Max Weber argued, the Calvinist ethos contributed to Western rationalism and through its ethics of frugality to the emergence of capitalism.[22]

Meanwhile, emerging in the cities of Italy first and in those of North-Western Europe later, the social and cultural renewal movement, called the Renaissance, also besieged the cosmic-Thomistic world view. Despite their theological differences, the one being biblically inspired, the other being secular and aesthetic in character, the Reformation and the Renaissance placed the human individual on a pedestal. Moreover, both placed man in a historical perspective. The Renaissance, inspired by the rediscovery of Greco-Roman culture, defined man in terms of secular history, while the Reformation, inspired by the prophets of the Old Testament, defined the human individual in the context of a history of salvation. Again, despite this important theological difference, the Reformation and the Renaissance broke open the circular, spheric *corpus mysticum* in favor of a linear, developmental history. The Enlightenment would finally define this evolutionary history in terms of Progress.[23] All this had, of course, great implications for man's self-understanding and his relations with the institutions around him. Burckhardt wrote in his classic study of the Renaissance, that medieval men, half awake and half in dreams, wore veils woven from faith, childish constraint and delusion. This veil disfigured their view of reality. The world to them was constituted by race, nation, corporation, family or some other abstract generality. But then, Burckhardt continued, in Italy for the first time, the veil is lifted, is blown away in the air. A more objective way of observing reality emerges, while man begins to experience himself as something private, as an individual with a mind of his own.[24]

These elements then are radicalized during the Enlightenment, once defined appropriately as a process in which paganism took hold of Western civilization.[25] Immanuel Kant saw this process as a fundamental secularization, and defined it aptly as man's emancipation from an enslavement which he had imposed upon himself in the past. But above all, the Enlightenment, emerging in consonance with the Industrial Revolution, opened up the medieval *syndesmos*, leaving individual man ever more to his own devices. These devices were believed to be rational and logical, and infinitely more reliable than the faiths, beliefs and fancies of the past.[26] Enlightenment Rationalism took two roads from this point on. There was the road, or better still the highway of empirical Science which was believed to be the only feasible way towards Progress. And there was the return of the Greek *logos* as a metaphysical principle, absolutized by Hegel and forged into a mythological, almost pantheistic principle, called Spirit, *Geist*. In both cases we are, of course, back again full circle, because the idea of Progress of the Positivists and the prime-moving Spirit of the Hegelians contained a spheric world view which was as cosmic and closed as Plato's or Aquinas's systems. Hegel's dialectical method, founded upon gnostic dualism (cf. his Manicheistic theory of *Entfremdung*) was a blatant attempt to neutralize history again. Marx and Marxism adopted the method, meanwhile demonstrating time and again in this century that it neutralized humanity and humaneness in the process. Likewise, the very influential positivistic world view in which Science and Progress were put on a pedestal, produced a technocratic and instrumentalist approach to the world. The approach was ahistorical, amoral ('value-free') and, if organized well, as for instance in the case of the holocaust, extremely violent and inhuman.[27]

The problem is, of course, that history is a Janus-faced phenomenon. It is riddled with unintended consequences, contingencies and strange elective affinities, as Max Weber has demonstrated many times. Inspired by the Enlightenment, successive political revolutions (1789, 1848, 1917) and scientific-technological innovations (Industrial Revolution, Atomic Revolution, ICT-Revolution) have attacked closed world views and their related closed political systems. But these revolutions and innovations have in their turn often given rise to systems of depressing closure. Indeed, despite the Enlightenment and often in the wake of the Enlightenment, we have witnessed time and again over the past three centuries that attempts have sucessfully been made to close society and culture, to neutralize history, to enslave the individual, to suffocate liberty and creativity. In the twentieth century various forms of fascism and communism in particular have demonstrated this trend of recurrent anomie. Institutions are then employed as instruments of totalitarian control. History, it stands to reason, is thus reduced to a chain of brutal controls and coercions, and tradition to a bone-dry, repressive, and cliché-ridden past. The slogan may be 'the future is ours, comrade!',[28] but in reality this future is the status quo of unequal power distribution directed and controlled by members of the single ruling party, in particular the top brass thereof.

Modernization and modernity

Yet, hazardous and contradictory as history may be, we need to consider the uneasy relationship between traditional institutions on the one hand, and the ongoing process of change and development, called history, on the other.

This is particularly necessary, given the fact that the institutional framework of a society changes drastically when it is subjected to the forces of science, technology, industry, bureaucracy, to the socio-economic and cultural impact of cities, to the policies of nationally bounded states, and to the forces of a market economy – i.e. if a society sets out to *modernize*. All these processes somehow began in the early-capitalist cities of Europe,[29] and continue to transform the world today. What is, maybe somewhat hyperbolically, referred to as 'the electronic revolution' is a late offshoot of this very complex set of socio-cultural, economic and political changes which Michael Polanyi once called the Great Transformation, and which Gehlen saw as the second 'absolute threshold of human evolution' (the Neolithic being the first threshold). It is in fact an extensive and intensive, very complex process of *modernization* that has fundamentally changed first Western societies, but after World War II increasingly developing nations as well.

There is much academic resistance regarding the concepts of modernization and modernity, since they allegedly simplify and generalize very complex, particularistic and idiosyncratic processes, developments, and movements. These concepts, it is claimed, also tend to be used in an ethnocentric manner, in particular when the world is divided into a modern part, the prosperous West and North, and a pre-modern part, the underdeveloped, if not primitive East (except for the Pacific Rim) and South (except for certain nations in South America and, of course, Australia and New Zealand). Formulated in such prejudicial terms, modernization and modernity are indeed useless, if not harmful concepts.

It has been proposed to abandon the terms altogether, and to rather speak and write in terms of *development* and *transformation*. But here similar objections can be voiced. Development, for instance, is closely related to the idea of evolution, and if evolution is understood primarily as progress, one is close to ethnocentrism again, since the normative model of a developed and truly progressive society is usually presented by Western nations. Transformation is of all the concepts the most neutral one, and is therefore quite useful. Yet, its conceptual disadvantage is that it has no equivalent for modernity which refers to the socio-cultural upshot of the transformation process. It is odd and awkward to characterize a fully developed society in terms of the neologism 'transformity'. Moreover, transformation may be too neutral. Change is a perennial and permanent process. Thus, everything and everyone is always involved in transformation. It is, in fact, as bleak and general as the concept of change which also lacks heuristic pith.

There is, of course, no valid objection to continue the use of 'modernization' and 'modernity', if one defines them clearly in advance, thereby demarcating their specific meaning. It is the same with 'society' and 'culture', or for that matter 'organization' and 'institution', which are also meaningless and senseless concepts if one does not demarcate their heuristic limits in advance.

If one then tries to define 'modernization' and 'modernity', it will not be very helpful to pile up various processes, tie them together and call the resulting conceptual heap 'modernization' and 'modernity'. This is, nevertheless, often done. Modernization is then viewed as the overarching concept of industrialization, urbanization, secularization, growing impacts of science, technology, bureaucracy, etc. All these processes have contributed to the emergence of modernity, but merely piling them up into one conceptual heap is not conducive to a better understanding of the phenomena and processes denoted by them. What is needed, is a concise model which in an ideal-typical manner lays bare the fundamental 'logic' or 'rationale' of modernization and modernity.

One can construct such a model after Talcott Parsons by combining two lines of socio-theoretical thought. Pursuing some basic notions of Durkheim modernization is then defined as a pervasive process of structural differentiation which started with the division of labor that is endemic to all social life. Structural differentiation is not absent in pre-industrial societies and indeed the seeds of modernization can be observed in many cultures that have not yet been influenced by industry, science, technology and the capitalist mode of production but still contain rather well-developed systems of divided labor. However, in Western societies, roughly after the Renaissance, structural differentiation accelerated steadily and became very dominant in the Industrial Revolution. The division of labor and the ensuing diversity of social roles has led in most Western nations to a steadily expanding socio-cultural universe of ever greater complexity.

While this structural complexity grew – and this is a conceptual line borrowed from Weber – the fundamental values, norms and meanings, originally tied to religion and the family, rationalized, i.e. grew ever more general and abstract. In order to span and cover the often widely divergent and differentiated structures of modernity, culture – i.e. values, norms and meanings – had to be stretched like a rubber band. In other words it had to lose its fundamental features and experiential contents. Religiously motivated and family-based neighborly or brotherly love, for example, generalized into class solidarity, and from there into bourgeois welfare state solidarity. This solidarity is supposedly expressed by sharply progressive taxations for the assistance and succor of the needy, the impotent, and the incapable in society. It is an attractive idea which was the core of the original ideology behind the welfare state. Yet seeing the many deductions from one's monthly paycheck, it is hard for any welfare state citizen to view, let alone feel and experience them as a token of one's solidarity with the less fortunate of society. In other words, solidarity has been rationalized in the welfare state into a very general and abstract kind of value and norm, called 'social solidarity'.[30] This too is modernization.

Independently from Durkheim and Weber, Georg Simmel developed a similar theory of modernization for which he laid the foundations in his book on social differentiation published in 1890.[31] In all societies, Simmel argued, the human individual is located in a web (network!) of intersecting group affiliations. As a result, while he socializes into society the individual develops an awareness of being more than just a cog in a machine, a particle of a larger whole. Playing different roles, changing as it were these roles as he changes the jackets of his wardrobe, he gradually develops the awareness of being in fact an individual: 'here I am, the player of various roles'. However, such an awareness of individual identity will be weak or even dormant, if the groups that people socialize into are limited in number, collectively adhered to, and strongly legitimated religiously. The same awareness is however radicalized, Simmel argued, in modern industrial society. Due to the increased division of labor in industrial society, group affiliations and role identifications will multiply and contribute to a heightened sense of distance between the individual and the various, often in substance quite different social roles that must be performed. Due to the intense social differentiation caused by modern division of labor, social structures become pluralistic and increasingly abstract, while human beings grow increasingly individualistic and conscious of their allegedly 'inherent' creativity and liberty.[32]

Modernity can thus be defined as the confluence of structural differentiation in which society is institutionally pluralistic and humanly individualistic on the one hand, and culturally generalized in which values, norms and meanings are increasingly vague and abstract on the other hand. The problem is, however, that these processes do not necessarily run parallel. A society can be highly differentiated structurally, yet 'lag behind' culturally since the values, norms and meanings are still relatively concrete and distinct. This is often the case when there are scores of voluntary associations in which people interact in a meaningful manner, tying their interactions to relatively stable traditions.[33] The USA, the 'nation of joiners', the society of many voluntary associations, is usually presented as an example. In terms of technological development and socio-structural differentiation American society is a leader in modernization. However, due to its many mediating structures, such as the voluntary associations in the first place, its culture, i.e. its values and norms, are less advanced in modernity, that is to say, they are less generalized and abstract. Some social theorists and commentators claim that America's mediating structures and their 'social capital' are in decline. Sociologically, that would indeed indicate a 'catching up' in cultural modernization.[34]

It is, however, also possible, that structural differentiation lags behind in terms of the generalization of values and norms, as was demonstrated by the Soviet Union in its last days. The society and the economy were ruled by a monolithic, poorly differentiated state bureaucracy, whereas the communist ideology consisted of highly abstract and generalized Marxist conceptions in which nobody believed anymore. It may be a strange conclusion at first sight but this abstract Marxist ideology fits the previous definition of modernity: in the last years of the Soviet Union, Marxism was a generalized, empty, very abstract, uninspiring and in that sense modern ideology. Actually it was as modern as the 'The Third Way' professed by today's European social democrats.[35] The only difference is that Marxism functioned as a repressive instrument in the hands of old-fashioned tyrants who tried to keep hold of their power in a thoroughly anti-democratic state apparatus. 'The Third Way', on the contrary, is a soft ideology which will not repress or oppress anybody. On the contrary, precisely because it is vague, general, and abstract, it has the flexibility that suits the highly developed structural differentiation of today's society. Moreover it is not employed by tyrants who cling tightly to their undemocratic power.

The dynamics of progression and regression

The model of modernization contains yet another pitfall. It easily degenerates into a rather simplified evolutionism, suggesting that modernization is a linear and teleological process, driven by some sort of Aristotelean *entelechy* or Christian *telos*. Usually such teleologies preach the doctrine of Progress which is an idea that might be useful politically but in general bears little fruit analytically. One must therefore add another element to the model. I call this element, for the lack of better concepts, the dynamic interplay of progression and regression. These concepts are used analytically, i.e. as ideal types, and thus not politically or otherwise normatively.

Wherever and whenever human beings set out to do things collectively, they will, as we have seen, set up divisions of labor. The specialization of tasks is in a sense unavoidable and becomes very predominant under the regime of industrialization, causing an ever-expanding and in this sense progressive differentiation of structures. Sooner or later this will be accompanied by an equally progressive cultural generalization. In this respect modernity is the result of a progressive socio-cultural generalization.

But throughout the ages of human evolution contrary, regressive forces have also been at work: people searching collectively for integration and for holistic structures which bind them together. There is also a search for fundamental values and norms believed to be stored up in sacred traditions, rituals, symbols and texts, containing the alleged basic truths of life and death. In pre-modern societies the regressive impulses are stronger than the progressive ones, as is testified by relatively low degrees of role specifications and work specializations. The present sharply distinguished roles of father and teacher, for instance, were not really differentiated in pre-modern societies: teachers treated their pupils paternalistically, and fathers approached their children at home in a didactic manner. Often as patriarchs at home they also performed certain religious functions and rituals, which in a stage of more advanced modernization are usually exercised by specialized religious professionals, that is, if they are still performed at all. In the early 1950s I witnessed at the dinner table of a sternly Calvinist family in Holland how the *pater familias* opened each dinner by reading a passage from the Bible, using the antique version approved by the Dordrecht Synod of 1619. He started at Genesis 1, read through the entire Old and New Testaments up until the Apocalypse of St. John (which was deemed to be too enigmatic), and then began a new cycle at Genesis 1 again. He also said a prayer after each Bible reading. In my present, thoroughly modernized and agnostic mind, this memory belongs in some sociological museum.

In a pre-modern setting, values and norms will be concrete and felt to be fundamental, if not true in a taken-for-granted manner. They are institutionally fixed and do not remain open to reflections and relativizations. They are, in fact, held to be 'normal' and deemed to be 'natural'. These fundamental values and norms of the group are represented in sacred symbols, and enacted in rituals. They are also enshrined in a sacred, metaphysical tradition which is handled with great care and circumspection. In a pre-modern setting this cultural regressive impulse is a predominant one, which is precisely why we call it a traditional society and a traditional culture.

In the pre-modern world, structural and cultural regression, in the sense of structural holism and cultural fundamentalism, is the predominant impulse, whereas the progressive impulse of structural differentiation and cultural generalization is in most cases not totally absent but definitely secondary. In modernity things are just the other way around. The progressive impulse is very dominant, while structural and cultural regression may not be totally absent, but is still rather residual. In fact, the moment structural differentiation is radicalized to a point that it becomes dysfunctional, as in the case of scientific specialists who even within the same discipline are unable to communicate with each other scientifically or otherwise, the regressive impulse begins to operate. Another example is the case of an over-formalized and differentiated bureaucracy in which competence is compartmentalized to such an extent, that the very same tasks are being duplicated, and the general efficiency is seriously impaired. In such a case the call for integration and integrative approaches will sooner or later be heard. It is a call for interdisciplinarity, integral management, overall de-differentiation, and deregulation. This regression can even be radicalized to the point that atavistic, pre-modern modes of acting, thinking and feeling are propagated, as in the case of New Age holism, libertarian communitarianism, and (crypto-) fascist forms of nationalism and ethnicity. Similarly, the search for supposedly fundamental values and norms – as, for instance, in the search for corporate culture and corporate identity ('what is our mission?') – can also be radicalized. It may eventually result in sheer fundamentalism which uncritically embraces supposed basic truths laid down in holy books and how-to bestsellers. In other words, radicalizations of the structurally and culturally regressive impulses may be easily debauched in pre-modern states of mind, emotion and action. Gehlen's concept of primitivization comes to mind, of course.

Yet, such radicalizations do not necessarily need to occur. It is actually quite normal for the progressive structural differentiation and cultural generalization to be decelerated, or softened rather, by the regressive impulses which then function, so to speak, as the drag chutes of modernization. When it is decided to slow down the forces of radical progression, as is often the agenda of (neo-)conservatives, this does not necessarily mean the embrace of an all-out, radical regression. Conservatism is, of course, not the same as reactionary fascism, communitarian libertarianism, or New Age holism.

This consideration is relevant for the theory of institutions. Gehlen's institutionalism, for example, came quite close to a reactionary type of conservatism in which the regressive impulse was heavily emphasized at the expense of the progressive impulse which was in fact decried and ridiculed by him as a decadent, subjectivistic decline of the traditional institutions. On the other hand, there are liberal and libertarian post-modernists who proclaim the post-institutional network society, which supposedly herald the end of institutions such as the state, marriage, the family, the church, the school, the university, etc. They over-emphasize the progressive impulse at the expense of regressive forces. In the next chapter I shall try to arrive at a better balance, introducing the distinction of 'thick' and 'thin' institutions and networks. But we must first complete our present considerations of the historical nature of institutions and their often strained relationships with modernization and modernity.

Rationality, subjectivity and modernization

It is helpful to emphasize two dimensions in modernization and modernity: first, the supersession of substantial rationality by functional rationality; second, the inherently de-institutionalizing impetus of modernization which may end up in an anti-institutional mood couched in subjectivism. Rationalization and subjectivization are the two most conspicuous and intrinsic components of modernization and modernity. Both have a rather problematic relationship with history.

Weber, as we saw earlier, described modernization in terms of a pervasive disenchantment of the world by which he meant the victory of first religious rationality and next scientific rationality over irrational magic. Once more, modernization is in his view first and foremost rationalization. This rationalization began in Ancient Judaism where prophetic religion based upon revelation attacked and dislodged natural religion based upon irrational magic. This type of rationality, as was mentioned earlier, re-emerged in the Reformation, in particular in its Calvinist and Puritan forms. It was a precursor of the secularized, pagan rationality of the Enlightenment which laid down the foundations for scientific rationality. From then on modernization consisted of the victory of chemistry over alchemy, of astronomy over astrology, of geology over geomancy, of science over magic, and of empirical sociology over metaphysical social philosophy.

Weber's conception of rationalization and rationality has been duly criticized and should indeed be corrected. It is helpful, I think, to view rationalization as a far more ambiguous and less linear process. In fact, rationalization is a gradual supersession of substantial rationality by functional rationality (cf. chapter one). In functional rationality all emphasis is placed on means, methods, and procedures developed for the effective and efficient realization of certain goals. As has been observed by various social theorists, in modernization these means tend to acquire the status of goals, in which case functional rationality becomes irrational. Goal displacement is, of course, the dilemma of the sorcerer's apprentice, which is so apparent in our predominantly technological society and culture.[36]

The predominance of functional rationality in modernity fosters, as we have seen in chapter one, the domination of the organizational dimension in society, and is rather detrimental to the institutional dimension which is geared towards substantial rationality. In fact, the replacement of substantial rationality by functional rationality as the hard core of the modernization process, is a replacement of the institutional dimension by the organizational dimension. Karl Mannheim observed this inherent paradox astutely.[37] The more rational a society grows *functionally* (i.e. in terms of methods, procedures, and means), the more irrational it will become *substantially* (i.e. in terms of values, norms and meanings). It is like with communicating vessels: the increase of efficiency and functionality coincides with a growth of generality and vagueness in substantial values, norms and meanings. The church, the university and the army, to give three arbitrary examples, modernized into efficient organizations that are managed by the principles of modern business administration. In fact, it is quite possible for a high ranking officer in the American army to become, after retirement, president of a university, and next move on to the top management of a church. Despite their institutional differences the army, the university and the church can be managed equally successfully by the same type of (functionally rational) manager. Yet, at the same time it has become less and less clear what exactly the meaning and destiny, or to use business administration jargon, the mission is of these institutions. Mission statements are usually very vague and general, and as a result rather similar. That means, their substantial rationality is in decline. It is no wonder that the historical dimension becomes blurred as well. The vague values, norms and meanings tend to deteriorate into manageable and functional commonplaces that embody an abstract and cliché-ridden past, not an inspiring and goal-setting tradition.[38]

However, as we have just seen, this is only one part of the process, namely the progressive one. There is also a regressive impulse at work in modernization which consists of a search for fundamental values, norms and meanings, i.e. a search for substantial rationality, for an institutional *nomos* which shows people what their meaningful position in the cosmos is or could be, and beyond that, what the ultimate ends and goals of their individual and collective lives are or could be. Modernization and modernity are not nonlinear phenomena. They are spread out between the poles of function and meaning, between organization and institution, between functional rationality and substantial rationality. The moment institutional meaning and substantial rationality is overshadowed by organizational function and functional rationality to the extent that man's *nomos* is endangered, one will witness sooner or later that the progressive impulse is pushed back by the regressive impulse. People will then search for fundamental values, norms and meanings that help them to direct their actions and interaction towards individually and collectively defined aims and goals. Here is the paradox again: by focussing on basic values, norms and meanings, the regressive impulse enables us to formulate aims and to set goals, and thereby to orient ourselves to the future.

To give the example once again, when in the 1980s corporate life was by and large dominated by the functional rationality of scientific management and purely quantitative economic considerations, it seemed to be the epitome of efficiency and effectiveness. Yet, not for metaphysical reasons, but due to mergers and take-overs, corporations were suddenly confronted with the phenomenon of culture, corporate culture. Previously culture had always been defined by managers and management consultants as a 'soft', irrational factor. But in most mergers and take overs corporate culture, i.e. traditional and tenacious patterns of acting, thinking and feeling, turned out to be a very 'hard' and rational factor. Culture is rational because it is the sum total of values, norms and meanings that gives the organization substance and direction. If it is vital, corporate culture enables management to design clear strategies. Indeed, we can call it cultural capital. Meanwhile, we have arrived at the same paradox again: the regressive impulse – the rediscovery of culture – is needed in order to design a clear and meaningful strategy towards the future.

Yet the personal computer, e-mail and the Internet has transformed the relationships between individuals and institutions. In this electronic world individuals are more autonomous, depending more than ever on their subjective resources, and much less on institutional directives and controls. But the institutions have not disappeared. They still exist but have changed considerably. For one thing, they have become less 'thick' and overbearing, as will be argued in the next chapter.

The search for legitimacy and trust

The complaint is often heard these days that organizations have 'short memories'. The knowledge and experience of earlier generations of managers is forgotten, or simply ignored, with the obvious result that the wheel of efficient management must be re-invented time and again by successive, new generations of managers. Indeed, when organizations modernize to the extent that their institutional dimensions become vague and abstract, the past, and thus the fund of knowledge and experience, evaporate and vanish. The institutional dimension gives an organization history, i.e. durability and stability, and a strategic sense of direction and purpose. It may be old-fashioned to formulate it this way, but it is not any less pertinent: the institutional dimension contains wisdom from the past, and thereby provides specialized knowledge and functional expertise with profundity, sincerity and foresight. Indeed, the institutional dimension gives an organization legitimacy and trustworthiness.

Moreover, as several studies of corporate culture have demonstrated, the institutional dimension gives the workers of an organization in all echelons and units a sense of meaningful participation and solidarity. If the institutional dimension disappears, the destructive forces of anomie lie in waiting and cultural capital will dwindle. Institutions are able to incorporate and radiate trust and mutual understanding. If they disintegrate, disappear or are abandoned, paranoia and hatred will run rampant. Superficially, organizations may seem to be efficient and effective, but under the surface forces of disintegration are at work. If we are really heading for a post-institutional society, as some post-modernists claim, serious disasters in public and private organizations can be expected.

In this and the previous chapters Gehlen's warning of de-institutionalization and his pessimistic predictions as to the rise of subjectivism and the concomitant decline of Western civilization (ideas that were very similar to those of Durkheim) were taken seriously. Yet, the inherent reactionary and at times rather cynical type of *institutionalism,* as expressed by the idea that man ought to let himself be consumed by institutions (the state in the first place), was not embraced as an acceptable and meaningful alternative. Moreover, such cynical pessimism is not realistic, if one heeds the simple fact that institutions cannot be destroyed as long as the human species is still in existence. They are universal, probably biologically grounded patterns of behavior. A historically grounded institute, such as the Nazi state, can collapse, but it will be succeeded by another configuration, such as the democratic *Bundesrepublik,* simply because state formation is a universal institution. The democratic *Bundesrepublik* is a historical institute and as such a particular, historically specific and empirical realization of the universal institution 'state'. This is not *Institutionsabbau,* institutional destruction, but *institutional transformation.*

Finally two tasks should be undertaken when tackling the moral dilemma of institutionalism and subjectivism. First, we must come to terms with the idea that we live in a post-institutional society of flexible networks and informational flows. We must decide what in this idea is realistic and empirically valid and thus must be incorporated into our present rethinking of institutions. We can then also determine what in this idea is fallacious, and in terms of a normative philosophical anthropology, objectionable. The next chapter will be devoted to this task. It will be argued that institutions and networks are not at all mutually exclusive concepts. If one wants to maintain the notion of modernity, one should realize that former limits or borders, and former centers or nuclei have indeed largely lost their formerly strong hold over acts, thoughts and emotions. We will not let ourselves be consumed by them. Fully modernized individuals live these days in the context of 'thin' institutions.

Second, we must get a clearer picture of the type of society and culture we have moved into in the past couple of decades. Chapter five attempts to present a phenomenology of the post-modern society and culture, without yielding to the anti-institutional mood which is so typical of most post-modern philosophers and ideologues. I shall try to focus on aspects of contemporary society and culture which Gehlen and certainly Durkheim could not have foreseen, when they designed their institutionalist theories. Meanwhile, although I am not sure about Durkheim, I am quite confident that Gehlen would decry today's post-modern staccato culture and network society as further proof of his prediction that Western civilization was heading for decline and degeneration. Its pervasive de-institutionalization, he would repeat, would eventually incapacitate the motor that keeps the human species vital and alive – *Handeln*, i.e. behavior, action, and production. It must be obvious by now that this will not be the conclusion of this book.

1. Dandyism is a perfect example of this type of 'spoiled anomie'. Cf. César Graña, *Modernity and its Discontents*, 1964, (New York: Harper Torchbooks, 1967), pp.148-154. Otto Mann, *Der Dandy. Ein Kulturproblem der Moderne* (The Dandy. A Cultural Problem of Modernity), 1925, (Heidelberg: Wolfgang Rothe Verlag, 1962). Naturally, Scott Fitzgerald's novel *The Great Gatsby* comes to mind as well.

2. This is, of course, a reference to Karl Mannheim's idea of the *Standortgebundenheit* of human knowledge, i.e. the innate relatedness of knowledge to socio-economic interests. It is a neo-Marxist redefinition of the neo-Kantian notion of *Wertgebundenheit,* i.e. value-relatedness which Max Weber employed in his methodology, since it refers to the socio-economic infrastructure as causal determinant of the cultural and ideological superstructure. However, Mannheim himself indicated that he was rather tributary to Ernst Troeltsch's theory of *historicism*. See Karl Mannheim, 'Historicism' (1924), in: *Essays on the Sociology of Knowledge,* (London: Routledge & Kegan Paul, 1952), pp. 84-133, in particular pp. 97-124. This is not the place to discuss the ensuing philosophical problem of relativism which Mannheim tried to avoid with the notion of 'relationism'. His attempt to expand historicism into an encompassing world view was severely taken to task by Karl Popper in his *The Poverty of Historicism,* 1957, (London: Routledge & Kegan Paul, 1969).

3. Cf. Maurice Halbwachs, *Les Cadres sociaux de la mémoire,* 1925, (Paris: Presses Universitaires de France, 1952).

4. See for instance Michael Ignatieff, *The Russian Album,* (London: Penguin Books, 1987), in particular chapter 1: "The Broken Path", pp. 1-20.

5. Emile Durkheim, *Pragmatisme et Sociologie. Cours inédit prononcé à la Sorbonne en 1913-1914 et restitué d'après des notes d'étudiants par Armand Cuvillier* (Pragmatism and Sociology. Unpublished course given at the Sorbonne in 1913-

1914, and reconstructed from student course notes by Armand Cuvillier), (Paris: Vrin, 1955).

6. Gnosticism was an important element in the so-called cultural revolution of 1968 and the succeeding years. I discussed this in my *The Abstract Society*, (Garden City, NY: Doubleday, 1970), chapter 4: 'The Spirit of Protest', pp. 92-136. See also the literature used and mentioned in the endnotes.

7. See Theodor Adorno, *The Jargon of Authenticity*, 1964, translated by K. Tarnowski and F. Will, (London: Routledge & Kegan Paul, 1973).

8. See Barry Bruce-Briggs (ed.), *The New Class?*, (New Brunswick, NJ: Transaction Publishers, 1979); Hansfried Kellner, Frank W. Heuberger (eds.), *Hidden Technocrats. The New Class and New Capitalism*, (New Brunswick, NJ: Transaction Publishers, 1992).

9. Obvious examples are Francis Fukuyama, *The End of History and the Last Man*, (New York: The Free Press, 1992) and Jean-Marie Guéhenno, *La Fin de la Démocratie*, (Paris: Editions Flammarion, 1994).

10. For 'nomos' as a meaningful order see Peter L. Berger, *The Sacred Canopy*, (Garden City, NY: Doubleday, 1967), pp.19-28. Berger: "the most important function of society (c.q. the institutions, AZ) is nomization." *Ibid.* p. 22. And: "every nomos is an edifice erected in the face of the potent and alien forces of chaos." *Ibid.*, p. 24.

11. Richard Crossman (ed.), *The God That Failed*, 1949, (New York: Harper & Row, 1963). The contributions of Arthur Koestler (pp.15-75) and André Gide (pp. 165-195) are of special interest, I think. See also Koestler's famous novel *Darkness at Noon*, 1946.

12. This section is an English version of an article I published in a Dutch sociological journal: "Instituties en geschiedenis", in: *Mens en maatschappij*, September 1967, pp. 277-298. A few sections of that article were also used in my *The Abstract Society*, (Garden City, NY: Doubleday, 1970), pp. 64-70.

13. Karl R. Popper, *The Poverty of Historicism*, *op. cit.* And Karl R. Popper, *The Open Society and Its Enemies*, 2 volumes, 1945, (New York: Harper Torchbooks, 1962.

14. Romano Guardini, *Das Ende der Neuzeit*, (Würzburg: Im Werkbund Verlag, 1950). Guardini (1885-1968) was a German theologian and cultural philosopher of Italian descent. He initially studied physics, chemistry and political economy, but decided after a religious crisis to switch to theology and to enter the priesthood. He was ordained in 1910 and received his theological doctorate in 1915. After five years of pastoral work he entered into a university career. He was dismissed by the Nazis in 1939, but took up his professorship again in 1945. In theology he focussed on liturgy, in philosophy he tried to integrate the thoughts of philosophers and writers. After the war he engaged in cultural analysis and cultural criticism. 'Das Ende der Neuzeit' belongs to this part of Guardini's vast intellectual legacy.

15. *Ibid.*, p. 13. My translation, AZ.

16. Cf. H. D. F. Kitto, *Greek Tragedy,* 1952, (Garden City, NY: Doubleday Anchor Books, 1954).

17. It is still worthwhile to read N.D. Fustel de Coulanges, *The Ancient City,* 1864, (Garden City, NY: Doubleday Anchor Books, n.d.) in which he warns us not to romanticize ancient Greece's democracy.

18. Karl Loewith, *Meaning in History,* 1949, (Chicago: The University of Chicago Press; Phoenix Books, 1962), p. 6. Cf. also Rudolf Bultmann, *Geschichte und Eschatologie* (History and Eschatology), (Tübingen: Mohr-Siebeck, 1959). On p. 16f Bultmann discusses Thucydides's conception of history: 'Historical processes are understood in the same way as cosmic processes; it is a movement in which despite the alterations always the same happens in new formations.' My translation, AZ.

19. Joachim of Fiore died as the abbot of the Cistercian monastery Fiore, Calabria in 1201. He was the founder of a prophetic movement, called *Joachimism* which was taken up by the Franciscan Order. History, according to Joachim, was divided in three stages. There is first the Era of the Father (the Old Testament, domination of the married laymen), next the Era of the Son (the New Testament, domination of the priests), and third the Era of the Spirit (the Present, domination of the monks). The third stage began with Benedict (480-543) and the Benedictine Rule, but received its full deployment in the Cistercian Order in 1260. The movement bore early reformatory elements, was increasingly anti-papal and stood in opposition to the ruling German emperors. Cf. Karl Heussi, *Kompendium der Kirchengeschichte,* 1907, (Tübingen: Mohr-Siebeck, 1956), para 61v, p. 232.

20. Mircea Eliade, *Cosmos and History. The Myth of Eternal Return,* 1954, (New York: Harper Torchbooks, 1959) develops the interesting argument that the myth of eternal return could save modern man from 'the terror of history'. Like Popper, but from a totally different point of view, Eliade attacks historicism and makes an attempt to eliminate history and historical consciousness in the process.

21. R. G. Collingwood, *The Idea of History,* 1946, (New York: Galaxy Books, 1961), p. 55.

22. Along to to Max Weber's well-known essay on Protestantism and the spirit of capitalism, one should consult Ernst Troeltsch, *Die Bedeutung des Protestantismus für die Entstehung der Modernen Welt,* (München-Berlin: Mohr-Siebeck, 1911). Unlike Weber Troeltsch emphasizes the pre-modern, medieval components of the thought of Luther and other reformers.

23. See Robert Nisbet, *History of the Idea of Progress,* New York: Basic Books, 1980). A very critical essay on the Enlightenment ideology of Progress is Albert Salomon, *The Tyranny of Progress,* (New York: The Noonday Press, 1955).

24. Jacob Burckhardt, *Die Kultur der Renaissance in Italien. Ein Versuch* (Renaissance Culture in italy. An essay), 1860, (Stuttgart: Alfred Kröner Verlag, 1976).

25. Peter Gay, *The Enlightenment: An Interpretation. The Rise of Modern Paganism,* 1966, (New York: Vintage Books, 1968).

26. In its infancy the Enlightenment 's rationalism was ahistorical and caught in gnostic dualism, as was exemplified by Descartes's opposition of the *res cogitans* vis-à-vis the *res extensae,* i.e. subjectivity versus objectivity. The ensuing anthropology was taken to task by the remarkable Giambattista Vico (1668-1744) who emphasized man's integrality (not just mind, reason, intellect, but also emotion, passion, fantasy) which should be viewed at all times in terms of his social and historical nature. Cf. his *On the Study Methods of Our Time,* 1709, translated by E. Gianturco, (New York: Bobbs-Merrill Company, The Library of Liberal Arts, 1965). The translator's introduction gives insight into Vico's attempt to reconcile the two worlds of the sciences and the humanities. As in Neo-Kantianism (cf. Rickert and Simmel) the study of history is what gives the humaniora their special and legitimate place.

27. Cf. Zygmunt Bauman, *Modernity and the Holocaust,* (Ithaca, NY: Cornell University Press, 1989).

28. Cf. Joseph Novak (alias Jerzy Kosinski), *The Future is Ours, Comrade,* 1960, (New York: E. P. Dutton & Co., 1964).

29. See my *A Theory of Urbanity. The Economic and Civic Culture of Cities,* (New Brunswick, NJ: Transaction Publishers, 1998).

30. This evolution was discussed by Benjamin Nelson, *The Idea of Usury. From Tribal Brotherhood to Universal Otherhood,* 1949, (Chicago: The University of Chicago Press, 1969).

31. Georg Simmel, *Ueber Sociale Differenzierung,* (Leipzig: Duncker & Humblot, 1890). Photomechanic reprint by Liberac NV Publishers, Amsterdam, 1966. See also Georg Simmel, *Conflict & the Web of Group Affiliations,* translated by Kurt H. Wolff and Reinhard Bendix, (New York: The Free Press of Glencoe, 1955).

32. See also my *The Abstract Society,* (Garden City, NY: Doubleday, 1970).

33. Cf. Peter L. Berger, Richard J. Neuhaus, *To Empower People. The Role of Mediating Structures in Public Policy,* (Washington, DC: American Enterprise Institute for Public Policy Research, 1977). Reprint with various comments in Michael Novak (ed.), *To Empower People. From State to Civil Society,* (Washington, DC : The AEI Press, 1996), pp.157-214. See also Robert W. Hefner (ed.), *Democratic Civility. The History and Cross-Cultural Possibility of a Modern Political Idea,* (New Brunswick, NJ: Transaction Publishers, 1998).

34. See e.g. Robert Putnam, "Bowling Alone: America's Declining Social Capital", in: *Journal of Democracy,* 6:7 (January 1995), pp. 65-79. This is not the place to discuss the debate that this article stirred up. It is, of course, questionable if America's social capital has degenerated to the extent Putnam has indicated. It is interesting to note that the social capital in European societies which formerly were organized in terms of a comprehensive welfare state, has been revitalized after policies of decentralization and privatization were applied. Cf. my contribution 'Civil Society, Pillarization and the Welfare State' to Hefner (ed.), *o.c.,* pp. 153-174, and my *The*

Waning of the Welfare State. The End of Comprehensive State Succor, (New Brunswick, NJ: Transaction Publishers, 1999).

35. If one reads Anthony Giddens, *The Third Way. The Renewal of Social Democracy,* (Cambridge: Polity Press, 1998) one wonders what is actually left of the ideological legacy of Social Democracy. There is in this manifesto precious little that a Liberal, or for that matter a Conservative, could disagree with. In that respect this treatise is quite modern. Some may even say post-modern.

36. See chapter 1, section 'institution and organization', and the endnotes 7-9 of that chapter. Cf. Hans van de Braak, *The Prometheus Complex. Man's Obsession with Superior Technology,* (Amersfoort, the Netherlands: Enzo Press, 1995).

37. Karl Mannheim, *Man and Society in an Age of Reconstruction,* 1940, (London: Routledge & Kegan Paul, 1960), pp.51-57.

38. See also my *On Clichés. The Supersedure of Meaning by Function,* (London: Routledge & Kegan Paul, 1979)

CHAPTER FOUR

Traditional Institutions and Flexible Networks

Sociology of knowledge

Prior to World War II the sociology of knowledge was a European affair. Its main message was that human knowledge is embedded in socio-economic and political structures, but it is in a sense also *a priori,* i.e. in origin and essence an inborn and natural capacity. It thus wavered between mainly Marxist materialism and neo-Kantian or neo-Hegelian idealism, and struggled with the problem of relativism. Karl Mannheim was in effect the embodiment of this European type of sociology of knowledge. He placed man's *Standortgebundenheit* – i.e. his being positioned in a socio-economic and political infrastructure – at the center of his sociology of knowledge. This reminds us of Marx's notion of *Unterbau* (economic infrastructure). But he also, in a more phenomenological manner, emphasized the importance of historical structures of meaning which have a distinct momentum of their own and are not a mere reflection of socio-economic and political circumstances, like the Marxist *Ueberbau* (cultural, ideological superstructure). In this part of his sociology of knowledge he paid tribute to Max Weber who always emphasized the autonomy of *Sinngebilde,* i.e. meaning structures or institutions. Mannheim tried to avoid relativism by what he called 'relationism' which he saw as a perpetual relating of knowledge to socio-cultural, socio-economic and political circumstances. Mannheim clearly struggled with these problems and did not solve them smoothly. This is the reason, I think, why reading his books and essays is such an intellectual challenge. Many, however, will disagree and take him to task for the obvious inconsistencies in his thinking, as did Robert K. Merton and Karl R. Popper in the 1950s.[1]

After the second world war sociology in general, and the sociology of knowledge in particular, has been mainly an American affair. 'Modern sociology', as it was often called, remained, until roughly the 1970s, American sociology. The discipline was in general held hostage by functionalism in theory and by operationalism in research. In this approach sociology of knowledge was reduced to the sociology of education and science, focussing primarily on their organization. That is, notwithstanding the influential treatise *The Social Construction of Reality* (1966) by Peter L. Berger and Thomas Luckmann which presented a phenomenologically inspired sociology of knowledge,[2] the sub-discipline remained predominantly a sociology of educational and scientific organizations. This was a regrettable reduction. In this chapter the sociology of knowledge is viewed instead as a sociological approach which analyzes and interprets knowledge – scientific as well as non-scientific, everyday knowledge or common sense – within the context of institutions. In other words, sociology of knowledge not as branch of organizational sociology but as a specimen of institutional sociology.

Mannheim distinguished two basic types of knowledge: *ideologies* which re-interpret and distort objective facts in order to maintain an existing constellation of power (the *status quo)*, and thereby to defend and promote distinct individual and collective interests; and *utopias* which also re-interpret and distort objective facts but do so in order to establish a better society in the future.[3] In our terminology, ideologies are regressive, utopias progressive thought structures. In focussing on these thought structures the sociology of knowledge according to Mannheim has a critical function to perform. It should help to separate the false and negative ideological components of knowledge from the correct and positive utopian components. That is, the sociology of knowledge should enable us to separate the ideological chaff from the utopian corn, after which the norishing spiritual bread of the future can hopefully be baked. He entrusted this task in particular to well-educated academicians, journalists, and artists. These people are the new intelligentsia which, he believed, has transcended the various class origins of its members. They are in that respect not classless but rather socio-economically free-floating. In other words they will not adhere to the ideas and sentiments of their class of origin in a fundamentalist manner. They are, we could add, thoroughly modernized. That qualifies them to scrutinize class-based ideas, and to separate the ideological chaff from the utopian corn. Incidentally, these ideas remind one of the Critical Theory of the *Frankfurter Schule*. Indeed, Mannheim who after his collaboration in the aborted Bela Kun regime fled Budapest, settled down in Frankfurt am Main, where he began his sociological studies. In a sense he stood at the cradle of Critical Theory.[4]

However, the sociology of knowledge in Europe has still another origin which is not to be found in the Hegelean-Marxist tradition, but rather in the neo-Kantian tradition as exemplified by Max Weber's 'interpretive sociology'. 'Critique' is in this neo-Kantian tradition not seen as a normative evalu-

ation of facts in terms of 'good' and 'bad', 'positive'and 'negative', 'beautiful'and 'ugly', 'nice' and 'nasty', etc. These are after all value judgments.
Critique is in this tradition rather a systematic and ideal-typical analysis of
empirical reality, which abstains from value judgments as much as possible.
Kant's 'Critique of Pure Reason' was not, of course, a normative criticism of
analytic reason but a detailed and fundamental analysis of our cognitive
competences which are transcendental, i.e. prior to sensual experiences of
reality. 'Critique' in the neo-Kantian sociology of knowledge is the equivalent of 'analysis'. This was systematically elaborated by the aforementioned
introduction to the sociology of knowledge by Berger and Luckmann. Inspired by Max Weber, but also by Alfred Schutz, George Herbert Mead ,
and Arnold Gehlen, Berger and Luckmann designed this brand of sociology
as a *Kultursoziologie* (cultural sociology) in which the dialectical tensions
between and the mutual relationships of individual (inter)actions and collective institutions occupy the central point of analytic attention.

The sociology of knowledge thus conceived enables us to interpret critically common sense knowledge as well as scientific or semi-scientific knowledge. In fact it opens venues to subject sociological concepts, theories and
theorems to critical scrutiny. They can, for instance, be confronted with actually occurring, empirical processes and structures. What is, for instance,
the connection between a sociological concept like *community* and socio-
cultural processes and structures? Such a concept is not hanging up in the
air. It is not a free-floating concept. It has been prominent in European Romanticism, as exemplified by socio-philosophical and sociological theories
of the *Gemeinschaft* vis-à-vis the *Gesellschaft*. The concept was again
prominent in the tradition of American 'community studies', and recently
again in so-called communitarianism. Why and how does such a tenacious
concept come and go?

Changing primacies of concepts

I find it fascinating to observe how certain sociological concepts suddenly
become fashionable, not just in academic sociology but also in journalism
and in politics. They acquire a fixed position in a rather general jargon and
are no longer defined in more or less precise descriptions. Apparently, everybody knows what is actually meant by them. They have acquired the status
of infallible clichés.[5] Dawkins would probably call them 'memes' and emphasize their replication power. In the 1970s, for example, the concept of
culture was not much in use outside cultural anthropology, because it was
considered to be 'vague', 'abstract', 'soft' and thus hard to operationalize.

106

Certainly among sociologists in those days, it was not academically correct to speak and write about culture. In fact, it was even considered a politically incorrect concept. In leftist circles culture was associated with conservatism. In a heated debate among anthropologists and sociologists the concept 'culture of poverty' was forthrightly rejected. Although I always found it difficult to understand because it expressed the institutionalization of poverty as a fact, the concept was (very normatively and politically) seen as an instrument of domination and control. In the 1980s, however, culture suddenly became a widely used and generally accepted concept. For example, concepts such as organizational culture or corporate culture are nowadays used in the social sciences, politics, public policy and business administration. Nobody asks anymore how to define it accurately. It has become an axiomatic cliché. In fact, 'culture' seems to have taken the place of 'social structure' which was widely used in the 1970s.

Inevitably, the sociologist of knowledge will then raise the question of what actually happened in society and culture for such a conceptual change to occur. It has been suggested that the wave of corporate mergers and takeovers in the 1980s and 1990s bear the brunt of responsibility for this conceptual change.[6] When a business corporation merged with or was taken over by a more powerful corporation, it was learned, usually the hard way, that it was not enough to take merely the financial aspects and the formal organizational structures of the two companies into account. In a merger or takeover not just assets and profits, structures and functions but above all human beings are being put together and forced to cooperate. These human beings bring into the new company their own idiosyncratic ways of acting, thinking and feeling, their own patterns of doing things, their often tenacious *modi operandi* with the emotions, sensitivities and awarenesses that go with them. Culture, it was learned, is not 'soft', 'vague' and 'abstract', but quite 'resilient', 'outspoken', and 'concrete'. All of this meant of course that the institutional dimensions became more prominent.

In the 1960s and 1970s socio-scientific concepts such as 'system' and 'planning' were widely used, far outside the realm of the social sciences from where they originated. Many social scientists as well as politicians and civil servants held to the belief (and indeed a mere belief it was) that the existing 'social structures', the so-called *status quo,* could be changed radically. Maybe they should not be overthrown in a Marxist revolution, but the least one could do was to try to re-structure them as radically as possible. The 'social system' which Talcott Parsons introduced in the 1950s as an analytic (ideal-typical) concept, now acquired a firm ontological status, and was demonized as the source of all social ills and problems.[7] These were years of discontent but, certainly in Western Europe, that did not prevent the spectacular rise of the comprehensive welfare state. If there was ever a regulating and controlling system, it was this welfare state. It led to the idea that society could be made and constructed according to rational, pre-conceived plans or scenarios. Actually, many of the left-of-center New Class who fought 'the System' at the end of the 1960s and the beginning of the 1970s, became civil servants in the welfare state and experts in planning and control. The idea of contingency which, of course, runs counter to the belief in rational planning and control, was whisked aside as a romantic and thus irrational vestige of the past. Incidentally, Mannheim's theory of planning was usually discarded, as it defined planning in terms of a substantially rational 'planning for freedom'. That is not what the politicians, civil servants and social scientist of the 1970s wanted or intended, when they propagated planning as the main tool for social policies. They had a functional-rational, instrumental type of planning in mind. But then, it is indicative that nowadays in Europe very few still talk and write about planning and control, while the concept of system has also become remarkably rare. In contrast, concepts such as contingency, differentiation, fragmentation, deregulation, innovation and flexibility nowadays hold a firm grip on the minds of many social scientists, politicians and civil servants. In public policy, business administration and social sciences one rather thinks and speaks in terms of flows and processes instead of in terms of structures and systems. Risks and experiments seem to have taken the place of planning and control. Apparently, important and decisive changes occurred in society and culture during the 1980s.

As the waning of the comprehensive welfare state set in, the belief in the 'makeability' of society and the rational planning of the future weakened.[8] The neo-liberal call for a free market, less regulated and controlled by an overbearingly bureaucratized state, was paired with the call for a decrease of corporatism on the part of societal organizations, the unions first and foremost (cf. Reaganomics and Thatcherism). Individual citizens, not collectivities, became the basic units of this neo-liberal order. The jargon of the market spread vastly and quickly. Thinking in terms of business administration and of management techniques took hold of the socio-scientific, the political and the bureaucratic minds and actions of people working in the public sector. This would have been unthinkable in the 1970s, when it would have been denounced as nefarious capitalist thought.

Thinking, speaking and writing in terms of the market and market forces took a remarkably strong hold of the public sector, where state services were now named 'products' and citizens 'consumers', or even 'customers'. They were presumably the customers of 'service producing' civil servants. In order to promote competitive forces many services and former government activities were contracted-out, a few of them were even privatized. Despite the fact that the state's core business – guaranteeing safety and security, defending constitutional rights, controlling and stimulating the national economy, watching monetary stability, etc.– is not a matter of production for a market simply because there is no real competition here. Moreover, although citizens are not consumers but bearers of constitutional rights, the jargon of the market has deeply penetrated into the public sector. What was literally unthinkable in the 1970s, became normal parlance in the 1980s and 1990s.

But the 1990s again witnessed some changes which are interesting from the point of view of the sociology of knowledge. After *die Wende* of 1989 it became increasingly evident in Central and Eastern Europe that the market would not revitalize and thus the economy would not prosper, if society did not also revitalize and evolve into a truly *civil* society, i.e. a society in which scores of organizations and institutions constitute a semi-autonomous field in which citizens are enabled to deploy their initiatives, realize their private and collective interests, and link their civil rights to public duties. It was indicative that the 'velvet revolution' at the end of the 1980s actually began with the call by Polish workers for a free union in a free society. It slowly dawned on Western Europe and North America as well, that an autonomous civil society constituted the necessary feeding ground for mutual trust and fruitful cooperation. Where trust is absent, the economy is impaired since distrust always inflates transaction costs, such as legal advice, expensive contracts, long and exasperating meetings and negotiations, etc. In short, the jargon of the market still prominent in the 1980s was, if not pushed aside, certainly mitigated by a *moral jargon* in which concepts such as responsible citizenship, corporate governance, trust, social capital, and civil society began to occupy a central position. The concept of community and the idea of communitarianism belong to this important change as well. As they are closely related to the concept of insitution and the idea of neo-institutionalism we must subject them to closer scrutiny.

Community – a hazardous concept

Over the past few years the concept of community has experienced a remarkable comeback in socio-scientific, political and bureaucratic discourse. In fact it has acquired a rather fixed position together with the socio-philosophical and normative-political idea of *communitarianism*.[9] If a concept acquires such notoriety, it is imperative for social scientists not to accept it thoughtlessly, but to subject it to rational scrutiny for which the sociology of knowledge offers the appropriate conceptual tools. There are some serious analytical and normative disadvantages connected with the concept of community and the idea of communitarianism. They call for a concise critique and an acceptable alternative. We should stick to the basic tenet of the sociology of knowledge that concepts and their changes over time are related to socio-cultural realities and their changes over time. Just as there is some method in most madness, there is always some empirical reality in jargon and popular clichés. What is the empirical reality behind this remarkable return of the nineteenth century concept of community?

To start with, there are two distinct meanings of the word community. It is often used superficially as an administrative concept: the Middletown community as a legal and administrative entity. In this sense it is comparable to the German word *Gemeinde*. But then there is also the sociological concept of community, comparable to the German word *Gemeinschaft*. In this sociological sense, community refers to a configuration of human beings who live, work, act and interact together in face-to-face relationships within the context of distinct moral values and norms. Community will be used here in this second sense of the word. But a warning is in order here: the Anglo-Saxon, American concept of community is not the same as the German, continental-European word *Gemeinschaft*. To start with, *Gemeinschaft* has, ever since Ferdinand Toennies's classical treatise, an opposite, called *Gesellschaft* which is a type of society in which the interactions are not face-to-face, in which there is distance and organized coldness between people. It is not morality as in *Gemeinschaft*, but functional expediency which moves and drives a Gesellschaft. The English concept 'community' does not possess such an opposite since the meaning and connotation of 'society' is definitely not *Gesellschaft*.

Sometimes an American community in the real social world may indeed come close to a *Gemeinschaft*, but that, I shall argue, is in fact a sort of degeneration. The core of the meaning of 'community' is in my view very different from that of *Gemeinschaft*. This difference, it should be stressed, is not merely semantic, but very much socio-philosophical and political. As to the latter, in terms of democracy the notion of *Gemeinschaft* is, unlike that of community, a hazardous one.

It is my contention that when Americans speak of community, usually more explicitly expressed as *our* community, they actually mean something else than Germans talking about *Gemeinschaft*, rarely expressed by the way as *unsere Gemeinschaft*. Community in America is the concrete social and cultural environment of a distinct group of people. The community, it is firmly believed, should remain safe and wholesome, particularly in view of the next generations. A phrase one rarely hears in continental Europe, is always very prominent in America: 'We want our community to be a good place for our children to live and grow up in!' The phrase is certainly in use in non-urban communities, but also in (big) cities where people will often claim that they want to keep up their neighborhoods as communities that are safe and socio-culturally wholesome.

Naturally, these are normative and often utopian ideals which in the real world can not and will not always be realized optimally. Urban slums subjected to poverty and physical deterioration are, of course, far removed from the community ideal. But that is the sociologically customary distance between ideals and reality. The point I want to emphasize here is the rarely observed fact that there is an essential difference between the original American concept of community and the German concept *Gemeinschaft*. What then is the difference?

To start with, even the most community-minded Americans remain rugged individualists who are very sensitive as far as their privacy is concerned. They will not easily immerse themselves in a collective 'we feeling' that supersedes or engulfs their individuality. *Gemeinschaft*, on the contrary, is very much a collectivist concept. The individual is expected to be absorbed by the *Gemeinschaft*, to experience a dizzying 'we feeling' that actually destroys individuality. It is but a small step to define it in terms of *Volk*, or, even more fatefully, *Rasse*. It then represents an exclusive collectivity which easily views itself as being superior. In fact, *Gemeinschaft* nowadays often stands for ethnicity. Religion is also a *Gemeinschaft* building force which strongly inclines towards a rather closed type of collectivism. The history of monastic orders in the Roman Catholic Church presents many examples of such often exclusive and closed communities.[10] In any case, *Gemeinschaft* is a collectivity that supersedes individuals and their private and material interests. It is wholesome precisely because it is collective.

Secondly, the community is for Americans not an end but rather a means – a way to help individuals, and in particular their children, to advance in life materially, to participate in close cooperation with others in the project of Progress. That is in the end what America is all about for most Americans. *Gemeinschaft* has a very different sociological and socio-psychological content and connotation. It is not a means, an instrument for the advancement of individual and material interests and progress but an end – in fact, an ultimate end in itself! Individuals should let themselves be consumed by the *Gemeinschaft*. This coincides with two different types of ethics. In the American community the ethic of responsibility prevails. It is a sober and rational ethic (*Verantwortungsethik*). The European *Gemeinschaft* aspires to an ethic of ultimate ends driven by irrational inclinations and aspirations (*Gesinnungsethik*).

Obviously, and this is a third difference, a *Gemeinschaft* is a potentially closed collectivity. It is rather exclusive because the strong 'we feeling' is necessarily linked to an equally strong 'them feeling'. The European idea of community has always been exclusive, if not in terms of nationality (c.q. *Volk*) or ethnicity (c.q. *Rasse*), then certainly in terms of socio-economic class and socio-cultural status group (*Stand*). The American idea(l) of community, on the contrary, is in principle (that is, *de iure*, in terms of the Constitution, not *de facto*, i.e. in reality) an open and inclusive collectivity. America unlike most European nations, is a land of immigrants. Ethnic differentiations and fragmentations into separate 'ethnic communities' have aggravated in the last decades, but still the notion of community is a much more inclusive and open notion than that of *Gemeinschaft* which tends to be exclusive and closed. The 'ethnic cleansing' practices of the 1990s in the former Yugoslavia present a bizarre and cruel example of this point. Only the lunatic fringe in America would incite an 'ethnic cleansing' for the benefit of a particular community. Together with collectivism this dimension of exclusivity of *Gemeinschaft* is crypto-fascist.

Fourthly, while Americans tend to think about their community in a bottom-up (*anascopic*) fashion, Europeans are much more inclined to conceive of community in a top-down *(katascopic)* manner. The anascopic conception of community can be radicalized and eventually end up in libertarianism. But if radicalized, the katascopic conception may easily end up in authoritarianism and even totalitarianism. These are, of course, extremes. Yet, we do encounter in them another, little observed difference: American communitarianism is originally a neo-liberal and progressive philosophy, whereas European communitarianism (notably, *Gemeinschaft* cannot offer a useful noun similar to communitarianism) remains in essence conservative, regressive and often reactionary, if not fascist.

Once again, we should not be naïve. There are, of course, many forces at work in America which run counter to this picture. Many communities position themselves as separate, usually ethnic entities. In the name of ethnic community some aspire to the breakdown of the multicultural mozaic that this society has been until now, or close themselves off from the rest of society. For example, increasingly the wealthy in the suburbs literally put walls around their community, and employ private guards to take care of their safety. Such communities resemble internment camps, although the incarceration is a self-imposed one. In such cases community degenerates into an exclusive and closed phenomenon. Yet, on the whole, as threatening as such paranoia is to the American notion of a wholesome community, this and similar closures are still the proverbial exceptions to the general rule. The general rule is that unlike *Gemeinschaft*, which in origin and nature is closed, katascopic, collectivistic and essentialist, community is in origin and nature open, anascopic, individualistic and functionalist.

Lately, America witnessed the emergence of a movement, called *communitarianism*. Proponents and leading ideologues view it primarily as a social, not as an intellectual movement which may explain why its theoretical foundation has been so shallow up until now. What is worrysome in particular is the fact that the notion of community is not clearly defined and comes suspiciously close to the idea of *Gemeinschaft*. References to *Gemeinschaft* are strikingly naïve.[11] This is, in view of some fundamental changes that will be discussed in the remainder of this chapter, regrettable. Communitarianism is meant as a response to socio-cultural changes and challenges, but its socio-philosophical and sociological conceptualization is not just shallow but in view of the predominant transformations inadequate. Since the 1980s or thereabouts, two global, socio-cultural and political transformations have emerged which run counter to the aims of the communitarian movement: firstly, the European concept of *Gemeinschaft* refers to a centered reality, whereas everwhere we can witness an ever increasing decentering of the world; secondly, this concept also refers to traceable limits and borders, whereas we witness everywhere the fact that limits and borders are becoming porous. Decentering and delimiting (or debordering) are two processes running counter to the notion of *Gemeinschaft* and its ensuing communitarianism. They must be discussed in some more detail, after which I shall argue that in view of these two processes we should substitute the concept community with two related concepts: *institutions* and *networks,* while communitarianism should be exchanged for *neo-institutionalism.*

Uniformity and differentiation

Before we discuss the two transformations mentioned at the end of the previous section, we must briefly deal with a paradox that has become characteristic of our late-modern, or post-modern world: there is a seemingly progressive uniformity but there is also a progressive differentiation, and the two seem to function as communicating vessels. Or phrased differently, on the one hand, the world is growing more and more uniform – economically, socially, culturally and in a sense also politically. It is often called *globalization,* or colloquially *McWorld*. But on the other hand, a strong case can be made for the opposite proposition that the world is progressively compartmentalized, fragmented, and differentiated.

The uniformity thesis usually presents variations of Max Weber's proposition that modernization is first and foremost a progressive rationalization, a disenchantment of the world brought about and exacerbated by bureaucracy, science and technology. A recent variation of this thesis is George

Ritzer's observation that the world is being engulfed by a pervasive *Mc-Donaldization*, which is a pervasive standardization of all the components of human life.[12] Generally popular theories about 'the end of ideology' and 'the end of history' also belong to this uniformization thesis. Allegedly the big ideological controversies belong to the past now that a general, vague and thus rather spineless liberality, economically borne by triumphant capitalism, has supposedly overtaken mankind – or at least that part thereof which is socio-economically and socio-culturally developed (modernized), and economically well-off.

Post-modernists usually put forward the contrary idea that the opposite of such a generalization and uniformization has occurred and is still taking place. We witness everywhere processes of individualization, differentiation, fragmentation, specialization, and parcelling which are fostered and globally distributed by the Information and Communication Technology (ICT). Far from promoting the uniformity and stagnation of communication, Internet enables a world wide interaction of individuals who in former days would never have exchanged anything among each another. Processes, flows and perpetual change, not fixed structures and systems are the idiosyncratic characteristics of the electronic age and the cyberspace it has brought about. Likewise, it is not totality but individuality, not systemic convergence but individual divergence, not generalization but differentiation, not rational causality but irrational contingency, not necessity but chance which moves and inspires this electronic age. It has altered globally our societies, cultures, polities, and economies – and thus, of course, our consciousness and style of life.

Robert Reich has argued that in corporations the days are over in which 'Fordism' massively poured out products, while through sophisticated marketing the passive market was manipulated to absorb this mass production. Also, 'Fordism' knew a top-down command structure which allotted preset positions to people who were in fact one of a kind – workers. This too is a thing of the past. We allegedly now live in the day and age of 'Toyotism' which is a production system in which products are tailor and custommade. Computers enable us to produce products according to the individual wishes of the customers. Mass production is increasingly being set aside by differentiated production. Moreover, the 'Toyotistic' organization is not a hierarchical, top-down command structure in which uniformized workers are allotted preset positions. They are, on the contrary, flat and informal organizations in which workers are partners with individual capacities which are the organization's best assets. They are the valuable human resources which are evaluated and then used in the production process. Meanwhile, due to the ICT many tasks can be performed by the individual partner at home. The uniformizing time schedule of 'Fordism' is in many organizations set aside in favor of an individual time schedule. The individual output per capita not the hours spent in the office is after all what really counts.[13]

However, it is not very useful to distinguish sharply between a uniformity thesis on the one hand and a differentiation thesis on the other hand. Such oppositions usually manage to warm up ideological hearts, but rarely enlighten clear thinking minds. In fact, while they reject the legacy of the Enlightenment most post-modernists dramatically derail as far as clear analyses and interpretations of reality is concerned. This is particularly true of their rather romantic flirtations with differentiation, individualization, chance and contingency. (It is indeed remarkable how much most post-modernist philosophers resemble nineteenth-century romantics.) On the other hand, the defendants of generalization, uniformity, causality and necessity are as ideologically misguided and misguiding. They stick to a past in which coherence and limits were still dominant and influential. We rather have to draw the somewhat paradoxical conclusion that developed societies these days increasingly exhibit a global tendency towards uniformity, whereas we witness at the same time a widespread differentiation and individualization on the grass roots level. On the European continent, for example, there is a progressive transcendence of national borders, economically (cf. the *euro*, and the borderless job market), culturally (cf. numerous educational and artistic exchange programs), and socially (cf. transnational leisure activities and vacations), while in these areas globalization is also rapidly on the increase. It is even claimed that the nation-state with its distinct national borders and its distinct sovereignty is in decline, and may soon be a thing of the past.[14] Yet, at the same time we can witness the rise of regions and cities, often merging into urban regions, which function as the main engines behind Europe's economy and material welfare.[15]

Some, like the elder statesman Jacques Delors, the authoritative former chairman of the European Commission, believe in the traditional – in origin Roman-Catholic – subsidiarity principle. Subsidiarity means that higher levels of authority, say the European Commission in Brussels, should not engage in policy ventures which can be better dealt with by lower levels of authority such as regions, counties and municipalities. Others may want to go one step further and embrace the old Calvinist principle of 'sovereignty within one's own circle'. The nonconformist founding fathers of America embraced this radically decentralized principle which left a still visible imprint on the political culture of this country. In any case, such theories and theorems, but also ideas about regional and urban culture as well as organizational or corporate culture, indicate that people are not prepared to identify themselves with very general and abstract entities such as 'the welfare state' or 'a unified Europe', let alone 'the global system'. They identify themselves individually and collectively with concrete entities such as the family, the neighborhood, the city and the region. These are, in fact, essential institutions which no politician can afford to ignore.

Against this background we must investigate the differentiation thesis in some more detail. For clarity's sake I shall focus this discussion on two processes which have led to a multiplicity of centers and a porosity of borders. We must return to a point briefly made in the Introduction, i.e. the decentered and borderless world of today.

Multiple centers and porous borders

We can witness these days that politically, socio-economically and culturally there is no longer a single center or demonstrably coherent group of centers that direct and stimulate our individual and collective endeavors. In particular the areas of power (politics) and spirit (culture) which until recently possessed determinable cores giving direction and guidance to the populace at large, have been pemeated by this process of decentering. One does not have to embrace post-modernism to realize that as regards centers the situation has changed dramatically. Centered elites which in relatively small numbers determined the contents and main directions of human behavior – in religion, politics, economics, entertainment, fashion, and so forth – and which possessed some sort of durability and tenacity, are difficult to find these days. There rather is today a multiplicity of such centers which generally lack durability and tenacity. This is a process of *decentering* which, needless to add, is something else than decentralization of power, since it affects much deeper layers of human action, thought and emotion.

To give an obvious example of decentering, the days are gone in which the church, visibly located in the geographical center of the city or the village, constituted in conjunction with a relatively small societal elite the very center of politicial, socio-cultural and sometimes even economical events. As could be witnessed in most Western-European countries, in the twentieth century the primacy of the church was taken over step by step by the central government. Poor relief, succor of the sick and destitute, care of the elderly, leisure programs for youth and youngsters, and so forth had often been voluntary services offered by the various churches and sects. They were successively taken over by the increasingly comprehensive and lavishly subsidizing welfare state. It is, for instance, significant that the notion of charity gradually has acquired a bad reputation.[16] Through numerous subsidies and policies central governments emitted financial impulses to which, naturally, many (bureaucratic) strings were attached. It meant a considerable loss of autonomy because, after all, who pays the piper chooses the tune. In a sense, the state thus acquired a providential status, because while the church lost its grip on society, the state took over its place. The French word for welfare state is revealing in this respect: *état providente*. Even if, as in the case of a pillarized society such as the Netherlands, various organizations in the fields of education, sciences, health care, arts and media maintained their statutory autonomy vis-à-vis the central state, they changed under the impact of the comprehensive and centralized welfare state into state organizations.[17] In this sense, the central government was indeed a powerful center upon which public and private organizations and individual citizens depended increasingly.

Yet, the rather spectacular waning of the comprehensive welfare state after around 1980 put an end to this centering of socio-economic, socio-cultural and socio-political energies and impulses.[18] We live today in a multiplicity of economic centers (not just one market but a global plurality of markets), of socio-cultural centers (not just single sets of values and norms, clustered around single institutions but a great variety of values and norms and a vast variety of institutions), of socio-political centers (not just nationally bound sets of social policies but national boundaries transcending social policies). This brings us to the increased porosity of borders.

Cognitive and moral borders not just the geographical borders between nation-states have become increasingly porous since the 1980s and increasingly vague and abstract, which is inherent to the process of modernization. The end of the Cold War, the ensuing globalization, the growth and expansion of the single European market, the consolidation of the markets of Canada, America and Mexico, and the so-called ICT-revolution have contributed to the emergence of a kind of world in which geographical borders and moral and cognitive limits loose their importance and relevance.

Take for example the limits and borders of cognition. They indicated in former days what in all sensibility could and could not be thought, lest the difference between mental health and insanity be obfuscated. Today these limits and borders are, to say the least, rather vague and often porous. So-called deconstructivists often publish texts which must strike the naive reader as simply being insane. In the world of the arts and performances concepts such as absurdity and insanity have become obsolete, while artistic expressions in the world of pop culture could be labelled 'crazy' or 'mad', if one were to apply traditional, 'old-fashioned' criteria. While dadaism was still shocking in the roaring 1920s, today it is old hat. The madness it had to offer in protest against an alleged establishment, seems to have become quite normal in today's museums for modern art and on the stages of the performing arts. It may not make much sense to still use and apply such criteria, but one should note also that there are no altogether clear criteria anymore to make sound evaluations. Beyond the simple anything-goes stance there are only multiple and rather flexible criteria by which human expressions can be evaluated that is, if one still cares to assess them at all. Rather strict assessments were still needed in the heyday of the comprehensive welfare state which subsidized cultural productions according to certain uniform standards and criteria. However, with the steadfast progress of modernization such evaluations have become more and more problematic and arbitrary. In the Netherlands, many negative evaluations regarding art subsidies have been brought to court by the artists concerned. The judge is, of course, only qualified to review the procedures by which the evaluation came about, but evidently the lack of clear aesthetic criteria has facilitated this choice for litigation on the part of artists. In any case, this indicates that values and norms cannot be defined in a clear manner any longer. They are in that sense decentered and their boundaries are porous.

The multiplicity of centers and porousness of borders is demonstrated in an exemplary manner by universities and the sciences. Obviously, the university as the institutional home of the sciences has profited from the Enlightenment and the Industrial Revolution. They provided them with an influential, clearly delimited and quite central position in modern society. But now that the Enlightenment and its rationalism are losing ground in postmodern society and the ICT Revolution is changing the world of cognition dramatically, it may well be the university's turn to suffer from the loss of influence and power that the church has suffered in the past decades. In fact, it is observable that 'faith in science' is in decline.[19] The borders between science and para-science (astronomy-astrology, psychology-parapsychology, medicine-paramedicine, etc.) have become increasingly porous, while the traditional borders between the natural sciences and the humanities (C.P. Snow's sharply distinguished 'two cultures'), and the traditional borders between scientific disciplines and specialisms are increasingly becoming obsolete. There is beyond and outside these scientific obfuscations a growing porousness of the borders between rationality and irrationality. Businessmen, for example, who during the day are working with highly rational, computerized and statistical models after working hours visit their astrologers, or are subjected to bizarre physical exercises and various psychotherapies. Vague New Age philosophies, larded with popularized versions of Jungian depth psychology, Buddhism or other Oriental world views, complement these physical and psychic ordeals. In this way, corporate culture gurus claim, the bodies and the minds of managers are liberated from stress, anxiety and other generally hard to determine ailments. No wonder that a rather ancient figure reemerges in the post-modernist scene, gains notoriety, and reaps the material fruits he has always been after: the charlatan.[20]

Although it is not a dominant phenomenon transsexuality is an interesting case of border porosity. Not long ago it was impossible for persons who had been born in a wrong body gender-wise to cross the biological borderline that separates the two sexes. Today surgical, pharmacological and biological technologies have advanced to such a degree that these formerly impenetrable barriers have opened up. Likewise, the formerly very hard biological limit of the female climacteric beyond which it was impossible to bear children, can be transcended these days through the technique of *in vitro* fertilization. The freezing of fertilized eggs enables people to choose the moment of pregnancy. Even the death of the father, not long ago the absolute limit for passing on life, is no longer an impediment for giving birth to his child.

Needless to say, all this raises ethical questions and problems which are not at all easy to answer and to solve. It stands to reason that morality (the totality of values and norms that ought to guide human actions and interactions) and ethics (the group-specific, normative rules and regulations to which people adhere in their actions and interactions) are again very prominent in today's discussions and debates. The days of philosophical neo-positivism and functionalism that deemed such issues metaphysical and thus senseless and useless, belong indeed to the past. But in a world with multiple centers and porous borders the search for solutions and answers to the problems and questions of morality and ethics is painful and extremely difficult, particularly if one realizes that a return to the traditional, solidly institutionalized values and norms of former days is not feasible. Fundamentalism which tries to re-establish ancient centers and borders in a dogmatic manner is not an adequate answer to the issues raised by late- or post-modernity.

Institutions and networks

In the light of these two processes – decentering and debordering – the call for communitarianism is not a very adequate one, certainly not if community is taken in the European sense of *Gemeinschaft*. Community in this sense, as was argued earlier, demands a directive center and rather clear boundaries. In the debates on civil society the concepts of institution and network have meanwhile become more prominent. In economics and political science there is these days much discussion about *neo-institutionalism*, while the post-modernist idea of a *network society* has gained prominence in sociology, public policy and political science also. It makes sense to link these two concepts.

Institutions are, as we have seen, traditional patterns of behavior, passed on from generation to generation, changing slowly, if at all, in traditional societies which view them as God given or natural norms from which one should not deviate as they are strongly tabooed. Individuals are called upon to accept the institutions of their forefathers as authority structures that are not to be questioned. In a sense, traditional institutions 'consumed' the individuals who were born into them and will eventually die out of them. When modernization sets in, institutions will change, often rapidly as they lose their sacred and tabooed status. They are rationalized and looked at in a more instrumental and functional manner. Yet, they are and remain more or less objective structures in the context of which individuals are able to realize their individuality, their personality, and even their liberty. Emile Durkheim gave a pertinent definition of institutions as 'ways of acting, thinking and feeling, exterior to the individual and ingrained with the power of coercion by which they impose themselves on the individual'.

The 'objectivity' of institutions – i.e. the fact that we are born into them and will eventually die out of them, while they continue to impose themselves on successive generations – has always been judged positively as well as negatively. Sociologists such as Durkheim and Gehlen emphasized the importance of 'objective', taken-for-granted institutions for the survival of the human species, whereas others, more inspired by Marx and Freud, focussed instead on the alienating and neuroticizing functions of 'reified' institutional structures. The ensuing discussion which quickly gets stuck in the opposition of conservative versus progressive stances, is theoretically and analytically unfruitful.

Institutions as patterns of behavior are not, of course, empty shells. They are first and foremost patterns of values, norms and meanings. They are, in fact, what Max Weber called *Sinngebilde* (i.e. meaning structures), and what according to the writings of George Herbert Mead can be called structures of *meaningful interactions*. Institutions incorporate the values, norms and meanings that give contents and directions to human actions and interactions. It is particularly important to stress that institutions render behavior – one's own actions, interactions, thoughts and feelings as well as those of others – meaningful and thereby understandable. Moreover, people will define the individual and collective identitities of themselves or of others in terms of the institutions they or the others live by. (Identity can be seen as everything that answers the question 'who am I? or 'who are we?')

Georg Simmel has been one of the rare sociological theorists who integrated the notion of networks into the notion of institutions. Like Max Weber, Simmel realized that institutions do not really exist ontologically but consist in the final analysis of human actions and interactions. If one wants to study the institution of marriage empirically, one must study the actions and interactions, the thoughts and feelings of married people. But unlike Weber and most of his contemporaries, Simmel realized also that the predominant character of these actions and interactions was what he called *Wechselwirkung*, reciprocity or interplay. Each individual is a player of various roles that belong to different institutions. These roles entertain various reciprocities and thereby constitute a web or network enacted by the individual role players. Moreover, the individual actor belongs to different, intersecting groups, is as it were taken up in a web of affiliations. In addition, Simmel realized that in modern, pluralistic societies these webs of social roles and group affiliations are very complex and numerous which poses many problems for the individual but also many challenges and opportunities. The awareness of being an individual, we saw earlier, is heightened in such a situation, and it also requires active and conscious management on the part of the individual to deal with these complexities.[21]

In most theories of institutionalization the fact remains underexposed that people engage in scores of reciprocal relations and exchanges within the institutional framework they grew up in. Functional and business-like exchanges not just bonds of friendship and love, are in existence which sometimes can be very durable, transcending many years in a semi-institutional fashion, then again remain temporary and fragile. In other words, in traditional, thoroughly institutionalized societies people also relate to each other in *networks* which can remain informal and fragile, but are often also rather formal and institutional. Such networks secure a measure of flexibility within the otherwise thoroughly institutionalized framework of social bonds.

It is not easy to define the concept of network, maybe because it is, unlike the institution, such an ephemeral phenomenon. I see *a network as a set of reciprocal, usually informal, often rather anonymous bonds between actors (individuals or collectivities), which is set up and maintained for the promotion of private interests, and usually lacks a fixed, vertical hierarchy of power.* The actors in a network are often individuals, but collectivities, like business corporations or universities, can also enter into network-like, strategic alliances, if that serves their mutual interests. In fact, in many cases such alliances appear to be more efficient and effective than mergers or take-overs. In any case, network-like reciprocal bonds between either individuals or collectivities can span the entire globe. They are often virtual realities as in the case of Internet connections between individuals who are antipodes.

Networks are not usually inherited from previous generations, and thus lack tradition. On the contrary, they have been set up voluntarily by the involved actors and maintained as long as they function well and remain mutually profitable. Their voluntary nature is important. In contrast to traditional institutions which are not set up but historically 'grown' and 'inherited', flexible networks are in general the result of rational choice. They usually lack, certainly in the beginning, the feelings and emotions that institutional bonds generally carry and convey. However, unlike institutions which are closely linked to formal, in particular legal norms and controls, networks are in principle free, open and informal. A network usually presents a horizontal structure in which power is equally distributed. In a democratic environment a network will function best, if it is based morally on taken-for-granted trust. There are exceptions though, as is illustrated by the mafia, an example of a network organization, which is notorious for its unequal distribution of power, and which operates via fear and distrust. As is well known, this and other specimens of organized crime function optimally in societies that lack democratic institutions or suffer from a severely weakened institutional democracy.

The Italian *mafia* is an interesting case. It is indeed a perfect example of a network organization which is also thoroughly institutionalized, yet consists of countless informal ties, bonds, exchanges, partnerships, and above all dependencies. Outsiders can hardly make sense of this complex maze of network relations which, of course, protects them against the law and possible police interferences. Incidentally, post-modernist proponents of a radically de-institutionalized network society should take into account that such a society would present a prime breeding ground for mafia-like organized crime.

Thus, networks and networking are not really new forms of behavior and social structure, as is often claimed or suggested these days. They are not typical of the post-industrial ICT age and its related cyberspace of flows. Yet, what has changed in the last couple of decades is the character of institutions and the character of the process of institutionalization. To sum up this point briefly, when a society modernizes, we will witness that institutions grow vague, in a sense superficial. They no longer touch and influence people deeply, but remain ephemeral, functioning on the surface of their behavior. There is, in other words, *thick and thin institutionalization*, and in a fully modernized society, certainly in an ICT-society with scores of virtualities, flexibilities and contingencies, institutions will be thin and ephemeral rather than thick and traditional. However, I shall argue also that in such a late- or post-modern society networks will gradually become thicker than thinner, if they are to be functional and useful at all. We are thus moving towards a society and culture with thin institutions which in a sense carry thick networks.

Thin institutions, thick networks

Arnold Gehlen, whose theory of institutions we discussed in chapter two, believed that modernization entailed inevitably a process of ever increasing subjectivization which would endanger the institutions as it proportionately weakens their objectivity and taken-for-grantedness. Modern people no longer take their traditional institutions for granted, enter in endless and, according to Gehlen, utterly fruitless debates and discussions about what to do, think or feel. All this talking, which Helmuth Schelsky once nicely called *Dauerreflexion* (permanent reflexion),[22] impairs action and production, and contributes to the weakening of culture. We are living, he warned like a prophet of doom, in an era of late culture – *Spätkultur* – and it constitutes in fact the end of history – *post-histoire*.

Gehlen's institutional theory must be taken seriously, something which is done in chapter two and throughout the following chapters. It presents an impressive analysis of the anthropological necessity of institutions, and provides moreover a clear insight into the nature and functions of institutionalization. Yet, his theory of modernization as a progressive de-institutionalization is much less attractive. It led, as we saw, to a cultural pessimism whose rather reactionary conservatism precluded any idea of cultural development, innovation and progress. Institutions in Gehlen's theory lack any degree of flexibility. They are objective patterns of acting, thinking and feeling that are totally locked in and caged by tradition, and thus by the past. Individuals are called upon to let themselves be consumed by the institutions they grew up in, the state in the first place. In his theory of modernization there is no room whatsoever for the fact that historical institutions (i.e. in my terminology institutes) change over time, and do so very rapidly and very intensively in modern times. What he bemoans as institutional destruction and institutional loss – *Institutionsabbau, Institutionsverlust* – constitutes in effect a fundamental transformation of institutions on the institute level. These changes affect the very nature of institutionalization.

In the pre-modern world institutions were religiously motivated and magically driven structures which men were admonished not to alter as they had been handed down by God or the gods. What God unites, man should not separate – that was the idea behind the institution of marriage. But not just marriage and the family, also the church, the monarchy, the state, the nation were conceived and ideologically defended as god-given institutions against which one should never rebel, lest grave individual or collective disasters should befall men, women and children. Sure enough, in pre-modern times there were regular revolts against the powerful institutions of the day, as is demonstrated by the recurrent peasant revolts in the Middle Ages. Naturally, they were labelled as sectarian and sacrilegious. After the Enlighten-ment the place of (non-rational) God was assumed by (rational) Nature which was subsequently defined as the ultimate legitimacy of the existing in-stitutions. Even today patterns of behavior that are clearly 'cultural', are de-fined as being 'natural' and 'normal'. Consequently, behavior that deviates from these patterns is labelled 'unnatural' and 'abnormal'.[23] It is indeed in-teresting to note that people have the tendency to call the institutions they grew up in 'natural'. Asked why they do things the way they do, people often reply 'naturally we do this so.' The word 'naturally' is the equivalent of 'of course'.[24]

Traditional institutions are usually 'greedy'. Lewis Coser introduced the helpful concept of *greedy institutions* which demand from people complete loyalty and undivided commitment. One serves the greedy institution and is, as it were, totally consumed by it. Coser discussed three historical cases: (a) the serving of the ruler by eunuchs, Court Jews and Royal Mistresses; (b) the serving of the family by domestic servants and traditional housewives; (c) the serving of the collective by religious sectarians, Jesuits and Leninists, and people living in celibacy.[25] These are extreme cases. Most traditional in-stitutions bear greedy features as they impose on the individual strict and demanding norms and values which are binding. Traditional institutions re-quire a loyalty and a commitment which in modernity are rather rare and very hard to come by.[26]

Indeed, all this has changed, or is still changing. Institutions are no longer believed to be god-given or natural. The idea that they have been socially constructed and are handled by human beings according to their needs and interests has become widely spread in contemporary society. Notions of construction and beyond that deconstruction of social and cultural reality have become very popular over the past decades. They have led to a perva-sive sense of cultural relativity and, as we saw before, to an equally pervasive anti-institutional mood. Moreover, apart from some isolated fundamental-ist groups and sects, in most Western societies of today there are no greedy institutions left which demand from individuals undivided commitment and complete loyalty. On the contrary, in most organizations commitment and loyalty have become rather rare virtues.

Tradition borne by institutions provides societies with *cultural gravity*. It prevents people from floating around without direction, and it halts the ten-dency to change aimlessly and recklessly. Moreover, institutional tradition maintains in the present the bond between past and future. These functions are not to be taken lightly, as often happens in anti-institutionalism. How-ever, tradition can easily become a cumbersome burden when it is seen and experienced as a sacred and magically tabooed phenomenon. Sacred and magically tabooed traditions hold societies in a stifling grip, and preclude change and innovation, even if they are needed for survival. They tie the present to an ideologically venerated and celebrated past as a period of glory, as a golden past which, of course, is supposedly always better than the present. The future, on the other hand, is feared as a threat, as the abode of uncertainties and contingencies. In such a pre-modern situation the process of institutionalization is heavy and cumbersome, the institutions 'greedy', 'heavy' and 'thick'. They are not seen and experienced as semi-objective, historical and social constructions but rather as metaphysical, eternal and ahistorical entities. These 'heavy' and 'thick' entities maintain a sacred *status quo* in which change and transformation are to be precluded as much as possible. These traditional institutions are not only 'greedy', 'heavy' and 'thick', as we will see, but also 'closed'. They hold people hostage, as in a fatal embrace.

Modernization which entered a decisive phase after World War II, has changed all this. With innovations such as ICT, genetic manipulation, nanotechnology, and space research we have entered a new phase in a process that has developed over more than two centuries. The impact on institutions has been of great significance, because the further and the deeper modernization advanced, the 'thinner', the 'lighter', the more 'open' and 'flexible' they have become. This is not a demise of institutions, this is not *Institution-sabbau* as Gehlen believed, but an intensive transformation of the very nature of institutions and institutionalization. Modern, or late-modern institutions are less and less hampered by a traditional past and its cultural gravity. They are thinner, lighter, more footloose, more open, and as a result morally less binding. And there is no room left for greedy institutions which would absorb or even swallow individuals. Yet, institutions have not collapsed, they have not disappeared, they have not been deconstructed radically. Obviously, prime institutions such as marriage, family, neighborhood, school, state, law, and so forth, are still present and functioning. Yet, they are no longer the thick, greedy, grave and closed institutions they were not that long ago. On the contrary, today institutions are thin, light weight, open and not at all greedy.

Moreover, outside and adjacent to the core institutions we inherited from the past, alternative patterns of behavior have been and still are in development. They emerge in modernity easier and faster than in the pre-modern days of institutionalism and traditionalism. Marriage, for example, was in the pre-modern set-up a thick and heavy, god-given institution which could only be ended with great legal and emotional problems. The institution was 'naturally' reserved for members of the opposite sex. Couples living together in a common law marriage, that is outside the institution, encountered grave moral opprobrium. Often the full forces of social control were set in motion, particularly if the alleged perpetrators belonged to the same sex. That has changed rather radically. Marriage has become a thin and open institution. Living apart together (LAT) or living together in a steady relationship with or without contractual arrangements, are widely spread para-institutions which often are used as a preparation for joining the formal institution of marriage. The acknowledgment of the homosexual marriage is widely debated. In some European societies it is already a legalized fact.

Once more, the conclusion should not be that the ancient institution of marriage no longer exists in late-modern societies, that it has broken down as the victim of *Institutionsabbau*. Instead there has been a flexibilization of this institution on the institute level. The weight of tradition has decreased considerably. The formerly rather closed and greedy institution has become an open and flexible institution. It is much the same with other institutions. Indeed the formerly thick institutions of pre-modern days were transformed, engulfed as they were by a typically late-modern process of thin institutionalization. As a result, individuals possess more choices and options, are no longer bound by religiously and magically tabooed obligations, are in principle able to impress their own stamp on institutions, and receive opportunities to provide institutions with contents that are meaningful to them. There is still room for commitment, responsibility, loyalty, and trust but these virtues are no longer taken-for-granted (i.e. 'natural'). They are no longer religiously and magically, collectively and socially conditioned. They are rather voluntarily and individually negotiated, accepted and enacted. Unlike traditional institutions, late-modern institutions are voluntary patterns of behavior. They are no longer parts of a top-down and coercive command structure in which the allegedly correct forms of behavior are being dictated. They instead belong to a bottom-up configuration in which behavioral alternatives are being negotiated. The Dutch sociologist Abram de Swaan calls it a transition 'from management by command to management by negotiation.'[27]

Meanwhile, we should bear in mind that the difference between institutions and networks dimishes in proportion to the flexibilization of institutions, changing from authoritarian and closed ('thick') to democratic and open ('thin') patterns of behavior. Moreover, as I have mentioned earlier, networks did exist within the context of traditional institutions, but they were 'thin' and restricted severely by scores of formal and coercive rules and regulations. In contrast late-modern networks have ample opportunities to emerge and develop outside and around institutional frameworks, as in hardly professionalized paramedical therapies outside the official medical establishment, in informal bonds of friendship outside and around formal marriage, or in religious (e.g. evangelical) movements outside the church. They were almost always viewed as *liaisons dangereuses* in the thoroughly institutionalized past. Today, however, they are experienced and enacted as flexible opportunity structures.

Such networks will eventually, when they develop durability and density, become 'thick' networks and gradually grow into institutions or para-institutions. The sociological development of sects outside and often in competition with established churches is an old example of para-institutionalization. If such a 'routinization of charisma' (Max Weber) occurred in pre-modern times, it is to be expected *a fortiori* that it will occur in the context of a late-modern society in which network relationships stimulate and inspire people to act, think and feel as they themselves, and thus not one or the other authority, deem meaningful and functional. These flexible networks will then easily institutionalize into 'thick' networks. As such, they will, of course, subsequently easily function also as transitions to established institutions, such as the church, the sect, or marriage and the family. They may remain para-institutional, but they may also function as stepping stones to the traditional institutions and thereby contribute to their own transformation. They may even evolve into new institutional patterns. However, it will not be easy to come up with convincing examples of such totally novel institutions. Apparently, the institutional repertoire of mankind is limited. Meanwhile, it is obvious that these traditional, established institutions are affected in turn by these networks. They will become less cumbersome, less 'thick', more flexible, and more network-like.

Education presents a good example. In pre-modern times formal education was limited and restricted in time. Upon graduation one entered society with a distinct occupation for which one had been educated within a distinct institutional and organizational context. In contrast, today there is a lifelong learning which is not constantly taking place within the context of formal institutions such as the highschool, the college, or the university. To begin with, there is a lot of informal experiential education such as travelling the globe for a while, or taking a sabbattical leave. It can be intermittent and then complemented again by periods of formal education in established institutions. Indeed lifelong learning is a flexible process in which informal networks (perhaps established on the internet) and formal institutions are being alternated according to the wishes, needs and commitments of the learning individual.

In sum, it is apparent that a sharp distincton, let alone opposition between institutions and networks, as in the post-modernist notion of post-institutional networks, is rather senseless these days. Nor should one lament late-modern networks as being the beginning of the end of institutions and institutionalization.

Conclusion

The concept of community, I argued, should be handled with care and circumspection. Its connotations are ambiguous and thus confusing which is demonstrated by the rather different meanings of the concept in America and in Europe. Communitarianism might be understandable and even useful socio-politically in the context of American society, but it rapidly loses its democratic bent and direction, when it is applied in the sense of *Gemeinschaft* building. Even in the American context community might easily degenerate into a closed and ethnocentric idea and ideal, as the past of ethnic minorities and white middle-class groups has amply demonstrated.

What I propose here is to substitute the concept of institution with that of community, and to think and act socio-politically in terms of neo-institutionalism rather than communitarianism. It is necessary in this scenario to reconsider and to rethink the concepts of institution and institutionalization and to re-evaluate them in the light of the process of modernization which has deeply altered their nature and their functions. Today thick, greedy and closed institutions, conditioned by a heavy handed, often religiously and magically tabooed, coercive tradition, have been superseded by thinner, more voluntary, more open, and looser institutions which in the behavior of people are often alternated or temporarily suspended by flexible networks. I propose conceptual distinction between thick and close institutionalization on the one hand, and thin and open institutionalization on the other. The distinction between institutions and networks becomes opaque, to say the least, when networks grow dense and durable over time, and in that sense thick. The differences between thin institutions and thick networks are negligible.

This process is not the deconstruction of institutions, nor the end of civilization but a remarkable transformation that has taken place in the latest phase of the modernization process – a phase in which the developments of medical, biological and communicational technologies have played a predominant role. *In vitro* fertilization, prenatal technologies, genetic manipulation techniques, nanotechnology, and above all the ICT revolution of the past decades have transformed our lives and the world we live in. This transformation requires a fundamental rethinking of human behavior and of the patterns of behavior we pass on to subsequent generations. These patterns are the institutions and the networks that human beings need to provide their lives with a sense of meaning, need for their orientation in the world, and for the directions to guide their acting, thinking and feeling.

1. 1 See Robert K. Merton, *Social Theory and Social Structure,* Revised and Enlarged Edition, 1949, (New York, London: The Free Press of Glencoe, 1964, 9th printing), pp. 490-508. Karl R. Popper, *The Poverty of Historicism,* 1957, (London: Routledge & Kegan Paul, 1969), pp. 67-102.

2. Peter L. Berger, Thomas Luckmann, *The Social Construction of Reality. A Treatise in the Sociology of Knowledge,* (Garden City, NY: Doubleday, 1966).

3. Karl Mannheim, *Ideology and Utopia. An Introduction to the Sociology of Knowledge,* translated by L. Wirth and E. Shils, 1936, (New York: A Harvest Book, n.d.).

4. Cf. David Kettler, *Marxismus und Kultur. Mannheim und Lukács in den ungarischen Revolutionen 1918/19* (Marxism and Culture. Mannheim and Lukács in the Hungarian Revolutions 1918/19), (Neuwied und Berlin: Luchterhand, 1967).

5. See my *On Clichés. The Supersedure of Meaning by Function,* (London: Routledge & Kegan Paul, 1979.

6. Anton C. Zijderveld, *Bedrijfscultuur. Fantoom en feit* (Corporate Culture. Phantom and Fact), (The Hague: Stichting Maatschappij en Onderneming, 1983).

7. A perfect example of this is Alvin W. Gouldner, *The Coming Crisis of Western Sociology,* 1970, (London: Heinemann, 1972), in particular Part II: 'The World of Talcott Parsons', pp. 167-340.

8. See my *The Waning of the Welfare State. The End of Comprehensive State Succor,* (New Brunswick, NJ: Transaction Publishers, 1999).

9. See the communitarian manifesto of Amitai Etzioni, *The Spirit of Community. The Reinvention of American Society,* 1993, (New York: A Touchstone Book,1994). Also Amitai Etzioni, *The New Golden Rule. Community and Morality in a Democratic Society,* (New York: Basic Books, 1996). See also Robert Nisbet, *Community and Power,* (formerly 'The Quest for Community'), 1953, (New York: Galaxy Book, 1963).

10. In his classic, small study on monastic orders Adolf Harnack emphasized their paradoxical nature. See Adolf Harnack, *Das Mönchtum: seine Ideale und seine Geschichte* (Monastic Orders: their Ideals and their History), (Giessen: Verlag Alfred Töpelmann, 1907), p. 7f: "Monastic orders saved the individual from the bonds of society, and ordinary routines. They liberated the individual and elevated him to noble autonomy and humanity. But the same orders shackled the individual with petty-mindedness, mindless emptiness and slavish dependence." My translation.

11. See, for instance, Etzioni, *The Spirit of Community,* chapter 4: 'Back to We', o.c., pp. 116-133.

12. George Ritzer, *The McDonaldization of Society,* (Newbury Park, California: Pine Forge Press, 1993).

13. See Robert B. Reich, *The Work of Nations,* 1991, (New York: Vintage Books, 1992).

14. See e.g. Jean-Marie Guéhenno, *La Fin de la démocratie*, (Paris: Editions Flammarion, 1994).

15. This is also a global phenomenon. See for America Neil R. Peirce c.s., *Citistates. How Urban America Can Prosper in a Competitive World*, (Washington, DC: Seven Locks Press, 1993). Also my monograph *A Theory of Urbanity. The Economic and Civic Culture of Cities*, (New Brunswick, NJ: Transaction Publishers, 1998).

16. See Robert Whelan, *The Corrosion of Charity. From Moral Renewal to Contract Culture*, (London: IEA Health and Welfare Unity, Choice in Welfare Series No. 29, 1996). IEA is the Institute of Economic Affairs, London.

17. This was discussed in more detail in my 'Civil Society, Pillarization, and the Welfare State,' in: Robert W. Hefner (ed.), *Democratic Civility. The History and Cross-Cultural Possibility of a Modern Political Ideal*, (New Brunswick, NJ: Transaction Publishers, 1998), pp. 153-174.

18. See my *The Waning of the Welfare State. The End of Comprehensive State Succor*, (New Brunswick, NJ: Transaction Publishers, 1999).

19. See John Horgan, *The End of Science. Facing the Limits of Knowledge in the Twilight of the Scientific Age*, 1996, (New York: Broadway Books, 1997).

20. The social and cultural history of the charlatan is given by Grete de Francesco, *Die Macht des Charlatans* (The Power of the Charlatan), (Basel: Benno Schwabe Verlag, 1937).

21. See Georg Simmel, *The Web of Group Affiliations*, translated by Reinhard Bendix, in: Georg Simmel, *Conflict and the Web of Group Affiliations*, 1955, (New York: The Free Pres sof Glencoe, 1964), pp. 125-95. Also Erving Goffman, *The Presentation of Self in Everyday Life*, (Garden City, NY: Doubleday Anchor Books, 1959) and *Interaction Ritual: Essays on Face-to-Face Behavior*, (Garden City, NY: Doubleday Anchor Books, 1967). A perceptive and lucid study of Simmel's sociology presents Anton M. Bevers, *Dynamik der Formen bei Georg Simmel* (Georg Simmel's Dynamics of Forms), (Berlin: Duncker und Humblot, 1985). On *Wechselwirkung*: pp. 76-88.

22. Helmuth Schelsky, 'Ist die Dauerreflexion institutionalisierbar?' ('Can permanent reflexion be institutionalized?'), 1957, in: Helmuth Schelsky, *Auf der Suche nach Wirklichkeit*, (Düsseldorf-Köln: Eugen Diederichs Verlag, 1965), pp, 250-275.

23. The conception of nature has, of course, a long and complicated history which cannot be discussed here. See R. G. Collingwood, *The Idea of Nature*, 1945, (New York: Oxford University Press, 1976).

24. On 'of-course statements' see Alfred Schutz, 'Common-Sense and Scientific Interpretation of Human Action', in: Alfred Schutz, *Collected Papers I*, (The Hague: Martinus Nijhoff, 1962), pp. 3-26, in particular p. 13.

25. Lewis Coser, *Greedy Institutions. Patterns of Undivided Commitment*, (New York: The Free Press, 1974).

26. Coser warns not to mistake greedy institutions for what Erving Goffman called *total institutions*. Unlike greedy institutions, Goffman's total institutions, also called *asylums,* are physically separated from the rest of the world by walls, barbed wire, locked doors, high walls, etc. Examples of total institutions are mental hospitals, jails, concentration camps, army barracks and boarding schools. In fact, such total institutions do not really demand commitment and loyalty to their values and norms. They demand obedience and submission. Greedy institutions, Coser emphasizes, do not physically separate their servants from the world at large but rather create social distance through undivided commitment and absolute loyalty. Moreover, as Goffman indicated, within asylums the ordinary barriers between sleep, play and work are lifted. This is not necessrasily the case with greedy institutions. See Erving Goffman, *Asylums,* (Garden City, NY: Doubleday Anchor Books, 1961). Coser, *op. cit.,* p. 5f.

27. Abram de Swaan, *The Management of Normality,* (London: Routledge, 1990), pp. 150-160

CHAPTER FIVE

Life without Limits:
Staccato Culture and Flexible Society[1]

Moral rules and authoritative limits

An important function of institutions is to impose limits on human behavior. In modernity we tend to deplore this fact. We are autonomous individuals who prefer to view and experience our lives as open fields of expression, exploration and realization. This is, of course, one of the main reasons for the previously discussed anti-institutional mood. Institutions, after all, impose limits on our expressions, explorations and realizations. Even if they are but 'thin' institutions, institutions do prevent the full materialization of the idea(l) that 'anything goes'.

In his book on moral education Emile Durkheim developed an interesting argument about this. Whether we like it or not, he writes, the essence of all morality is discipline based upon authority. Morality sets rules and regulations which restrict human behavior, imposes limits on our actions, thoughts and emotions, and it does so in an authoritative way. These rules, Durkheim continues, can be seen as a kind of repressive and authoritarian discipline, like a police force which tries to prevent certain undesirable acts and actions. But they can also be considered, and this is Durkheim's view, as autonomous instruments of moral education which instill in individuals a moral character. Only when they possess a moral character, are human beings able to master and regulate themselves. Self-control and self-regulation, Durkheim adds, are the essence of liberty: *la liberté est le fruit de la réglementation*. The problem is, however, that most of us these days deplore such rules and limitations. Modern man has an *appétit de l'infini*, an appetite for the infinite which Durkheim also calls, maybe with a reference to Charles Baudelaire, *le mal de l'infini qui travaille notre temps*, the malady of the infinite which afflicts our time. This malady is wrought by limitless aspirations. Typically modern rebellions against the limits imposed on human life by moral institutions are driven by oceanic desires and wishes which can never be satisfied adequately. Modern man will therefore be plagued constantly by feelings of inadequacy and injustice. The world is to the eternally longing romantic by definition an inhospitable, meaningless place. Spleen and a sense of pervasive *anomie* will then be his fate.[2]

Institutions, as we have seen, contain values and norms passed on from generation to generation. They will, of course, change during the course of this transference which is *a fortiori* the case in a (post)industrial, thoroughly modernized society. Fully modernized institutions are therefore not unalterable straightjackets and possess a considerable degree of flexibility. Yet, one should stress that modernized institutions also impose limits on our thoughts, emotions and actions. Within an institutional context anything simply does not go. Being married, being a citizen of a nation-state, resident of a particular municipality, staff member of a university or a museum, manager in a corporation, teacher in a school, one cannot simply do, feel and think whatever one would like to do, feel and think. Institutions restrict the range of behavioral alternatives and thus the range of options and choices. Yet institutions also constitute a set of routines which enable us to save mental and emotional energies, and to develop new ideas, new feelings and new thoughts. Durkheim adds that these institutional limits are in fact moral limits which do not smother liberty but on the contrary enable it. Moral freedom is not total and absolute liberty, but freedom within the context of obligations and restrictions. This is a crucial paradox which for most people who are thoroughly modern, is hard to swallow. Most of us find it hard to accept that we must develop and realize our creative abilities, our plans for the future and even our Self (our personal identity, our moral character) within the limits of institutions and their inherent moral rules and regulations. Both Durkheim and Gehlen would add that institutions allow us to respond adequately to the requirements of our environment. Moreover, they keep our feet solidly on the ground. Life, Durkheim once wrote, should not be suspended, should not float in thin air, lest death or illness result.[3]

But this argument is still too voluntaristic, as if motives and intentions of modern individuals were the only forces which run counter to the paradox of restrictive moral rules enabling the full operation of liberty and creativity. It is not just the anti-institutional mood as a kind of modern ethos which contests it. From the point of view of the sociology of knowledge we should also emphasize that it is the idiosyncratic nature of late-modernity itself – its flexibility, its transcience, its permanent flows, its global impact – which fosters a basic transformation of the position and functions of traditional institutions and their inherent morality. It is not only man's desires and longings, but late-modern society and culture as a whole that have become infinite, limitless. In the present chapter I shall discuss this late-modern state of affairs.

The main focus will be on the fact that contemporary, decentered societies with their porous borders have gradually given rise to indeed a life without strict and authoritative limits. Moreover, 'decentering' and 'debordering' have led to the emergence of a type of society that is driven by a peculiar *pace* or *rhythm* that differs from the pace or rhythm of pre-modern societies founded solidly upon traditional, 'thick' institutions. Modernization, I shall argue metaphorically, is a transition from a *legato* to a *staccato* type of culture. Incidentally, there has been very little sociological thought about the pace or the rhythm of specific societies and cultures. What follows is inevitably but an initial attempt to deal with it.

The functions of ceremonial caesuras

The notion of flexibility is widely spread in our late-modern day and age. We live, supposedly, in a post-modern society in which everything seems or ought to be possible, technologically as well as morally. After all, we are very close to making life in the biochemical laboratory, and we already manipulate it technologically. We put, if deemed necessary, an end to it, and euphemistically call that 'a good death'. We decide to 'make' a child, or to postpone its arrival, putting the fertilized egg literally on ice. We transform male bodies into female bodies, and vice versa. In addition, we network and correlate at our heart's desire, not much hindered by differences in age, class or status group, or by distances in time and space. As to the latter, the voice-mail saves messages for later, the Internet embraces the entire globe. In a very concrete and empirical sense, life has indeed become borderless and limitless.

Even the limit of death, which is probably the most absolute of all limits, is presently being tampered with, albeit with mixed results. In earlier days most people accepted this unconditional end to their earthly existence as fate or destiny, often consoled by religious doctrines about an afterlife and by collectively performed *rites de passage*. Today, most of us can and will not accept death, thus we put up a fight with the assistance of scores of medical or para-medical professionals. Medical technology has advanced to such a degree that death can be postponed even when the prospects of survival are nil. Dying is in such cases a torturous process which is hard to bear for the patient and to behold for next-of-kin and close friends. One of the most recent experiments in genetic manipulation apparently aims at a deceleration of the aging process. If successful, it is claimed, future generations may continue to live far beyond the present average lifespan of men and women.

Inherent in the de-institutionalization of the world of medicine is the re-emergence of various quacks and charlatans who offer their magical therapies and medicines to their often desperate clients. A mixture of crude psychologism, Eastern philosophies, and theories about purifying Nature is often presented as a valid alternative to the medical science learned in universities and practiced in hospitals. Putting living people to sleep and freezing them for the sake of cosmic journeys through the universe, or just for the fun of waking up thousand of years from now, is still science fiction. In some rare American cases dead bodies are frozen in the hope that future generations will be able to bring them back to life. Better than anything else such fringe phenomena seem to demonstrate the contemporary desire to temper with the absolute limit of death.

However, the most striking feature of modern life-without-limits is the fact that it hardly knows any ritual transitions and ceremonial caesuras, with the result that we are continuously confronted by all sorts of often unconnected, or but loosely connected people, objects, sounds, sights and events. This, it will be argued now, has given late-modern society and culture a very peculiar pace or rhythm which affected institutions in a very peculiar way.

In poetry a *caesura* is a pause, a resting point in the middle of a line of verse of five or six metrical foots. In music caesuras are rhythmic resting points which separate musical phrases. Thus a caesura is not, as is often believed, an interruption or a break in a sentence or in a melodic line, but a wordless or toneless connection between parts of a sentence or of a melodic line. Caesuras promote the fluent course of a line of verse or a musical phrase. A caesura is in fact a brief silence which gives speech or music a floating, legato cadence. When the poetic phrase is sung as in a *Lied* by Schubert, the caesura is the appropriate moment to take breath. Without caesuras poetic verses and musical phrases are restless, hurried, nervous, and ill-balanced.

We can fruitfully apply the metaphor of a caesura to life in society. Societal processes have a certain rhythm, pace, or cadence. The pace of the stock exchange, for instance, is much more hectic than that of a convent or a university; the rhythm of an airport or railroad station differs considerably from the cadence of a city hall or shopping mall. Caesuras, like the coffee break in the office, the party at the end of theworking day celebrating a memorable event in the organization, or the gong which ends the day of buying and selling in the stock exchange, present moments or periods of rest and inner restoration. They are not breaches in the ongoing stream of life and consciousness which Henri Bergson so fittingly called *la durée*. On the contrary, like the caesuras in a poem such ceremonial events provide life, as it were, with a legato character. In all societies, whether traditional and rural, or modern and industrial, there are recurrent, collectively celebrated ceremonies or more or less ceremonial events during which the normal stream of activities and enterprises is halted for a certain length of time. They enable people to catch their breaths. As much as the original religious meaning has evaporated for most of us, we celebrate Christmas and Easter *en famille*, or Chanuka and Ramadan, if only because we have affixed holidays to them. Even the summer vacation, or the weekend carries for many of us an almost ritual character. It enables us to step out of our daily routines, if only for a couple of days. Although Sunday has lost much of its religious luster and momentum which it had in rural society, the weekend is a repetitive caesura bearing a somewhat ritual character.[4] Meanwhile, our vacations and weekends are, of course, but weak reflections of the ritual caesuras which in pre-industrial times gave order and structure to the lives of men, women and children. As to societal rhythm, these ritual caesuras provided pre-industrial lives with a distinct *legato* character. Let us dwell on this subject for a while.

When life was not yet dominated by science and technology, by bureaucracy and advanced industries, when the world still resembled an enchanted garden full of surprises in which not the rational laws of natural science but the belief in a supernatural God or a capricious Fate determined the observations and experiences of men, people celebrated various transitions in life by means of collective ceremonies and rituals. They were often exceedingly elaborate and complex. For the transition from childhood to adulthood, from bachelorhood to marriage, for transitions like pregnancy, birth and death, complex ceremonies with elaborate rites and rituals were designed and executed. In a classic study which is still worth reading, the French anthropologist Arnold van Gennep called these rituals *rites de passage*.[5] Despite the enormous diversity and the great differences in detail among them, these rites exhibit a basic dynamic structure which he called the fundamental *schéma*. There is in each transition a scheme of three consecutive phases: first the *séparation* in which the individual is separated from his group or environment, next the *marge* in which the individual lives in a strange, transitional sphere between the 'old' and the 'new' reality, and finally the *aggrégation* which is the integration of the 'reborn' individual into the group. He or she lives from now on as a different being, a reborn person with a new identity.

In situations of crisis and danger which easily lead to one or the other existential breach or breakdown, the traditional and thoroughly institutionalized rites of passage ensure continuity. They maintain the fluent character of the stream of life, maintaining thereby, I may add, the legato character of the societal rhythm. Not only birth, death, marriage or puberty, but also the de-

136

parture from one's territory or the reception of strangers into the community are celebrated and ceremonialized through rites of passage. They are in this way integrated into the stream of life which is borne by the ongoing process of tradition and its institutions.

Incidentally, one should not romanticize these rites of passage, or think of them in a petit-bourgeois manner. In particular the second phase, that of the *marge*, is in many traditional cultures a period of extreme marginality in which boorish coarseness and foolish debauchery prevail. It is, as I argued elsewhere, a reality in a looking-glass which is psychologically as well as physically painful for the people subjected to them.[6] The *marge* itself is unpredictable: the 'old' reality has lost its vigor, the 'new' reality has not yet established its reign, everything is vague, capricious, boundless, illimitable, in short foolish. Indeed, anything goes. Anarchy reigns. It is sheer carnival. For the duration of this marginality people are outlawed, without duties but also without rights. There are no institutions and thus no values and norms, and, of course, no hierarchies of power and authority. There is very soon a dire need for the next phase, the *aggrégation* which is the much longed for return to an institutionalized order.

In my book on folly I discussed among others the late-medieval, early-modern Festival of Fools in which an almost tyrannical and well-organized foolishness reigned during the winter months. This was, after all, the season in which rural society enjoyed a much deserved, relative rest. It was experienced as a period of transition in which the 'old' year had 'expired', while the 'new' one was not yet born. Typically a marginal period. Residual magic and paganism survived in the foolish, carnival festivities, often conducted around and even within the church. Occasionally revolting mock ceremonies were performed in which the ecclesiastical hierarchies were reversed, usually under the inspired directions of the lower clergy. The higher clergy contested these foolish exploits, not so much for their coarseness and profanation, but because they exhibited a barely concealed paganism. However, even the severest threats failed to put an end to this massively supported folly. Eventually Puritanism and subsequently Enlightenment's rationalism would put an end to these foolish debaucheries, naturally in close conjunction with the capitalist mode of production which above all favors thrift and a stern work ethic, and abhors any sort of folly and irrationality. It was not the *marge* and marginal people but the *aggrégation* as a societal and cultural order of well institutionalized *burghers* which became the world modern people would inhabit.

However, as we have seen earlier, modernization itself unleashed scores of de-institutionalizing forces. So it also put an end to the legato character of traditional society. Modern society and culture began to lack well established and ceremonialized caesuras giving rise to a socio-cultural reality that was more and more driven by a *staccato* cadence. Contrary to the conventional wisdom about bourgeois culture as being passive, indulgent, and saturated, the *aggrégation* of the bourgeoisie after the French Revolution bore a restless character driven by a staccato pace which in fact was the motor behind its capitalist mode of production. This, of course, needs further discussion.

Bourgeois culture

Bourgeois culture which took hold of the Western world around the sixteenth century, has been an endless source of irritation, astonishment and admiration. One of its most striking features has been a recurrent stumbling block for revolutionaries of sorts: its capacity not only to *absorb* critique and opposition, to engage in what Herbert Marcuse has dubbed 'repressive tolerance'[9], but also to *generate* this critique and opposition. This is indeed a remarkable paradox. To state it somewhat provocatively, Karl Marx was indeed the prototypical product of the bourgeoisie of his days, but so were Proudhon, Flaubert, Wilde and similar anti-bourgeois philosophers and writers. Reading the joint lives of Sartre and Beauvoir, two prominent *gauchiste* bourgeoisie haters, one is indeed struck by the thoroughly (upper-) bourgeois character of their ways of thinking, feeling and acting.[7] Another perfect example of this is manifested by the self-styled Marxist playwright Bertolt Brecht (1898-1956) who from the *Dreigroschenoper* on in all his plays attacked the capitalist bourgeoisie viciously. After the war he lived and worked in East Berlin at the expense of the communist regime that put him on its ideological pedestal. But he lived the life of a *grand bourgeois*, drinking American whisky, smoking (pre-Castro) Cuban cigars, building a summer retreat in Denmark, and steadily filling his bank account in Switzerland. Perhaps the only non-bourgeois thing about him was his notoriously bad body odor due to the fact that he refused to bathe or shower regularly.[8]

Indeed, bourgeois culture does not only absorb quickly and thoroughly everything that comes at it, but also recurrently generates its own contradictions which it then quickly incorporates and institutionalizes. Thus, the negations, even those generated by itself, are neutralized in what Herbert Marcuse called a 'repressive tolerance'. However, it is questionable whether such a neutralization of negations is really repressive. Take the *avant garde* in modern art for example. When the first shock of an anti-bourgeois innovation, often called 'revolution', has been endured, the innovation is quickly defined as 'interesting', 'innovative', 'compelling' and 'fascinating', and then locked up in an institutional cadre, such as a museum for modern art. This has been the fate of most 'shocking' and bourgeoisie rocking *avant garde* art, from Salvador Dali to Andy Warhol. Rarely do these avant-gardists, their followers and their adulators realize that the desire to shock the bourgeoisie is itself, to begin with, typically bourgeois, and that these shocks are again rapidly absorbed and thus neutralized by the bourgeois culture. The representatives and products of anti-bourgeois *Dadaism* of the 1920s present a perfect example. After all, today dadaists and dadaist products are incorporated in the history of art. They are by now solid components of the established bourgeois culture, respected and respectable phenomena. Dadaistic art objects are auctioned, sold for high prices and exhibited in museums for modern art. In the end it is all a matter of economics. Artists after all do not generate wealth, and thus depend on rich people who can afford and are prepared to invest financially in art. Rich art collectors are usually bourgeois capitalists.[10]

However, at the core of this bourgeois culture lies the emphasis upon useful work, diligence, rational frugality, efficient management and rational planning of nature, society, culture and even history. To the bourgeois the world is no longer a mysterious and incomprehensible, enchanted garden, driven by the whimsies of a dark Fate, but rather a field of possibilities and potentialities which are to be explored and then exploited. Gradually the inscrutable God of Christianity is being pushed to the outskirts of bourgeois life, absorbed, as it were, by a vague and rationalist Deism, or succeeded by the inscrutable Invisible Hand of the market place. Bourgeois culture is no-nonsense, rational and calculating. The world is to be explored and exploited, constructed and manipulated in a rational manner. Even the future is to be planned rationally by means of scientifically constructed models and scenarios. Economically, the bourgeois is, of course, a capitalist and the true capitalist, embodied by the merchant first and the entrepreneur next, is a level-headed, functionally rational *no-nonsense workaholic*. His world view lacks magical enchantments, is rationalized and embedded in scores of mainly quantitative calculations, greedily applied in commerce, the sciences and technology.[11]

But what strikes us most in view of the present discussion and analysis, is the unceasing compulsion, the restlessness, and the lack of clearly demarcated, ceremonialized caesuras in bourgeois culture. In a sense, the legato cadence of the pre-capitalist and pre-industrial world with its traditional and often magically guarded and even tabooed institutions is steadily pushed aside by the frenetic staccato beat of a society and culture primarily focussed upon permanent production, permanent consumption, permanent progress, and permanent innovation. The latter is of special importance, because perpetual innovation is believed to stimulate the market and to open up new markets. In pre-modern, rural society innovation was met with distrust and fear, as it could endanger the tabooed, sacred order. In the modern, industrial and bourgeois world innovation is deemed to be essential and indispensable. That adds, of course, to the restlessness of bourgeois culture which requires a specific world view and a specific ethos.

Before we explore this further, it should be stressed once more that also in this respect the bourgeoisie generated its own contradictions, because in the nineteenth century in particular, bourgeois culture had given rise to complacency, indulgence, self-satisfaction and smugness. Often the *bourgeois gentil'homme* was the very opposite of the pro-active merchant and entrepreneur. He was the reactive, if not reactionary rentier who abhorred change and innovation. This complacency was in its turn again absorbed and neutralized and then pushed aside by enterprising innovators and innovative entrepreneurs who revived the core of the bourgeois culture.

We saw in the first section of the previous chapter how Karl Mannheim distinguished two types of knowledge which highlighted two types of culture. In *ideology* the facts are distorted in order to maintain the status quo and the power structure that goes with it. It is a weapon in the hands of the ruling class which is oriented towards the past in a reactionary manner. *Utopia* also distorts the facts but does so in order to transcend the existing order in the hope that a better, more just and free society will emerge in the future. It is a weapon in the hands of the powerless who look forward to the Good Society. But Mannheim – and this is rarely noticed – distinguished a third knowledge type which he found typical for our late-modern society and culture. He called it *neue Sachlichkeit*, i.e. *Matter-of-factness* or *New Functionalism.*[12] Here the facts are not distorted as in utopia and ideology, but on the contrary uncritically adored, venerated and embraced. From the point of view of matter-of-factness both ideology and utopia are summarily rejected as being unpractical and useless. It is, in other words, the prosaic attitude which demands practical, applicable, useful results, not speculations. It demands facts not theories. In this brand of functionalism values and norms which in ideologies and utopias have clear demarcations and often stand in mutual opposition, tend to become neutral, vague and general, thereby loosing their heuristic pith. New Functionalism is a no-nonsense ethos and as such is not interested in values and norms. If a value does play a role at all, it is efficiency – a rather thin value, that is.

New Functionalism, I hasten to add, is typically bourgeois. Neither the old feudal status groups – nobility and clergy – nor the working class would be a suitable social cadre for this *neue Sachlichkeit*. It emerged and prospered within the bourgeoisie. We may add still another characteristic. It actually carries a peculiar time awareness, and deals with time in a remarkably pragmatic manner. A society and culture bound to the New Functionalism will measure and partition time in terms of the clock and the stopwatch, while the seasons, religious festivals and the various rites of passage have lost their position in the awareness of time. In New Functionalism there are no longer institutionalized resting points, or ceremonial caesuras which enable people to organize their thoughts and feelings in an analogous manner. Instead, pragmatic, down-to-earth men and women believe that life can be rationalized and streamlined efficiently. Various ceremonial caesuras can actually be dispensed with as superfluous fuss. New Functionalists carry on their businesses relentlessly and restlessly. There are two dominant complaints: first, time seems to pass exceedingly rapidly ('time flies by'), and second, stress caused by the perennial fear that work will not be finished on time, seems to dominate all other experiences. This stands to reason because without institutional demacations and ceremonial caesuras days, weeks, months and years constitute successions of time units which with hindsight seem like one grey, indistinguishable fog. The past can barely be remembered and the future seems to evaporate to rather strict, rational time schedules. Time lacks the existential co-ordinates by which it can be measured in an analogous, substantially rational manner. Pragmatic people live by wristwatches, stopwatches and time-clocks.

All this may be illustrated by the following example. In a traditional society with clearly demarcated ceremonial caesuras a funeral is a collective ritual by which relatives and friends take leave of someone who has recently died. It is a rite of passage in which the emotions of grief and maybe even spite, regret and anger are canalized and collectively borne. The funeral rite itself and the succeeding period of collective mourning constitute a sort of *marge* for the members of the nuclear family. After the funeral rites the *marge* offers them an opportunity to return to society in the new role of widow, widower or orphan. Death is almost always a bewildering and deeply disturbing breach in the course of daily life. It is through the funeral rite and the period of collective mourning afterwards that this breach is mended, or at least made bearable. In that sense, the ceremonial internment and the institutionalized mourning afterwards constitute a forceful caesura. Compare this with a contemporary cremation. Here everything is professionally planned and rationally streamlined. Architecturally most crematoria radiate efficiency and functionality, i.e. a spirit of New Functionalism. They are 'death plants' in which people do not actually depart from their deceased loved ones, but in a sense dispose of them. It all happens within a strict time schedule, because while one mourning party is in the process of offering condolences after the cremation, the next party has arrived to participate in the following cremation session. It reminds one of the assembly line in industry. After the coffin has been removed to the incinerator, and after people have expressed their condolences to the next of kin of the deceased, a kind of hiatus emerges which is not closed or bridged by ceremonial rites and an institutionalized period of mourning. Grief must be emotionally processed in silence and solitude. There is no grave to which the bereaved can return with flowers, commemorating the deceased.

Incidentally, this rationalization of death has a paradoxical consequence: cremations are in general much more emotional events than traditional funerals, simply because the emotions of grief, spite and regret cannot be drained ceremonially and collectively. They are instead stowed up individually and privately. Solidly institutionalized rituals have, among others, the function of collectively channeling and processing emotions, feelings and experiences which in general are quite hard to bear individually and privately. Naturally, this has already been discovered as a blind spot in the market of professional assistance. Whereas in former days relatives, friends and neighbors, and in particular Catholic priests, Protestant ministers, or rabbis escorted a dying person and assisted upon death the bereaved relatives, today these support functions have in many cases been taken over by professionals who have been trained for this task in a rational, scientific manner. Naturally, these mourning professionals cannot answer the most essential question of all: what is the sense of dying and the meaning of death? Priests, ministers and rabbis have an answer. At least they used to have one, and should still have one. What good do religious professionals do, if they can no longer provide life and death with a meaningful purpose? In any case, the gap caused by death is no longer bridged by a traditional, collectively celebrated ceremony, but is instead filled haphazardly with the stowed up, private emotions of the bereaved, and at the same time also with the functional rationality of the funeral business and the mourning professionals.

I venture to generalize this observation and formulate it as one of the core features of our fully modernized world: our society based upon a functionally rational matter-of-factness has very few institutionalized, traditional ceremonies at its disposal which results in breaches, gaps, and hiatuses in our lives that cannot be bridged adequately. They are usually filled with unbridled emotionality on the one hand and professional rationality on the other. In short, our fully modernized society is as rational as it is irrational.

Loose people

Human relationships have undergone profound transformations since the 1960s. In 1984, a Dutch journalist described this change in an essay that bore the intriguing title 'A Little Bit Married'. He discussed – admittedly with a focus on Dutch society, but it bears on all late-modern societies – the extreme individualism of contemporary men and women. Society, he argued, has become a compilation of 'loose people' who are differentiated yet hard to distinguish: 'Our days exhibit the emergence of the grey shade. Everything one could or could not be in former days, one can be today a little bit, half of it, or a bit on the one hand and a bit on the other.'[13] Aesthetic and erotic preferences, for example, are no longer sharply demarcated within one single person.

This is illustrated well by the present state of affairs in the institutions of marriage and the family. Marital and familial relationships are no longer clearly demarcated and delineated. An anecdote may serve as an example. Recently, I embarrassed the head of the President's office of my university. I received an invitation for myself and, as stated, my 'partner' to attend a formal dinner. I answered that I did not have a partner, and asked respectfully, if I could bring my lawfully wedded wife along instead. This, of course, was a blatantly old-fashioned response. The gentleman, however, got the message loud and clear, and asked in his response for my understanding and sympathy since his job had become quite difficult lately. Some of your colleagues, he wrote in his letter which was interspersed with unsuspected irony, are like you indeed married, others are divorced but entertain a steady living-apart-together (LAT) relationship. Such LAT -partners again are usually of a different sex, but increasingly of the same sex as well. We may soon even expect the advent of legally wedded homosexuals. In order to offend nobody he, like so many these days, had lumped all relationships together under the general and grey category of 'partners'. By doing so he was, of course, both socially and politically correct.

There is these days a broad variety of partnerships, ranging from traditional heterosexual marriages to more recently homosexual, formalized partnerships. Due to the frequency of divorce many children grow up in a mix of families – the father's new family or the mother's new family, or some time in the former then in the latter, or alternating periodically between them. Naturally, flexibility is the only adequate concept to characterize these arrangements. We live more than ever before in a 'flexible society', with 'flexible families', 'flexible partnerships', and a 'flexible labor market'. There is a distinct decline in fixed and delineated categories. Needless to say, this poses serious problems for census bureaus and other statistical agencies. As a result, demographical statistical data has become rather inadequate, if not inaccurate.

The more modern a society is, the more the limits of institutions and the margins between institutional sectors will fade away and become blurred. Life is thus subjected to the overall grey shade, and people will become 'loose people'. Due to this fading away of institutional borders remarkable 'chemical' reactions and connections occur in the realm of values. One can observe this in religion where, as in the case of New Age, various religious, magical and metaphysical, Western and Eastern traditions are mixed into a sort of metaphysical hodgepodge, usually accompanied musically by 're-lipop' or otherwise religiously colored pop-music. Gender differences were not that long ago still distinguished in sharply different societal female and male roles which were binding. Today this is no longer the dominant pattern. One may celebrate this as the end of male dominance with its ingrained inequality of the sexes, but the socio-psychological dimension is usually not taken into account. Apparently, even if the ideal of 'unisex' could be practiced in a sensible manner (which, experience has taught, it cannot), children should still be confronted with the difference of male and female roles. In particular the roles of mothers and fathers ought to be differentiated – not necessarily, and preferably not, in traditional, patriarchical ways. Yet, it is hard these days to give a meaningful content to the roles of mother and father in the nuclear family.

In the ghettos of the big cities, where due to the absence of permanently present fathers the disintegration of the nuclear family has reached an advanced stage, it remains unclear to boys growing up what the male role in general and the father role in particular constitutes today. Most of these boys are in many respects, but certainly with respect to the male and father roles, in limbo. Increasingly, still very young boys, from the ages of six to twelve years old, engage in criminal acts. They are mostly led and inspired by youth gangs which in a sense constitute a substitute for the faulty nuclear family. The gang leader functions in many cases as a substitute for the absent family father.

In any case, social roles are becoming more and more fuzzy. The role of husband and father is increasingly blurred into an identity, according to which one is a little bit a husband and a little bit a father, while the former wife and mother ought to be a little bit of a wife and a little bit of a mother and, unlike most of her predecessors, a career woman as well. Time with the children is then organized rationally in so-called *quality time* which is usually a time of the day in which the kids are being spoiled thoroughly. Playing fuzzy roles as parents it is hard to educate children in a consequent manner, exercising the delicate balance of rewards and punishments, teaching the difference between right and wrong, between rights and duties. In short, it is not just social roles, but also morality that has become fuzzy.

Until recently transsexuals could not to change their bodies in accordance with their inherited gender and the social role socially adjudicated to it. To-day transsexual transitions occur in ever greater numbers, while societal resistance and aversion diminish. Converts to the Roman Catholic faith, it is claimed, have a tendency to become 'more popish than the pope'. If one applied this piece of folk wisdom to transsexuals, one could expect that the 'true' men and 'true' women of earlier days survive among transsexuals after they have successfully gone through their transition. One of my colleagues went through the long, socially, psychologically and physically painful and strenuous transformation in which her body was adjusted to her innate gender. She has become not only a beautiful lady but also a pleasant and impressive personality, while she kept the unusual intelligence and intellectual creativity she possessed before the alteration.[14]

When social roles were still clear and therefore narrowly defined, it was rather difficult to play conflicting roles. Today such conflicting roles hardly exist, simply because roles are no longer sharply defined and distinctly differentiated. One person can combine several, quite different roles. For instance, in today's call for and practice of ongoing education, educational furlough, in-service training, and so forth, it is feasible that certain individuals combine the two educational roles of teacher and student, being a teacher during working hours, and a student during extra-curricular or post-doctoral courses. These roles were strictly distinguished in earlier days, being complementary and sometimes, as many of us will recall, adversarial. If a teacher has a part-time position and engages in an in-service training program, he or she is in fact part (a bit) teacher and at the same time also part (a bit) student. The roles we play these days are actually a rather loose lot.

We can easily extend the list of examples. For instance, the fading and blurring of the formerly distinct limits and margins of work is an interesting case. It is increasingly difficult, if not impossible, to distinguish in most jobs between working time and leisure time, particularly when people, who are registered officially as being unemployed, engage in the so-called black, or informal, or grey (sic!) labor market, where neither they, nor their employers pay formal levies such as income taxes, welfare and insurance premiums. The traditional margins and borders of the labor market blur and fade away, when people are employed in part-time jobs, in flexible work schedules, or when early retirement is forced upon them, as was customary in Europe of the 1980s. These categories of people have in common that they are no longer employed in a regular job. The labor market has lost much of its former rigidity. Jobs require increasingly a flexible workforce of generalists rather than narrowly defined and demarcated specialists. Universities and vocational training schools have often adjusted their curricula accordingly, favoring multi- and inter-disciplinary courses instead of the more specialized mono-disciplinary courses of earlier days.[15]

It is customary in communication theory to distinguish between *analogous* and *digital* communication. The distinction, I realize, is problematic but, if not taken too literally, can be quite useful. Communication is digital when a single, clearly circumscribed, unequivocal message in terms of 0 and 1 is being sent. It is analogous, when there are one or more messages which are multi-interpretable and somewhat non-descript. If digital communication appeals to reason and cognition, analogous communication tries to invoke perception and emotion instead. Digital communication is primarily functional, while analogous communication works with values, norms and meanings. A military order, or the argot of technological experts is usually digital. A declaration of love, or the language of a poem or novel is usually analogous.

With the advance of the electronic revolution, people will internalize this functional, digital style of communication which incidentally is also favored by the media, as is demonstrated, for instance, by their predilection for the one-liner. People they interview preferably should not engage in lengthy expositions and intelligent nuances, but answer with simple, or even simplistic one-liners. Children these days grow up with the personal computer and are in a short time great virtuosos in the operation of its software. Certainly, subsequent generations will be well versed in digital communication, far more than those of us born before say 1970. Yet, analogous communication will not disappear, because it is a basic anthropological fact that feelings and emotions, values, norms and meanings will not disappear and cannot be solely communicated in a digital manner. A future of robotized human beings who communicate exclusively in this manner, is a science fiction scenario. To be sure, experience shows that people will indulge in subjective feelings and experiences, and yearn for values, norms and meanings, the more they are exposed to the functional rationality of the late-modern world. Moreover, the Internet does not kill emotions, but on the contrary provides the space to express them far beyond the confinements of personal space. Indeed, cyberspace is borderless and limitless, and offers undreamed of facilities for modern man's search for infinite aims and perspectives. They are by definition not digital but analogous.

In any case, the blurring of institutional limits generates not only loose people but also loose categories and loose concepts. And that is disastrous for a predominantly digital society which depends on precise bureaucratic categories and exact statistical data for its strategies. Late modernity generates loose categories and loose numbers. Statistics, Arthur Koestler once joked, are like a bikini: what they show is suggestive, what they hide is vital. When, however, statistics fall apart because of their looseness, they may still be presented as suggestive data, while neither concealing nor exhibiting what is vital. Instead they contribute to the existing grey shade in which true problems and crucial issues which can generally be communicated only in an analogous manner, can be obfuscated. It is probably for this reason that many politicians and managers throw produce data liberally and eagerly. This 'data' suggests digital clarity, yet they spread around politically and managerially analogous clouds.

Loose values

As to the values of incommensurable world views, merchants, bankers and entrepreneurs are in general tolerant as long as their interests are not threatened. They will usually be intolerant with regard to radical brands of socialism, since they interfere with their capitalist interests. The Calvinists among these businessmen shy away from starting a religious conflict with their Roman-Catholic colleagues or competitors, if only because, as Northern Ireland has demonstrated tragically, a fierce and prolonged religious conflict is capable of destroying the entire economy of a country. There are no winners in such a war. Tolerance in the world of business is a matter of well-understood self-interest.

Holland is in fact a perfect example. Its economy has always been primarily (though not exclusively) dependent on trade and commerce, and thus on banking and legal services. Despite grave differences of religious and political world views – Calvinism, Roman-Catholicism, Socialist Humanism and Liberalist Humanism, and recently also Islam – Holland's predominantly merchant culture has been generally quite tolerant. This has nothing to do with some sort of ingrained peaceful quality of the Dutch nation, but rather with its history and its geographic location at the estuary of two large European rivers (the Rhine and the Meuse), and between the North Sea and the European hinterland. The country has been predestined geographically to excel in trade, commerce and related services. In order to avoid civil war or similar disturbances religious and political oppositions have been institutionalized in a system called *verzuiling*, that is *pillarization* or *columnization*. The core sectors of society, such as education, health care, labor relations, and until recently also leisure activities in sporting clubs, brass bands, and various youth associations were organized perpendicularly (i.e. intersecting the various horizontal socio-economic classes and socio-cultural status groups) according to the different world views. Pillarized organizations were not voluntary associations. One was born in a pillarized setting in the context of which all of one's activities were organized. Pillars were until the 1960s ruled top-down by men of upper or upper-middle class families who ruled the nation as a rather powerful and authoritarian elite. Incidentally, identification with pillars accounted for the absence of severe social unrest in the Netherlands. After all, workers identified with their ideological pillar in the first, and with the working class only in the second place. In fact, worker unions too were pillarized: there existed until the 1970s a Social-Democratic, a Protestant and a Catholic union.

Needless to say, the system changed considerably in the 1960s when processes such as democratization, emancipation and secularization began to affect the core of these pillars. The amazing thing is, however, that the system did not collapse. There are still scores of Protestant and Catholic primary schools, one Calvinist, one humanistic, and two Roman-Catholic universities, Protestant and Catholic hospitals, a 'neutral' workers' union (a result of the merger of the Social-Democratic and the Roman-Catholic unions) and a Protestant workers' union. Although fundamental changes are on their way the media (radio and television) are also still pillarized. What has happened since the 1960s is the following: the values pertaining to these pillarized organizations have become vague, general, rather abstract – the opposite, so to speak, of fundamentalism. In the heyday of pillarization – from the end of the nineteenth century up until the 1960s – pillarized values were organizationally grounded and thickly institutionalized. After the 1960's these values were generalized, grew abstract, were only thinly institutionalized, hovering, as it were, over the various organizations.[16]

This process in which the world view and ethos of various pillars generated loose values, has been facilitated and exacerbated by the comprehensive welfare state which in the Netherlands emerged roughly after 1960. After all, the comprehensive welfare state with its numerous bureaucrats and professional experts functioning as a megasystem of 'distributive justice' is a pre-eminently functional-rational, digitally bureaucratic structure. Such a system is not, of course, much concerned with the substantial and analogous rationality of values. It operates by and large as a kind of value-free or value-neutral technostructure, driven, as it were, by Mannheim's New Functionalism. The moral dimension of this phenomenon – i.e. the ethos of the comprehensive welfare state – has rarely been analyzed and discussed in the social sciences. Most of the socio-scientific analyses of the welfare state, those of sociologists in the first place, have actually functioned as ideological justifications for the comprehensive welfare state – a function for which they were usually lavishly remunerated in terms of research money, consultancy fees, and jobs in the public sector. Elsewhere, I have argued that the value-neutral, amoral nature of the comprehensive welfare state entertained an elective affinity with an immoralist ethos that spread rapidly among the recipients of the welfare state's largesse. The focus of this immoralist ethos was on consumption, not on production, on rights, not on obligations, on entitlements, not on responsibilities.[17]

There was a remarkable paradox at work here. Most retrospective analyses of the 1960s and early 1970s focus on the so-called revolutionary student actions which brought turmoil to the streets, the corridors of power, and of course the universities. The year 1968 is usually considered as the summit of all the unrest. In that year the rebelling students in Paris affectuated the fall of President Charles de Gaulle whose authority was believed to be indestructible. However, usually little or almost no attention is paid to the remarkable fact that despite these often rather emotional rebellions and revolts against the Establishment, almost invariably borne by the irrational anti-institutional mood, a pervasive no-nonsense rationalism spread out over society under the aegis of the comprehensive welfare state. The comprehensive (intensive and extensive) welfare state is a pre-eminent example of the New Functionalism which obviously was not hampered by the protests and rebellious acts of the students. On the contrary, in most Western-European countries the welfare state expanded and intensified dramatically. Meanwhile many leaders of the student protest movements were absorbed upon graduation into the welfare state system in which many of them began to occupy influential positions. Naturally, the radical leftist values they embraced so whole-heartedly and often irrationally in their student days, were now dampened, generalized and softened. Today, Social-Democratic parties in Europe enter into political coalitions with former adversaries. Their matching ideology is called *die neue Mitte* in Germany and *The Third Way* in the United Kingdom. It is a vague, general and abstract ideology interspersed with loose values, serving the aims of New Functionalism and its no-nonsense *Realpolitik*.

Power ought to be legitimated in terms of values, so as not to degenerate into merely bureaucratic control, or maybe even coercive terror. In order to justify itself, i.e. to show itself as a just force, power must appeal to a higher authority. Max Weber suggested that there are idealtypically three such higher authorities. In pre-industrial societies power is often legitimated by *tradition* carried by institutions such as the papacy or similar religious leaderships, the monarchy or similar political institutions. Extraordinary personal qualities – *charisma* – is a second foundation for legitimate power which is quite normal in traditional society (cf. Jesus of Nazareth) but not absent in modern settings (cf. Adolf Hitler). In a fully modernized society, Max Weber believed, the legitimacy of power is best secured by the *formal rationality of laws and procedures.* In democracies, for instance, the power of rulers is legitimate because it is the result of elections and remains subjected to the rule of law. However, in a fully modernized, late-modern, or post-modern society traditional and charismatic values have become marginal and exceptional. Tradition is no longer a vigorous force in this day and age, whereas charisma has been transformed by the media into fame and performance. Pope John XXIII and Charles de Gaulle are by now old-fashioned. Instead we admire 'personalities' whose images of fame have been construed by media and communication specialists. Likewise, legality, Weber's third type of legitimation, is greatly neutralized these days, if solely because of a steadily growing legalism ('litigating society', 'contractual society', etc.). Due to this 'juridization' of contemporary society procedural justice, the cornerstone of a democratic society, has been subjected to inflation. As a result it has lost much of its legitimizing power.

There is still another source of legitimacy which is far more appropriate to the late-modern or post-modern state of affairs. Remarkably, more than a century ago Alexis de Tocqueville referred to this source of legitimacy which in his days was still in its infancy – *public opinion*. Politics, policies and power are increasingly dependent on this force which, of course, is nothing but a sophisticated, statistical construct of hundreds, sometimes thousands of individual opinions. In a society without distinct ceremonialized caesuras and institutional limits, and with a sophisticated media that can influence the minds and attitudes of people massively, Public Opinion can be quite unpredictable. More than anyone else public affairs experts know how capricious Public Opinion is. It is, in a sense, the modern variant of traditional Fate. It stands to reason that politicians and policy makers who set their course and strategies according to the results of the latest opinion polls, produce nothing but ad hoc policies, and a staccato type of politics.

This is maybe the reason why many these days yearn for the inspiring entrepreneur in the world of business, and for the inspiring statesman in the world of politics. Not surprisingly there is these days in the corporate and in the political world much discussion about the need for inspiring *leadership* – a topic by the way which was not long ago deemed to be politically incorrect as it reminded people of totalitarian regimes headed by an *il Duce*, a *Führer*, or an *el Leader*. Nevertheless, in the 1990s scholars and consultants discuss the need for leadership in times in which values and norms seem to be vague, abstract, footloose, and thus rather unreliable. The true entrepreneur and the true statesman, it is claimed, may surround themselves with functionally rational experts and consultants, but they themselves should not be specialists, nor functional, technocratic and digitally thinking rationalists. In these days of global and multiple competitions chief executive officers and leading politicians ought to be *virtuosos* in the legato and analogous design of middle- and longterm strategies. They should not let themselves be blinded by the staccato of the myriads of details and the vagaries of the periodical opinion polls. They should not be driven on the spurr of the moment by loose values, as men-without-qualities who are always busy. Making long hours in the Oval Office, knowing the many details of the many dossiers of government, keeping a close watch on everything that happens in and around this high office, keeping track of the opinion polls – all this is not sufficient for the making of a great American president. The truly great Chief Executive Officer of a corporation is not a Mannheimean New Functionalist, who keeps track of every single detail in his company, who refuses (or is afraid) to delegate power, who at all times wants to play safe. The truly great CEO focusses on middle-range and long-term strategies, is an inspiring example for people at all levels of the company, does not follow fads and fashions, and is not afraid to take high risks.

Two relativizing reflections ought to conclude this section. The first one is inpired by the previously mentioned playwright Bertolt Brecht who once exclaimed that a country is to be deplored, if it needs heroes. There is apparently something terribly wrong with a nation that needs heroes, and unavoidably also a Nietzschean *Herrenmoral* (morality of strong lords). When the over-bureaucratized, rigid, axiologically eroded Soviet Union collapsed economically, politically and morally, this ramshackle collection of nations and states was much in need of an inspiring statesman, a moral hero who would lead these devastated peoples through the darkness of general destitution and anomie towards a future of prosperity, security and safety. In the West it was believed for a while that Michael Gorbatchev would fulfill this exemplary role.We were, as we know now, mistaken. He was apparently too much infected by the bureaucratic ethos of the party whose secretary he still was when he launched his celebrated *perestroika*. He just produced many written and even more spoken words which direly lacked inspiring and useful visions, deeds and policies. Since his departure Boris Jeltsin has tried to don the cloak of a statesman, but all he demonstrates is a pitiful mixture of erraticism and despotism. One moment he plays the fool, the next he is a despotic tribune. Indeed, Russia is by now a pitiful and deplorable country. It desperately needs political heroes, but given its long history of despotism one must fear the day such heroes will emerge.

The second relativizing reflection stems from Alexis de Tocqueville. More than a hundred years ago he discovered a cultural law – quite an accomplishment, because laws are sparse in the world of culture. A democratic society, he claimed, offers liberty, equality and security but because of these three values democratic culture will necessarily lack passion and profundity. It remains particularly defenseless vis-à-vis the velvet coercion of bureaucracy with its procedures and formalities. Tocqueville believed that this law, as is in the nature of laws, is inevitable. It was senseless, he observed, to resist democracy, and to long romantically for the golden past of an aristocratic society, as many aristocratic compatriots in his day did. Despite his aristocratic upbringing he rejected the aristocratic world of inequality and lack of liberty. He accepted democracy *pour faut de mieux*, for lack of a better system and by that he accepted democracy's endemic mediocrity and general lack of *grandeur*. Today, more than one and a half centuries later, living in a late-modern society, we should heed this message. Liberty, equality and security, not heroism and Great Leaders, are the values we should cherish and defend. But lack of *grandeur* and profundity is the price we have to pay for it. Democracy is indeed destined to suffer from a 'terrible lightness of being'. Democratic values are constantly endangered. The greatest threat comes from within democracy itself, from forces which, driven by self-interest and by the emotional lure of gnostic subjectivism, seek to radicalize liberty into anarchy, equality into egalitarianism, and security into reactionary institutionalism.

Loose memories and loose language

Compared to our ability to remember and memorize, the memories of people in traditional, pre-industrial societies are generally phenomenal. Institutions are the storehouses of our memories, therefore when they are 'thick' people will easily remember, when they are 'thin' people will easily forget. In pre-industrial, traditional societies institutions are 'thick' and thus memories are strong. Often amazingly strong. Anthropologists, for instance, who conducted research on the kinship relations in so-called primitive societies, usually expressed their amazement at to the almost inconceivable complexity of these networks. Their amazement increased when they discovered that many of their respondents knew and reproduced these intricate systems by heart. We would need a computer, they in contrast were able to reconstruct all these interwoven networks from memory, and to tell in addition scores of stories and legends related to them. Also the fund of orally transmitted legends, myths and anecdotes, and the many stories and little histories that these 'primitives' could recite, would fill a library in our society. Who exactly is 'primitive' here?

Maybe the Jewish Talmud is the most impressive example of the traditional ability to remember and memorize. The Talmud contains not only the Jewish laws, but also Jewish morality, and the records of theological debates on these laws and the morals. This enormous corpus was passed on orally from generation to generation for six centuries. When around 200 AD the unity of Jewry was endangered by the diaspora, this massive oral legacy was codified and put into writing. In the following centuries it was not uncommon for rabbis to know not only the Pentateuch but also the entire Talmud by heart as well. Before the Second World War the Jewish professor of the 'Old Testament' at the University of Amsterdam, Juda L. Palache (1886-1944) who perished in Auschwitz, drew attention and great admiration because he knew the entire 'Hebrew Bible' by heart.[18]

In short, these were memory structures and competences compared with which even the most retentive memories of modern people are definitely primitive. Several factors were and still are at play here. To begin with, ever since the invention of the art of printing and the erection of private and public libraries we have been storing information in books. The computer has reinforced this trend. Actually, we do not have to memorize much, because we have library stacks and computerized databases at our disposal which, without much physical and mental energy, can produce the needed information instantly. In other words, we have actually transferred our memory to libraries and computers. Needless to say, this weakens our historical awareness, because in the process our capacity or competence to remember declines. Even in the case of auto-biographical facts and data, late-modern people remember bits and pieces in a general and vague manner. In this sense our memories have become loose.

Moreover, because of the staggering developments in communication and information technologies we are bombarded constantly by large amounts of disconnected data and fragmented information. Due to the power of tradition and the restricted means of transmission pre-modern information, as voluminous as it often was, possessed a great deal of coherence, and a fluent, legato character. Or in other words, traditional information was much more substantial-rational and analogous than our information which is rather functional-rational, digital and ephemeral. It stands to reason that our memory has few points of support and orientation, when the information we have to process is predominantly funtional-rational, digital and fragmented. It goes, as we say, in one ear and goes out the other ear. Who remembers today what he heard on the radio, saw on television, or read in the newspaper yesterday? Add to that the disconnected informations of books, weeklies, billboards, meetings, daily discussions and so forth.

However, the most pertinent difference between pre-modern and modern dissemination and reception of information is the fact that today information must be processed individually because it lacks solid *cadres sociaux* (Maurice Halbwachs). Pre-industrial information was, as it were, embedded in a venerated and time-honored tradition which was embodied by institutions. It was received and digested collectively, not individually. Halbwachs, as we saw in chapter three, argued that memories and reminiscences are not just individually carried about, but always socially grounded.[19] Within the context of social interactions parts of the past, which we thought we had forgotten, may suddenly be remembered again. Daily experiences can easily illustrate this observation. How often do we suddenly remember (and much to our surprise) facts and events from the past, while talking with someone or interacting with people in other ways. Often, Halbwachs also claimed, that often the memory someone else relates to us, triggers a memory on our part which we had forgotten. Halbwachs drew two main conclusions: firstly, human beings do not really forget what they have experienced in the past; memories are put into the storage rooms of our consciousness. Secondly, memories are essentially not individual but collective by nature. They constitute a *mémoire collective*.

In the light of this theory it stands to reason that problems will emerge in the area of memories, when social cadres lose their demarcations and individualism increases to the effect that society develops into a compilation of loose people. The social cadres which Halbwachs raised as the prerequisites for our memories, are in this day and age weakly, 'thinly' institutionalized. The social contacts between late-modern individuals take place in multiple and flexible networks, which are, of course, quite a shaky ground for memories to be based upon. In such a situation, memories will easily become blurred and remain dormant in the twilight of consciousness. Or they may pop up associatively and in a staccato manner at unforseen and unpredictable moments as disconnected snatches that cannot be properly processed. In consequence they are usually emotionally drained off. In sum, loose people with loose values in a flexible society and culture with 'thin' institutions and multiple, flexible networks generally have loose memories and a weakly developed ability to remember people, things, events, and experiences from the past.

Needless to say, words too will become loose. It is remarkable that loose babbling which is and always has been characteristic of children, and which was allegedly also the prerogative of women in pre-modern society, has become a predominant trait of modernity. Because of the massive amounts of decibels produced by modern stereo-installations a discussion with some substance is simply impossible in most contemporary social gatherings. One is forced to twaddle on, now with this and now with that person. Gossip and party chit-chat are the appropriate forms of loose words and loose thoughts. It is a loose form of communication which incidentally can be employed functionally, since it is the ideal climate for loose contacts – one night stands and flexible, interchangeable networks.

In the days before telephones, word processors, e-mail, fax and the Internet, people often communicated with each other by means of handwritten letters. Correspondence in those days was a time consuming activity which required considerable concentration and attention, because thoughts and emotions had to be weighed and considered carefully before they were, as it was called, 'entrusted to paper'. Letter writing often developed into a literary art form, as the volumes of the collected letters of great authors demonstrate. Oscar Wilde and Thomas Mann, to give two arbitary examples, really composed letters.[20] They were probably quite aware of the fact that these literary products would appear in print posthumously. Today people rarely write letters. We do not entrust thoughts and feelings to paper. We pick up the telephone and chat, or we sit down at our personal computer and jot down lines of loose words for the fax or the e-mail. Incidentally, as an avid user of these marvellous pieces of modern technology, it has struck me how carelessly e-mail letters are being put together. Knowing that all these words will soon vanish by a single press of the delete-knob, we do not care to edit and proof read our messages. They are sent out with typing errors and all. This too is, of course, loose language and loose babbling. Telephone and Internet chats are usually, and probably also unavoidably, incoherent and associative – loose thoughts, loose emotions and loose words. Once more, some will call this 'the unbearable lightness of being'. Is it really that unbearable? We return to this question later.

Loose language – as *langue* and as *parole* – occurs everywhere these days. In bureaucracy for instance, when people conduct meetings. Often so-called discussion papers are presented which must entice people to 'brainstorm'. In such sessions loose ideas and loose words are strung together associatively. Free associations are believed to be creative. And then there are the so-called talk shows in which people chat freely about everything as long as it is without substance, weight and relevance. Famous movie or television stars love to chatter on about the least interesting subject there is: their personal life and world view. In such television performances 'personalities' are being constructed. Needless to say, all this loose talk generates semantic and heuristic inflation. After a while, one forgets to ask the simple question of what all these words and sentences actually mean. Inflatory chatter has been institutionalized rather solidly in the (often syndicated) newspaper column. If one is contractually obliged to fill one's weekly column with personal thoughts and observations, one cannot avoid eventualy producing merely loose words and sentences. Thoughts and reflections roll as marbles through the pages of most columns. They are in fact the favorite staccato of the contemporary intelligentsia. The readers of these columns assess not so much their substantial rationality as their ability to entertain. The few columnists who do manage to produce pieces of substance and value are, I am afraid, out of step with our late-modern society.

Naturally, loose language flourishes in the world of politics. In fact, it is often elevated here to an art form. Politicians who refuse for whatever reason to reveal the real motives of their political course and actions, cannot afford in this day and age of mass media to simply hold their tongues. With a microphone in front of their mouths and a camera zoomed in on their faces, they must say something, no matter what. If they are experienced political professionals, they will start talking, smoothly, rapidly and superficially. Clichés will roll freely over their tongues. Critical listeners will conclude that they not are not really meaning what they say. However we have been massaged by loose language in the media to such a degree that only a few of us are still able to listen critically. Critical listeners are, of course, the last thing loose-talking politicians want.[21]

No way back

When a society modernizes, it can be observed that the institutional borders and limits of earlier days blur, while caesuras in one's biography, such as death, birth, puberty, and marriage grow into gaps which are filled by irrational emotions on the one hand and rational sciences and techniques on the other hand. Staccato culture is the result, as are loose people, loose values, loose emotions, loose thoughts, loose words and loose memories. This phenomenal change should not, however, seduce us into engaging in cultural pessimism, and decline-of-the-West philosophies. The warning is not superfluous, because in my experience people often draw the conclusion from the previous analyses that I am evaluating the discussed phenomena and processes negatively, putting the past with its 'thick' institutions on a pedestal. This is not and never has been my intention.

One should not forget that traditional, ceremonialized caesuras with those rites and myths embedded in allegedly God given institutions, put a very heavy burden on the shoulders of individuals. Likewise, the clear and distinctive institutional borders and limits with their sharply separated roles, competences and power differentiations, have always kept people apart, and suppressed the weak ones among them. They have set human beings against each other, individually and collectively. Let us not forget, for instance, that rancorous feuds between clans or similar closed groups constituted a well-established, very 'thick' institution in many pre-modern, traditional societies! In these thickly instituted feuds people hated other people passionately, often without really knowing why. The feud grew into an autonomous, 'objective' institute which simply ordered new generations to take up the hatred of their parents and grandparents, and to engage in acts of irrational and bloody revenge. There was, to be sure, no 'unbearable lightness of being' in those pre-modern days, but the weight of a tradition rich in taboos, of 'thick' institutions, and of an elitist morality must have been unbrearable, certainly for those living in the lower strata of these usually undemocratic, thoroughly hierarchical societies. Certainly, values, emotions, words and actions were not loose. On the contrary, they were generally very solid, severe, and in some cases very savage.

Moreover, creativity, liberty and security were not defended and safeguarded by a constitutional state in those pre-modern and traditional days, but had to be gained and maintained laboriously, often with very heavy personal sacrifices. Moreover, usually only a small and select group of extraordinarily gifted or privileged individuals was able to escape the chores, toils, and routines of daily life. Everyday life was for 'normal' people cumbersome, and heavily imbued with mediocrity and depravity. The immortal names of a few creative individuals shone through this often dark and tradition-directed cosmos: Newton, Bruno, Galilei, Michelangelo, Rembrandt, Vermeer, Augustine, Luther, Pascal, Bach, Mozart, Beethoven, *e tutti quanti*. Even today their lights have not been extinguished. But what we should not forget, is that the large masses of people remained locked in institutional cadres which were the fruits and bearers of a magically tabooed, cumbersome tradition.

There is also little reason to put the legato rhythm of traditional culture on a pedestal. More often than not it led to dull resignation. Certainly, there was more cultural vitality in the medieval countryside than the historical studies of Burckhardt or Huizinga suggest, and also politically there was more unrest and rebellion among the peasants of the Middle Ages than most romantic accounts of this age have surmized. But due to the absence of the printed word and of mass media this peasant culture could never acquire dominance. Moreover it remained locked up, restrained and disciplined by the forceful estate structure of feudalism. It is true that the cities began their assault on the closed, medieval *syndesmos,* as early as the ninth century. Indeed they were the seedbed of modernity, of the arts and sciences, and of political democracy. But it took several centuries to liberate the urban economy and polity from the shackles of feudalism and its inherent species of despotism. In short, there is no valid reason for adopting a nineteenth-century brand of romantic conservatism in yearning for a return to the pre-modern past.

On the other hand, there is also little reason to applaud modernization as the Great Liberation of the Individual, and as the Great Progress of Reason. In our highly flexible, 'thinly' institutionalized world, inhabited by loose people with loose thoughts, emotions, words, acts and memories, liberty degenerates easily into a non-committal and complacent attitude that focusses exclusively on safeguarding private interests and on stimulating subjectivist emotions. In addition, modern individualism often molds human beings into herd-animals who thoughtlessly follow each hype and fashion deemed interesting and emotionally rewarding. And although reason and rationality have undeniably progressed in modernity, mainly under the aegis of science, technology and bureaucracy, we have also witnessed that time and again new forms of irrationality and unreasonableness have emerged and played havoc with human civilization. Mass destructions, such as the nazi and Stalinist genocides, were accomplished by means of a thoroughly rational organization. Mainland Europe has in the past centuries repeatedly testified to this distressingly paradoxical fact. Albert Salomon captured this paradox in the observation that 'the logic and tyranny of progress gave to the world the progress of total tyranny.'[22]

In sum, a return to a past of traditional caesuras, to the days in which there were strictly defined and demarcated 'thick' institutions, is unfeasible and undesirable. Fundamentalism, to use this much abused term for lack of a better one, is such a movement that yearns for the days of an allegedly golden past. It does not try to destroy modernity, if solely because modern technology, like the mass media, can be employed successfully for the dissemination of fundamentalist ideas. Fundamentalism instead tries to curb modernity's secularizing tendencies by disseminating traditional, and often ancient values and norms. Usually a holy book, the Bible or the Koran, is proclaimed to be the God given and therefore infallible guide for life in all its many facets and compartments. What most of us find hard to swallow about fundamentalism is its inherent intolerance and parochialism. While this was being written the Taliban in Kabul who deny all women access to formal education, organized in the local football stadium a public feast in which a convicted burglar was beheaded. During the same event a physician cut off a thief's right hand after a local anaesthesia. The beholding crowd shouted the praise of Allah in whose sacred name these atrocities were performed. One wonders what is going on in the heads and minds of these people. It is like a collective mental disorder. Fundamentalists of all convictions are devout and disturbingly fanatic enemies of what Karl Popper called 'the open society'. As we have witnessed in the past and regretfully still witness today, fundamentalists of various religious and political persuasions often engage in acts of terror which are not only utterly cruel, but also, if one applies basic human virtues such as compassion, decency and fairness, are utterly unreasonable.

In view of all this *a moderately conservative stance* seems to be the most reasonable one. It will be branded, I realize, as neo-conservatism. But then, neo-conservatism is another container concept which is usually filled with things both Liberals and Socialists abhor. However, there are a restricted number of distinct qualities, or *virtues* rather, which form the core of conservatism.[23] To begin with, conservatism rejects the egalitarianism that is endemic in the left-of-center specimens of modernity. Most conservatives will defend the societal need for socio-economic stratification, since its absence, as radically communist experiments have demonstrated, will take away the basic motors of socio-economic advance, namely competition and the possibility of upward social mobility. Moreover, people are simply not equal, which then causes egalitarian regimes to operate in a tyrannical, i.e. murderous manner. Conservatives are not averse to elites, especially if they are seen as *qualitative* elites, and if there are procedures and mechanisms in the social and political systems to rotate or circulate elites. In any case, there is in conservatism a deep aversion of egalitarianism which it shares with liberalism. Equality should always be and remain an equality of opportunities, never, as in socialism, an equality of results. Incidentally, as is not the case in liberalism, in conservatism this aversion to egalitarianism is based upon moral convictions. Egalitarianism in the view of a conservative breeds an immoral ethos which fosters consumption, rights, and entitlements at the expense of production, responsibilities and obligations.

Next, conservatives believe in an institutional imperative, i.e. they emphasize the biological and sociological need for institutions embedded in tradition. The family, the church, the neighborhood, the school, the university, the state, and so forth will, of course, change, maybe even radically change, but they should not (and actually cannot) be declared outdated and superfluous. Institutions are, whether one likes it or not, anthropologically indispensable configurations. Moderate conservatism as advocated in this book will not, against the odds of modernity, cling desperately to the past which, as has been stressed, is not something to be celebrated and emulated to begin with. Yet, it will not lose its head and follow the post-modernist crowd that declares the advance of the post-institutional network society. There is, I have argued, a rather intriguing continuum between two opposite poles – 'thick' institutions and 'thin' networks and we have been moving lately in the direction of a convergence, where institutions grow 'thin' and networks grow 'thick'. This is an altogether different picture of contemporary society and culture, than the customary conservative return to the past.

Conservatives do not, of course, reject modernity. But they will be keen to curb modernism – in particular the thoughtless embrace of functional rationality – in favor of values, norms, symbols and meanings which are the essential components of substantial rationality, and enable a meaningful (analogous) communication between human beings. Or, in other words, functional rationality and digital communication are not rejected, as they are indispensable for an efficient organization of society. But they must be subordinated to substantial rationality and analogous communication. This communication will not be the communication of the days of 'thick' institutions and distinct, clear and concrete values, norms and meanings. It will be a much smoother, and in a sense also more superficial kind of communication. Yet, it will be indispensable for any modern civil society.

Although nineteenth-century conservatism was in general more of a cultural than an economic world view, focussing its attention and energy more on gentlemanly lifestyle and civil society than on the market and business enterprises, contemporary conservatism realizes that the capitalist free-market is society's only adequate and feasible economic foundation, and thus places strong emphasis upon entrepreneurship and business leadership. This, of course, accords with liberalism. However, it differs from liberalism in that it puts prime emphasis upon institutions as the foundations of a truly civil society. Liberalism's main focus is, after all, on the individual operating as producer or as consumer in the market, driven by his individual rational choice and the digital calculus. Conservatism's main focus, in contrast, is on the individual who interacts meaningfully with fellow individuals as in analogous communication, and who does so within the context of institutions, as 'thin' and as modern as they may be. Even 'thin' institutions provide the individual and his consociates with moral values and norms, and thus with direction, certainty, and meaningfulness. That is, they protect them against the destabilizing forces of anomie, without surrendering him to the alienation of ancient, overbearing and coercive structures.

Conservatives claim that a radically modernized society which sets out to sever the ties with tradition and the past, runs the risk of floating around in a self-congratulatory kind of aimless flexibility. It generates a staccato culture which is liable to stagnate morally, politically, and eventually economically. Radically modernized societies often embrace innovation as a sort of doctrine, while experiments are elevated into goals in themselves. In a staccato culture this strong emphasis on flexibility, innovations and experiments may even become a kind of restrictive and coercive tradition. Whoever refuses to innovate and experiment in a flexible manner because he treats institutions as a cultural heritage that ought to be handled with care, is considered a deviant person and is labelled as a politically and socio-culturally incorrect conservative. Paradoxically and ironically, it is the conservative who in the end may well be the truly innovative and creative individual.

1. This chapter is an English revision of an essay that was published in a Dutch volume of cultural critique. See Anton C. Zijderveld, *Staccato cultuur, flexibele maatschappij en verzorgende staat,* ('Staccato culture, flexible society and caring state'), (Utrecht: Lemma, 1991), pp. 25-44.

2. Emile Durkheim, *L'Education Morale,* (Paris: Librairie Félix Alcan, 1925), pp. 19-62. Charles Baudelaire's *Le Spleen de Paris* (1869) is, of course, a classic text. For a treatise on the broader sociological context see César Graña, *Modernity and its Discontents,* 1964 (New York: Harper Torchbooks, 1967).

3. Durkheim, *op. cit.*, p. 42: "la vie ne peut rester suspendue, sans que la mort ou la maladie en résulte."

4. See Witold Rybczynski, *Waiting for the Weekend,* (New York: Viking Penguin, 1991; Penguin Books, 1992). The author calls the weekend an institution (p. 14) and claims that life assumes in it a rhythm that differs from the rest of the week. The weekend which often starts on Friday afternoon is , however, not merely a time for lazing about, but usually filled with scores of activities, sports above all (p. 13). The following observation is quite perceptive: 'People used to "play" tennis; now they "work" on their backhand.' (p. 18).

5. Arnold van Gennep, *The Rites of Passage,* translated by M. B. Vizedom and G. L. Cafee, (Chicago: Phoenix Books, 1960).

6. In my monograph *Reality in a Looking-Glass* (London: Routledge and Kegan Paul, 1982) I have discussed several of such rites of passage in which ceremonial fools played the central role.

7. Annie Cohen-Sal, *Sartre: A Life,* translated by N. Macafee, (New York: Pantheon Books, 1987).

8. See Marianne Kesting, *Bertolt Brecht,* (Hamburg: Rowohlt Taschenbuch Verlag, 1959).

9. Herbert Marcuse, *One-Dimensional Man. Studies in the Ideology of Advanced Industrial Society,* 1964, (Boston: Beacon Press, 1968).

10. The economic dependence of modern artists on the international gallery scene was emphasized in the extensive sociology of art by Arnold Gehlen, *Zeit-Bilder: Zur Soziologie und Aesthetik der modernen Malerei* (Time-Pictures: On the Sociology and Aesthetics of Modern Art), 1960, (Frankfurt am Main: Vittorio Klostermann, 1986), in particular pp. 210-14: "Hausse, Baisse und Börse."

11. Max Weber, as is well known, highlighted the unintended, yet forceful impact of Puritanism on this rational world view. It was perfected by the Enlightenment of the eighteenth century. Werner Sombart portrayed this culture and mentality in his monograph *Der Bourgeois,* 1913, (München-Leipzig: Duncker & Humblot, 1923). See also Bernard Groethuysen, *Origines de l'esprit bourgeois en France,* (Paris: Gallimard, 1927).

12. Karl Mannheim, *Ideology and Utopia. An Introduction to the Sociology of Knowledge,* translated by L. Wirth and E. Shils, 1936, (New York: A Harvest Book, n.d.), pp. 256f., 262.

13. Herman Vuijsje, "Een beetje getrouwd" ('A Little Bit Married'), in: *Inter-magazine*, 11 November 1984, p. 130. The sociologist Hans J. van de Braak writing about "the splintering of our society" makes a similar observation: "In former days one was a believer or a non-believer, married or unmarried, man or woman. ... To-day there are married people living together, but also unmarried people living to-gether, or people who divorced and yet after some time have decided to live together again. There are people who are not simply man or woman. Some have altered their sexual status, and others who have not done this but dress in the clothes of the oppo-site sex. There are homosexuals who are united through marriage, and unmarried women who abhor men but want to get pregnant, and so forth." Hans J. van de Braak (ed.), *Taboo: Waarover we niet mogen spreken* ('Taboo: Things we are not allowed to talk about'), (Rotterdam: Ad. Donker, 1989), p. 31. My translation.

14. An early and still impressive account of such an adjustment of a male body to the female gender is given by Jan Morris, *Conundrum*, (New York: A Signet Book; the New American Library, 1974).

15. See for a detailed analysis of the flexibility of today's labor market under the aegis of economic globalization Robert B. Reich, *The Work of Nations*, (New York: Vintage Books, 1992), in particular 'Part Three: The Rise of the Symbolic Analyst', pp. 171-242.

16. See for a further exposition my contribution 'Civil Society, Pillarization, and the Welfare State' to Robert Hefner (ed.), *Democratic Civility: The History and Cross-Cultural Possibility of a Modern Political Ideal*, (New Brunswick, NJ: Trans-action Publishers, 1998), pp.153-74.

17. See my *The Waning of The Welfare State. The End of Comprehensive State Suc-cor*, (New Brunswick, NJ: Transaction Publishers, 1999), in particular chapter 3: 'The Ethos of the Welfare State'.

18. See the small and lucid introduction by Juda L. Palache, *Inleiding in de Talmoed* ('Introduction to the Talmud'), 1922, (Haarlem: Erven Bohn, 1954).

19. See Maurice Halbwachs, *Les cadres sociaux de la mémoire*, 1925, (Paris: Press-es Universitaires de France, 1952), in particular pp. 140-45.

20. Rupert Hart-Davis (ed.), *The Letters of Oscar Wilde*, (New York: Harcourt, Brace & World, 1962. Erika Mann (ed.), *Thomas Mann Briefe*, 3 volumes, (Frank-furt am Main: Fischer Taschenbuch Verlag, 1979).

21. I discussed all this in more detail in *On Clichés: The Supersedure of Meaning by Function*, (London: Routledge & Kegan Paul, 1979).

22. Albert Salomon, *The Tyranny of Progress*, (New York: The Noonday Press, 1955), p. 104. See also Carl Becker, *Progress and Power*, 1936, (New York: Vintage Books, 1949).

23. I am intrigued and thus influenced by Himmelfarb's argument that moderniza-tion has been in essence a development from virtues which commit people to values which are by and large non-committal. She views this as a process of de-moraliza-

tion. The Victorian virtues which in the conventional wisdom are usually dismissed as petit-bourgeois, stifling restrictions of human behavior, are re-interpreted by her. She places them in a new, refreshing perspective. See Gertrude Himmelfarb, *The De-moralization of Society. From Victorian Virtues to Modern Values*, (London: IEA Health and Welfare Unit, 1995). This is number 22 in the series 'Choice in Welfare' published by The Institute of Economic Affairs (IEA), London.

CHAPTER SIX

Institutional Conservation

A false contrast

Confronted by the question of what the role of institutions in contemporary society can and should be, one can distinguish for the sake of the argument two answers which are each other's opposites but have in common that they are both intellectually and morally simple and therefore deceptively attractive. Let us not fuss over names and rather call the two opposed positions simply *institutionalism* and *anti-institutionalism*. The former is generally held to be 'conservative', if not 'reactionary', the latter 'progressive', or 'post-modernist'. These labels are not altogether satisfactory either, but again let us not waste time discussing labels.

In *institutionalism* one declares the traditional institutions as the firm ground human beings have to stand on in order to survive as a species. The more a society progresses in modernization, the more human beings are in need of institutions grounded in tradition, since it is in the nature of modernity to upset, if not destroy ancient certainties and securities. Therefore, human behavior loses its steadfastness and orientation, which in the long run will endanger the survival of the species. The institutions passed on by former generations should therefore be kept intact, or, if need be, restored – even if the odds of modernity are against such a restoration. Instead of rebelling against institutions all the time, Arnold Gehlen once remarked, modern men and women would do well to let themselves be consumed by them. Naturally, this conservative stance is easily radicalized into a rather reactionary position, where we are called upon to turn our backs on the future, to preserve the past for better or for worse, and to do so with all the means of coercion available. Gehlen, we have seen, singled out the state as the superior institution which should maintain the basic order man needs for his survival. Its main capital is power, its main instruments the law, the police force and the armed forces. Democracy is not what this type of repressive institutionalism aspires to, and when it comes to morality it is very sympathetic to Nietzsche's *Herrenmoral*.

In the preceding chapters I have not whisked away this position, although I rejected emphatically any reactionary radicalization of it. Indeed for sheer biological reasons human beings need traditional (i.e. historically passed on) patterns of behavior which enable them to act, react and interact in a spontaneous and therefore efficient and effective manner. As much as they may constrain our liberty, and control our thoughts and emotions, the institutions enable us to save time and energy which can be put to use in a creative manner. Helmuth Plessner likened this to the actor on the stage. The actor plays a prepared role, but by playing the role he is able to demonstrate his artistic expertise and his unique creativity. Arnold Gehlen even claimed that we can only acquire and maintain freedom (and authenticity) through the alienation of institutions. He called it 'the birth of freedom from alienation'.[1] Moreover, Emile Durkheim's admonition should also be taken to heart: institutions are the bearers of morality which, if internalized through moral education, instills in human beings a moral character. Endorsed with moral character human beings will be able to recognize their own limits and responsibilities which are the hallmarks of true liberty.

In *anti-institutionalism* we may distinguish two currents. One is very old. It is the gnostic (or manichean) rejection of institutions as the ultimate realm of alienation. One turns away from these 'objective' structures and searches for authenticity, truth and pure identity in the inner abodes of one's soul. This type of subjectivism is a penetrating, free-floating and widespread anti-institutional mood. But there is also another type of anti-institutionalism: post-modernism as it is usually called, although this is something of a misnomer as it covers many different thoughts, sentiments and facts. Nevertheless, it argues against institutionalism *in* that modernization has by now progressed beyond the stage in which human beings are in need of institutional controls and restrictions. Actually, institutionalism is seen here as a contorted ideology which fails to take into account the fact that we have entered an Electronic Age in which the demarcations, limits, and centers of yesterday have lost their pragmatic functions. We supposedly live in a post-institutional society of multiple, rapidly changing networks, and incessant flows.[2] This society is ruled by flexibility and contingency, not by control and predictability. The idea that human actions and interactions are and should be structured by demarcated and centered institutions is old-fashioned and in view of the new realities of globalization, cyberspace and the Internet misleading.

With due respect, the anti-institutionalist will say, the social roles of Plessner and the institutions of Gehlen belong to a world of fixed structures, organized by rather fixed collectivities, in particular by elites invested with a fixed authority and a steadily increasing power. By now this world is out of date. We have moved far beyond it. The new world today and the coming century, is not one of inflexible institutions grounded in a traditional past. On the contrary, it is and will increasingly be a world of multiple and flexible networks which autonomous individuals construct and employ in a bottom-up manner according to their individual needs and interests. This, it is claimed by most post-modernists, is not a world of institutions and structures, but of networks and flows. If there were still an imperative at all – but the idea of an imperative is rather outdated – we would not speak of the institutional and traditional, but of the individual and flexible imperative. And as to Durkheim's morality, the post-modernist believes that in moral matters too things have become fluent and contingent. If there is a moral principle left at all, it is the dictum that 'anything goes'. This principle does not instill in us a moral character. Post-modernists live not only after but also beyond virtue.[3]

In this book I have examined this stance seriously, although I reject the gnostic-subjectivist variant without compromise. It cannot be denied that the process of modernization has entered a new phase with the spectacular rise of the information and communication technologies, the end of the cold war, the rise of the European Union, and the globalization of the economy. Under the impact of these spectacular changes structural differentiation which has always been essential to the process of modernization, has been intensified. All this has admittedly caused a fragmentation which was unknown in modernity's earlier stages. Political centers such as the nation-state, socio-cultural centers like the extended family, the church or the university, have lost much of their former impact and control. Today they must compete with alternative institutions – the nation-state in Europe with the European Union, the extended family with the one-parent nuclear family, the church with thinly institutionalized religious movements, and the university with the open and long-distance type of education offered by the Open University, and with scores of para-institutional courses, conferences and seminars.

However, as in the case of the opposite, institutionalist position, here too one should maintain a critical stance. To begin with, most anti-institutionalists are overtly or covertly rather manichean, although they admittedly lack the cumbersome sincerity of the gnostic subjectivists. In fact, irony and a facile play with contingencies are elevated by many post-modernists into a thought form and a style of life. Nevertheless, they often oppose demonized institutions with glorified networks which is not very conducive to a sound approach. It may warm the hearts of people, as is testified by its popularity, but it will rarely also enlighten their minds. This contrasting of institutions and networks is rather artificial, and rather ideological to boot. In order to be sustainable, networks need duration and will inevitably institutionalize. That is, networks will over time acquire weight, and become 'thick'. As was argued in chapter four, they are then but a small step away from 'thin' institutions. Conversely, institutions, as Georg Simmel argued convincingly, are structures of action and interaction in which *Wechselwirkung,* reciprocity, is endemic. This reciprocal nature of institutions will become more apparent when modernization advances. Late-modern, or post-modern institutions, we saw in chapter four, are indeed 'thin' institutions, and easily coincide with 'thick' networks. Certainly in view of the latest phase of modernization, the contrast between institutions and networks is a false one.

Moreover, the fragmented world of multiple contingencies and flexibilities which post-modernists applaud, may indeed be an exciting world full of challenges, opportunities and risks. This world is in all probability infinitely more exciting and entertaining than the traditional world of taken-for-granted institutions, but it is so only for the rich and powerful. To put it briefly, post-modernism is a rather luxurious philosophy suited for wealthy and rather spoiled people who can afford to take risks, and to frolic in contingencies and flexibilites. For the poor and vulnerable, however, this world is a dangerous and hazardous place, and it is so not because of contingency, but because of a lack of power, steady work and basic financial means.

De-institutionalization, crime and terror

There is a threat even the rich and powerful cannot escape these days – organized crime and international terrorism. Anti-institutionalists should realize that a truly de-institutionalized society presents a paradise for organized crime and for terrorists, because the fragmentation it entails makes it hard to be tracked down and controlled. And now that we brought it up, the mafia and international terrorism are prime sociological examples of network organizations. At the same time, they are solidly institutionalized. Their ways of acting, thinking and feeling (i.e. their institutions) are embedded in a strong tradition which is not based on democracy and the rule of law, but on naked power, dictatorial authority, and unscrupolous use of violence.

Institutions, after all, function as mechanisms which control man's impulses and dampen his emotions. If these inhibitions and control mechanisms break down in civil society, as happens for instance in revolutions and wars, people are at the mercy of the physically and/or politically powerful. One should not forget that societies with weak institutions, or, as seems to be the case in today's Russia, without adequately functioning institutions, are perfect breeding grounds for organized crime which has its own, non-democratic and parasitical institutions. Also such de-institutionalizing societies often offer home bases for terrorists, as was illustrated until recently by Lebanon. However, societies ruled by a totalitarian state which keeps societal institutions in a firm, dictatorial grip, and uses them as extensions of its power, are also attractive places for terrorists to operate from. Syria, present day Afghanistan and Libya are obvious examples. There can be no doubt that a constitutional state and a civil society with strong and autonomous institutions are, next to an adequately functioning market, the basic conditions of a decent, safe and secure life for all citizens. Anti-institutionalists should heed this basic fact. As to Russia, one does not need to embrace Gehlen's reactionary views concerning the state as the ultimate system of discipline and order, nor together with the remaining communists who long for a return of the totalitarian Stalinist state, to realize that the breakdown of Russia's central authority, and the absence of vital institutions as the corner stones of a vital civil society, bear grave consequences for the safety, the security and the well-being of ordinary Russian citizens. The political, socio-economic and moral destitution of this country presents a tragedy which will probably take many decades (and many victims) to end.

International terrorism may well be the most frightening consequence of the present borderless and decentered world. Due to globalization all of us are potential victims of terrorism. In the summer of 1998 *The Economist* carried an article on this issue. The article was as informative as it was disquieting.[4] There is, the article claims, an old and a new type of terrorism. Traditional terrorists have a political agenda which in the final analysis can be discussed and negotiated. As cruel as their actions can be and indeed have been, traditional terrorists are yet realistic and rational in the sense that they are being driven by an objective, an aim, an ultimate end, and thus by a political agenda which is negotiable. The IRA, the ETA, and the PLO have explicit political aims. Their ultimate aim is to acquire political legitimacy. The ANC of South-Africa is an obvious example. It was a terrorist movement during the reign of *apartheid*. It has now accomplished its goal – the end of *apartheid* and the rule of the country by the black majority. It also acquired legitimacy which to a considerable degree should be attributed to former President Nelson Mandela.

The demands of these old, traditional terrorists may strike their adversaries as utterly unreasonable, yet there is that desire to sit down eventually at the negotiating table. *New terrorism*, however, is quite different. Actually it is somehow rather post-modern. There is no distinct political agenda, and, the article in *The Economist* stipulates, 'its perpetrators have no realistic programme for taking power themselves. It is often just a cacaphonous cry for protest against the West in general, and American government in particular – fuelled by impotent rage over the Great Satan's cultural and geographical supremacy'.[5] New terrorists commit their crimes in the name of some vague sort of religious or metaphysical ideal. They are fanatically anti-American, anti-West, anti-government, anti-everything. The 'ideology' of the Oklahoma Bombers was non-negotiable since they were 'anti-government' period. New terrorists may even be simply insane, as for example the Japanese sectarian leader who some years ago incited his followers to strike at an unknown enemy by unleashing chemical poison in one of the tubes of the Tokyo subway system. In his headquarters the Japanese police found a supply of chemical weapons large enough to wipe out the entire population of Tokyo.

More dangerous and internationally threatening though are the new terrorists who are not insane. Take Osama bin Laden who operates a global network of terrorists from Afghanistan. He is, though little is known about him, apparently a wealthy, intelligent, Arabic islamist, who employs modern electronic technology for the communication with his multi-national, very flexible army of terrorists. It is said that he is driven by an amorphous, politically indistinct hatred against 'America' and 'the West'. He has allegedly proclaimed a *jihad* against the non-muslim world, which, of course, is quite an amorphous and oceanic program. It offers no room for reasonable negotiations, as it is hard to determine what he is after beyond 'the end of America', 'the end of Western supremacy', and 'the victory of world islam.'

The most disquieting thing about new terrorism is the fact that it is rather simple these days to acquire sophisticated (chemical, biological and nuclear) weapons with which targets can be hit indiscrimately and allover the world. A mini-atombomb can be transported nowadays in a small suitcase. Shady criminals from Central-Europe, Eastern-Europe and Russia sell weapons all-over the globe, and even trade in nuclear materials for the fabrication of nuclear bombs.

All this leads to a double conclusion. A world of 'thick' institutions to which individual human beings have to surrender, or, to use Gehlen's expression once more, by which individuals must let themselves be consumed, is a nightmare of control and repression. Soon man's freedom and creativity will be smothered, while the rich and powerful will view themselves as Nietzschean *Uebermenschen* who have the presumed right to reign top-down over whomever they deem to be weak and inferior. But then, in contrast, a radically de-institutionalized world of flexible networks in which people act and interact as loose people with loose values and norms, loose words and thoughts, loose experiences and emotions, may as easily acquire nightmarish dimensions. One may cling to the belief that authenticity, creativity and liberty are not only guaranteed but also fostered by such a post-institutional society of networks, but that is a tragic misconception. In such a radically 'open society' human beings will for their orientation, for their safety and certainty, easily turn away from reality and withdraw into the inner abodes of their subjectivity – often by using soft or hard drugs which notedly facilitate the repression of the reality principle. And that is the perfect environment for organized crime and terrorism.

One of the tragic consequences of the fascist, Nazi, and communist regimes in Europe has been the fact that a sensible brand of conservatism which searches prudently for a proper balance between traditional and collective institutions on the one hand, and individual thoughts, emotions and actions on the other, cannot acquire legitimacy and feasibility. In fact, the notion of an institutional imperative has in the past decades lost much of its appeal. Western democracies had learned their lessons in their struggles and fights with fascism, Nazism and communism. Ever since, the institutional imperative has been associated with an anti-democratic and reactionary type of conservatism. Beyond that it has usually been whisked aside by a pragmatic functionalism which after World War II focussed on organizational efficiency first and foremost. And when the Western world was restored politically, socially and economically – cared for safely and affluently by a comprehensive welfare state – a neo-romantic ideology, post-modernism, emerged in which the end of various institutions was announced and the advance of the post-institutional network society was proclaimed. In fact, as I argued in chapter four, pragmatic New Functionalism was fostered and cherished by the comprehensive welfare state, because it functioned as its appropriate ethos and mentality. This elective affinity next paved the way for the post-modern belief and trust in flows, fragmentations and flexible networks. Post-modernism presented itself as the appropriate ethos and mentality for the Electronic Age.

Yet, the hard facts of biological evolution, and the equally hard fact that organized crime and new terrorism prosper in a de-institutionalized environment, prove that the institutional imperative is unavoidable. It requires a rethinking of the nature and functions of institutions, since traditional institutionalism is as far as the contemporary world is concerned no longer adequate. To begin with, such a *neo-institutionalism* will have to incorporate the idea of networks. Starting from the conceptual premise that institutions and networks cannot be strictly separated, I developed in the former chapter a theorem in which I claimed that we are living in a world of 'thin' institutions and increasingly 'thick' networks.

Neo-institutionalism and communitarianism

Some cultural and political analysts claim that *communitarianism* is the appropriate alternative. I took exception to this idea. The movement originated in America and is propagated as a 'progressive', left-of-center answer to the right-of-center neo-liberalism and its one-sided market orientation. It is not the market, nor the state but 'civil society' viewed as a communal society, that is placed atop the communitarian agenda. But there is a big problem here, as I tried to demonstrate in the third section of chapter four. The notion of community reminds the European analyst immediately of the German concept of *Gemeinschaft*. In most communitarian manifestos this conceptual link is usually made rather thoughtlessly and naively. If it is not meant superficially as a purely administrative and legal concept, comparable to the German *Gemeinde*, as I argued in the previous chapter, community has in America rather different connotations from those that *Gemeinschaft* has in Europe. Once more, in America community is in essence and originally a bottom-up and functional concept. That is, driven by well-understood self-interests otherwise stern individualists band and work together in order to create and maintain a world which is safe and wholesome for themselves but above all for their children and grandchildren. In that sense, community is not collectivistic and it is not an aim in itself. Its nature is rather individualistic and pragmatic, and goes back to the days of the Puritan founding fathers. In addition, originally (but not always in actual fact) the American community was not exclusive but inclusive: whoever collaborated in and contributed to the community, was a member of it. On the other hand, *Gemeinschaft,* to phrase it bluntly, is essentially a crypto-fascist concept. If American communitarianists treat community and *Gemeinschaft* as synonyms, they should be aware that they are operating in politically and morally murky waters. After all, *Gemeinschaft* stands for a collectivity, run in a top-down, authoritarian fashion. It is expressedly exclusive because one is born into it, not integrated from the outside. The ultimate *Gemeinschaft* is the *Volk,* or, which is often identified with it, the *Rasse.* The practice of ethnic cleansing in former Yugoslavia is a recent and grim reminder of this fact.

Realities are, of course, infinitely more fateful than concepts. The American community has in its actual realization often moved suspiciously close to the European *Gemeinschaft.* Not only the Waspish suburbs of the 1950s and 1960s, but also the ethnic communities of the 1970s and 1980s were not inclusive but distinctly and increasingly exclusive. In fact, they have often come close to the actual realization of the pre-Mandela South-African policy of *apartheid.* It is tragic to hear Black Muslims in America condemn their supposed opponents in plainly racist terms and call for a separate development of their own *ethnos*. Their fanatical language testifies to an apparently deep-seated hatred and resentment, and comes dangerously close to the language of *apartheid* and ethnic cleansing. But then, the white middle classes also exhibit exclusiveness. In and around the suburbs communities emerge in increasing numbers which are surrounded by brick walls and supervised by armed guards. Apparently, people feel safe and protected within these compounds, but they are, of course, prisoners of their own paranoia. This is a community conception gone mad. Such walled in compounds of the well-to-do constitute the Gulag Archipel of the American white middle classes. This too is communitarianism and the involved community concept is very similar to that of *Gemeinschaft*. Reading about the philosophy of so-called New Urbanism reminds one of such a closed, exclusive, and exclusionary concept of community.[6]

In sum, I have tried to develop a theory of neo-institutionalism in which I followed the slippery road between traditionalist institutionalism on the one hand, and post-modernist anti-institutionalism on the other hand. In opposition to the adherents of the latter I have maintained the basic idea of philosophical anthropology that the human being for biological reasons is subjected to the institutional imperative, and I argued that a de-institutionalized network society would present an ideal environment for organized crime and new terrorism. Against the defenders of the former (luckily a rare breed these days) I have argued that in our present day and age – which is marked by the ICT revolution, has left the Cold War behind, and is part of a globalized economy – institutions can no longer be the 'thick' structures they have been for so long. In fact, we are moving towards a world in which institutions and networks merge, because institutions grow increasingly 'thin' and networks increasingly 'thick'.

A brief agenda

What we really need these days is a cultural, neo-institutionalist equivalent of the environmental movement. That is, we (young and old) should learn to practice *institutional conservation*. We learned over the past decades that the rather romantic conception of Nature as an extra-cultural, pure and pristine reality (Rousseau), or as a reality left to its own autonomous growth and development (Kant), is naive in view of the forces unleashed by technological developments and economic growth. Ever since the first report of the Club of Rome on the limits of growth (1972), we have been informed about and made aware of the dangers of environmental decay. Nature, this hazy concept of a past era, was redefined as Environment, that is as the very concrete reality of water, earth, and air. To ward off a progressive environmental decay on a global scale, the environmental movement, consisting of numerous formal and informal groups and organizations, demanded government policies and applicable scientific research. Most Western governments and especially scores of non-governmental organizations have designed such policies, while the environment has become a prime subject for interdisciplinary research in most universities. But research projects and policies are of no avail, if they are not borne by a sense of urgency on the part of the population at large. The past decades have indeed witnessed the emergence of such an awareness. Today environmental defense has become a taken-for-granted issue in most Western nations.

Like nature, culture is burdened with old connotations which are still in use but by now rather out of date. The romantic idea of culture as an immaterial Higher Order of eternal values and norms is the old-fashioned equivalent of nature as an immaculate world of authenticity and purity. Culture, as in organizational or corporate culture, is nowadays mostly viewed levelheadedly as a set of collective patterns of behavior – ways of acting, thinking and feeling, that is institutions. Such institutions contain values, norms and meanings which are far from eternal, let alone metaphysical. They are historical, socially constructed and socially carried on. In this sense institutions are relative. Whereas the Environment has become endangered by economic growth and technological development, or, if one wants, by Progress, culture as the Institutional Environment has increasingly and ever more vehemently, been threatened by modernization and modernity. Neo-institutionalism is in this sense the cultural equivalent of the environmental movement. Neo-institutionalism is *cultural environmentalism* aiming at *institutional conservation.*

Natural environmentalism, we all know, is plagued by two mutually opposed radicalizations. There are the so-called *eco-fascists* who overtly or covertly come close to a kind of blood-and-soil philosophy and embrace numerous alternative, supposedly pure and natural medicines and therapies. Politically they are a mixed bag. Some are left-of-center, others right-of-center. Yet, they are on the whole not politically organized, thus not very influential or harmful. There are also the politically organized environmentalists, like the influential *Grünen* in the German Federal Republic who in general profess a left-of-center course in politics. One can expect a similar situation in cultural environmentalism. There will be proponents of a reactionary defense of traditional institutions, proclaiming, as it were, the traditional culture as the historical blood-and-soil of a particular group of people. As I have mentioned earlier, after what has happened in Europe during the fascist, Nazi and communist regimes, we may expect that such reactionary institutionalists will be unable to politically organize themselves successfully. This is, for instance, demonstrated by the various parties of the Radical Right in Europe. They sometimes emerge alarmingly, as in France and Germany, but are usually unable to get a hold on the general electorate. Will there also be a parallel in cultural environmentalism of the left-of-center 'green movement'? One can expect such a parallel, certainly if post-modernists realize that networks will (have to) institutionalize in order to be sustainable and effective.

In any case, as in natural environmentalism there must be in cultural or institutional conservation a combination of rational policies and legitimating consciousness. Just as people have to be educated about the need to protect the natural environment against a progressive decay, they have to be made aware of the need to protect institutions against a progressive de-institutionalization. To begin with, people should be aware of the hazard of subjectivism and the anti-institutional mood that usually goes with it. Concrete policies on the part of governments and in particular a moral education within voluntary associations and non-governmental organizations are needed to maintain a sustainable cultural environment in the midst of the still ongoing processes of modernization. We must lose our innocence and naivety with regard to the instutitional environment, just as we had to become streetwise about the natural environment. Politicians, academics, teachers, businessmen, artists, and journalists should engage in multiple, public debates about the ins and outs of institutional conservation. Governmental policies, scientific research and above all moral education will be necessary in order to effect such a cultural environmentalism.

It is my contention that there are in particular six sectors which deserve prime attention: *family, state, religion, law, care* and *education*. These are the universal and basic institutions of humanity which constitute, so to speak, the solid core of the institutional imperative. This imperative, as we have seen in the previous chapters, is a *moral* imperative. Institutions embody morality. Through moral education they pass on to new generations the basic virtues needed to establish a truly civil society. Of these virtues I shall in the next paragraphs for the sake of clarity only discuss *responsibility*, i.e. the willingness on the part of individuals to pair at all times rights and duties, private interests and collective interests. The rights we possess in a civilized society are institutionally enshrined, in particular in the constitution. However, the duties which are the counterparts of the rights and which must be enacted in order to establish and maintain a truly civilized societal order, are to a great extent voluntary. Certainly in a fully modernized and democratic society, people are at liberty to claim their constitutional rights

174

and promote their private interests on the one hand, and to neglect their duties and negate collective interests on the other. Because the state in a democratic society is not totalitarian and is unable to exert dictatorial pressures on its citizens, there is little governments can do when citizens only heed their private interests and refuse to perform duties in exchange for rights. It all depends on the will and wisdom of the citizens, whether the civil society they inhabit together is just a matter of entitlements, or beyond that also a matter of commitments, loyalties and duties. It is in this sense that I see responsibility as the core of the institutional imperative.

The following reflections present but a rough outline of the main items of the neo-institutionalist agenda. But before that, I must refer once more to the last section of chapter one where (universal) institutions and (historical) institutes were conceptually distinguished. At the end of that section I noted it was awkward to maintain this distinction and proposed to use thereafter the concept of institution. This was deemed reasonable because institutes are after all historical and empirical specifications of institutions and thus in the end are not something so entirely different. In the ensuing discussion, however, I shall maintain the distinction between institutions and institutes, even if the concept institute is admittedly awkward. This, I feel, must be done because the historical, relative and socially constructed nature of the empirical institutes should be highlighted, if we hope to come to a program of institutional conservation that seeks to avoid the cultural pessimism of the alleged decline of institutions.

Nowadays, the traditional monogamic, heterosexual *marriage* is no longer the exclusive institute at the core of the nuclear *family*. This can be deplored as 'institutional decay' but it can also be viewed as an unavoidable component of the ongoing process of modernization, and thus as part of a historical transformation on the institute level that befell two universal, narrowly connected institutions, namely living in durable partnerships and living in bonds of blood relationship. Alternative set-ups have emerged and acquired legitimacy in most Western societies, such as living-apart-together arrangements, heterosexual and homosexual partnerships with or without legal contracts, and in some European countries fully legalized homosexual marriages. The crucial question is not whether this is all not simply decadence and decay, but rather how these alternative relationships shape and enact the novel mutual responsiblities, as well as the responsibilities both partners have with regard to biological and adopted children.

These are flexible arrangements but how flexible can one's values and norms be, if the issue of responsibility is raised? Human relations between adults and between adults and children are, as far as responsibility is concerned, never merely instrumental. In other words, the ultimate aim of such relations is not and cannot be the satisfaction of purely individual emotional wishes and desires. We are, of course, entitled to happiness but in the case of marriage and parenthood, happiness cannot be an exclusively private matter. It is, after all, limited by the others involved who are entitled to their happiness. That means, the pursuit of one's own happiness which as a value scores so high in this day and age of subjectivism, is severely limited by the responsibility to others.

Responsibility becomes concrete and practical in duties. The urgent moral question that emerges in the face of these new, flexible relationships between adults and between the generations, is what precisely the duties are all for the persons involved? These duties are, we must realize, no longer taken for granted and ascribed but rather voluntaristic and acquired. They will have to be discussed, spelled out, and negotiated. Is this a weakening of the marital bond? Yes, if people remain innocent and naïve vis-à-vis the institutional set-up they live in. No, it is even a moral strengthening of the marital bond if people are aware of the frugality of the institutional arrangement and keep working on its strength, resistance and durability. In the days of 'thick' institutions, duties were imposed by authorities, such as parents, grandparents, priests, ministers, rabbis and imams. Today, in a world of 'thin' institutions, we have to accost each other by ourselves about our respective duties. It is actually a situation of permanent, mutual, moral education. Often professional experts, such as psychologists and marital counselors, are called upon for advise and assistance. However, they cannot of course take over the mutual responsibiltiies and duties of the partners involved.

Let us take divorce as an example. In fact it has become such a widespread phenomenon in the Western world that one could call it an institution, or maybe better, a para-institution. Martin Luther once called the devil 'the monkey of God'. Divorce has become 'the monkey of marriage'. In any case, one of the reasons for this high divorce rate is the fact that marriage has become a very 'thin' institution. Without longing for the past in which this institution was 'thick' and based on the religious rule that what God had united, man could not separate, we should as married partners and parents more carefully consider and mutually discuss the consequences of a divorce for our children, as well as for each other. The responsibility one has taken upon oneself by putting children in this world should weigh infinitely heavier than one's individual right to happiness and emotional gratification. Research has established that most children suffer from the separation and divorce of their parents. Like the culture of poverty there also seems to be a culture of divorce, because children of divorced parents often repeat the divorce in their own adulthood. It can thus become a pattern, a habit – indeed an institution.

The allegedly old-fashioned position in which one decided, or more likely was told by moral authorities, to stay together as a couple for the sake of the children, is inimical to the subjectivist *ethic of ultimate ends*. But it did testify to the *ethic of responsibility* which is less outdated today than most of us (would like to) believe. In this ethic of responsibility the material and immaterial interests of others – the children who did not ask to grow up in this particular nuclear family first and foremost – are given priority over the interests of the parents. There are after all civilized ways in which parents can make a relatively decent living for themselves and maintain a gratifying nuclear family for their children, even if the emotional fire of their marital bond has been extinguished. It is in most cases a better solution for the children, than to split up the family. Marital problems become unmanageable though, when even a minimum of mutual respect is absent, and the children are witnesses to the mutual contempt and perhaps even to the vicious conflicts of their parents. In such a case separation and divorce are the only sensible solution. Yet it should be the last option, and it should be discussed thoroughly and sympathetically with the children. In many cases this last option can still be avoided. All it needs is a mature and open way of communicating with each other, a shared sense of responsibility and duty, and the willingness to relativize one's supposed right to private happiness and emotional gratification. This is, admittedly, a very tough order for late- or postmodern subjectivists.

The *nation-state* is an institute that emerged in Western nations in the eighteenth century and received its ideological justification in the ideas of the Enlightenment. It is one of the empirically visible specifications of the universal institution that whenever people live and work together some sort of political structure will emerge. The universal, non-empirical institution is 'politics', the historically specific realization of which is the Western 'nation-state'. Due to the radically decentralized federalism of the United States this institute has never reached the often rather overbearing and heavily bureaucratized character of most European nation-states. France's centralism is, of course, almost proverbial, but we should realize that also the comprehensive welfare state, as erected after the second world war in Scandinavia, the United Kingdom and the Netherlands, pushed the nation-state in the direction of an over-regulated, cumbersome centralism. However, the steady rise of the European Union, the spectacular developments in the areas of information and communication technologies, the collapse of the Soviet Union, and especially the globalization of the economy have altered the position and the nature of the nation-state dramatically. There has been a steady transfer of sovereignty from the various European nation-states to the European Union. The ICT-revolution has rendered the borders of the nation-state porous. Middle- and Eastern-European societies are searching, often in a painful way, for a manageable balance between a central government and ethnic regions. But also in Western Europe regions ('euregions') and cities ('eurocities') are engaged in an increasing competition with the central governments of their nation-state. Finally, multinational corporations may have their headquarters within the borders of a specific nation-state, but they operate in a footloose manner far beyond these borders and emancipated themselves a long time ago from each nation-state control. Some of them, incidentally, are economically and therefore also politically so powerful that they resemble nation-states. If Machiavelli could write his treatise on the management of absolute power today, he would probably focus his (ironic, if not cynical) attention, not on princes, but on the CEO's of multinational corporations.[7]

Is this then the end of the nation-state as a typically Western, historical institute upon which Western democracy has always rested? Is it the end of democracy, as has been suggested some years ago?[8] The neo-institutionalist admits that on the institute-level of institutional 'politics' decisive changes have indeed occurred, and are still taking place. The nation-state as a specific, historical institute has changed fundamentally. But these changes do not yet herald the end of this institute. Today, the state is no longer an overbearing, top-down ruling megastructure which controls society and the market through lavish subsidies and the bureaucratic strings attached to them. The state has increasingly become a partner in scores of networks with provinces, regions and cities, with corporate organizations and societal associations. The notion of public-private partnerships which are strategic alliances based upon agreements rather than formal contracts, is indicative. They are, in effect, typically late-modern networks with distinct institutional features. In a sense one can witness the previously discussed dynamics between institutional structures and flexible networks very clearly in and around contemporary nation-states. They have not disappeared, and they are not in the process of disappearing. But they have changed and they are still in the process of changing.

Meanwhile, as in the case of the family and its new, multiple partnerships, we ought to address the question what the core business of the modern state is today – a core, that is, which we must cherish and defend against assaults from within and from without. It seems to me that the most essential task of the state, its basic responsibility which it cannot delegate to other institutions, is its *constitutional mission*. The state should remain first and foremost a constitutional state which (a) defends our constitutional rights, the classic human rights in the first place, and (b) keeps and carefully guards its monopoly on the use of violence. I am prepared to define in addition to the classical human rights (freedom of speech, suffrage, integrity of the body, etc.), social rights as human rights too, albeit in a very strict sense, and certainly not in the oceanic sense of the comprehensive welfare state. It is a basic social and human right for people not to suffer from poverty, poor health, poor housing, poor care in old age, illiteracy, and unemployment due to circumstances beyond one's control and thus beyond one's responsibility, as in the case of severe physical and mental disabilities. In addition to these basic constitutional tasks of the state there are, of course, other core responsibilities of which two should be safeguarded in particular: (a) the state is responsible for the protection of our safety and property; (b) it is responsible for a proper functioning of the market, in particular for the freedom of competition which after all is the motor of the economy.

In the wake of the many privatizations that occurred in the 1980s the idea of privatization of the state's monopoly on violence has been proposed, and even practiced as in the case of private guards watching neighborhoods. The use of force which always is a matter of violence, should not be privatized but remain the solid and exclusive responsibility of the state. If the safety of the public realm is at stake, the police and the army should be armed, not private citizens and private guards. Particularly in the context of a but 'thinly' institutionalized world which is so vulnerable to organized crime and terrorism, the state, narrowly related, of course, to an independent judicial system, should be the firm and strong arm that ensures law and order. It is irresponsible and very naïve to believe that private individuals could effectively arm and then defend themselves against new terrorists and newly organized, very flexible and loose criminals. However, unarmed citizens still bear responsibility as to the safety of their neighborhoods. In close cooperation with the police and the politically responsible officials at city hall citizens can and should contribute to a socially viable, culturally vital and thus safer socio-cultural environment. The safety of the public domain is not and can not be the exclusive responsibility of the state.

An example may illustrate this point. One neighborhood in my city (Rotterdam) decided to take action against the growing inconveniences caused by drugs dealers and so-called drugs tourists from France and Belgium. It started as an uncontrolled, civic rebellion in which the residents took the law into their own hands. They were, incidentally, led by an inventive and forceful working-class lady. City hall stepped in and negotiated with a delegation of the residents, headed by this lady, a plan of combined actions of residents and the police. Patrolling the streets in shifts by day and by night the residents exerted pressure on the dealers and tourists to leave and avoid their neighborhood, while the use of force and violence was left to the police, when the need for it arose. At the same time the residents opened a home for the drug addicts of their own community where they are cared for on a voluntary basis. It is a demonstration of a collective sense of responsibility in which the (urban) government and the residents engaged in a public-private partnership. The neo-institutionalist sees here an example of a new sense of (public and private) responsibility.

Religion is a third universal institution. In contrast to America where despite modernization religion has remained solidly institutionalized, Europe has witnessed in this century, certainly since World War II, a steady decline of organized and solidly institutionalized religion. However, one should again bear in mind that this is not the end of religion as an institution. In the Netherlands, for instance, church memberships of the Roman-Catholic Church declined between 1966 and 1996 from 35 per cent of the population to 21 per cent. The Dutch Reformed Church declined in the same period from 20 per cent to 14 per cent. The stricter Calvinist church remained 8 per cent. People defining themselves as being 'non-church' increased between 1966 and 1996 from 33 per cent to 53 per cent. It is interesting though that in1996 40 per cent labelled themselves as being 'definitely religious' and 27 per cent as 'actually somewhat religious'. The belief of these people is very personal and many claim that it has in fact gained importance for them: asked if their belief has become more important 24% answered affirmatively in 1979 and 34 per cent in 1996. It is also remarkable that despite the obvious decline of church membership the churches are still in high esteem, and also religiously oriented schools are evaluated quite favorably.

Incidentally, in 1996 only 10 per cent of the Dutch population defined itself as atheistic ('there is no God or a higher force'). This was 6 per cent in 1966. 27 per cent defined itself in 1996 as agnostic ('I don't know if there is a God or a higher force') which was 16 per cent in 1966. In 1996 24 per cent as believers in a God who is concerned with people in a personal way. This was 47 per cent in 1966, but 39 per cent believed in 1996 that there must be a higher force which rules over life, up from 31 per cent in 1966. Asked if they saw themselves as believers 40 per cent of the Dutch population said 'Yes, definitely' (43 per cent in 1979), 27 per cent said 'Yes, somewhat' (25 per cent in 1979), 13 per cent said 'Actually not' (12 per cent in 1979), 20 per cent said 'No, definitely not' (20 per cent in 1979). That is, traditional faith in God has declined rapidly but vague religiosity and agnosticism rose, more so than distinct atheism which represents nowadays only 10 per cent of the population.[9] Once more, this is not *Institutionsabbau*, institutional decay, but a formidable transformation of a religious institute, the church as we have known it since the Middle Ages.

To illustrate this further, it is interesting to look at church attendance in the Netherlands. There is between 1966 and 1996 in the total Dutch population as to regular attendance (once a week) a considerable decline from 50 per cent to 21 per cent, while irregular attendance rose from 7 per cent to 13 per cent, and rare attendance from 8 per cent to 26 per cent. No attendance at all rose between 1966 and 1996 only 5 per cent, from 35 per cent to 40 per cent. The last figure remained stable since 1979. The attendance figures for church members is also indicative. Between 1979 and 1996 regular church observances on Sunday declined among The Roman-Catholics from 49 per cent to 27 per cent, and among the Calvinist protestants from 81 per cent to 68 per cent. But regular attendance in the Dutch Reformed Church declined from 49 per cent to 40 per cent between 1966 and 1979, but rose again from 40 per cent to 46 per cent between 1979 and 1996. The percentages of Roman-Catholics going sometimes to church rose from 22 per cent in 1979 to 40 per cent in 1996.

The religious picture of this supposedly rapidly secularizing society is, all in all, rather complex and somewhat confusing. Obviously, secularization is a decline of organized and historically instituted religion but apparently *not* a decline of religion as an institution. If the idea of 'thin' institutionalization is empirically observable anywhere, it is certainly in the present Dutch religious situation. Thomas Luckmann once called this fittingly 'invisible religion'.[10]

Here too the question about core business and core responsibilities should be raised. As to the still existing and functioning ecclesiastical institutes, one should realize that theologically quality is more important than the statistical quantities sociologists relish to report and ponder over. One could wonder, for instance, if the truly believing and participating core of the Roman-Catholic and Protestant churches were not equally small in the 1950s, prior to the 'secularization' of the 1960s, 1970s and 1980s. There was prior to 1960 a social coercion to go to the church and to be a church member, even if one did not really believe and participate with an inner conviction . 'Secularization' has been the rapid decline of this coercion, and it has, so to speak, 'cleansed' the churches of the outer rings of non-believers and internal non-participants, reducing them to the qualitatively 'superior' core. In other words, theologically 'secularization' should be defined and dealt with as 'purification'. It is then the responsibility of these quantitatively reduced, yet qualitatively purified churches to function in society – 'in the world' – as a spiritual elite, as the critical (prophetic) consciousness of late-modern, or post-modern men, women and children. They should not attempt to compete with the 'powers of the world', the media and the entertainment business in the first place, but design and execute their own, theologically authentic mission. To phrase it simply, the core business of Christianity is to speak, act and live in accordance with the Ten Commandments and the Sermon on the Mount, even if that is not at all entertaining.

It is not only theologically but also sociologically a distressing sight to behold (and hear!) a priest who in a desperate attempt to 'reach' adolescents, plays the guitar and sings popsongs in front of the altar, dressed in jeans. Is it really old-fashioned to think that it cannot be the mission of the Roman-Catholic Church to celebrate the mass in competition with the entertainment industry? One can in contrast also argue that it is theologically and morally more honest, and sociologically more sensible to stick to one's proper core business and to the responsibilities thereof. One may, for example, disagree with Pope John Paul II's intransigent stance on the hierarchy of the Roman Catholic Church, the exclusively male priesthood, birth control and abortion, but one cannot deny that he, in the end, faithfully executes the heavy responsibilities of the papacy. And he has until now done so in a remarkably modern way. He travels all over the globe, meets his fellow believers wherever they are, entrusts his ideas and policies to papal messages and books, and speaks his mind about various political conflicts in the world.

The most basic function of religion is its ability to construct a *nomos*, i.e. a meaningful order which provides human beings with a sense of security.[11] The other institution that creates such order is *law*. In fact, prior to modernization religion and law were indissolubly connected. Laws were in premodern societies religious laws and it was customarily believed that they were given by God or the gods. The Mosaic laws come, of course, to the mind immediately. It stands to reason that such sacred laws were magically tabooed. The idea of natural law comes, of course, very close to the idea of divine law.

Like religion it is not easy to define of law. In one of his witty poems W. H. Auden comes to the conclusion that law is as ephemeral and hard to catch as love. He lists several conceptions of law, of which the one given by a rather pompous judge is probably the most surprising one. The judge looks down his nose, he speaks clearly and most severely. He told us before, he says, what law is, but he is willing to explain it once more: 'Law is The Law'. Some say, Auden continues, that law is our fate, others claim it is the state, but then there are others again who believe 'Law is no more, / Law has gone away.'[12] The end of the institution of law? That would be as impossible as the end of religion.

Law is the Law, i.e. law is the court and the judge. It is, of course, as faulty as the idea that religion is the church and the priest. It is also an absurd radicalization of the *rule of law*. The essence of this rule is the simple fact that in a democratic society nobody stands above or outside the law. Even the most powerful have to obey the rules of the law, and even the most powerless are entitled to protection under the law. When, for instance, after the French Revolution penal law was introduced, the primary idea behind it was *not* to punish people for criminal acts, but to ensure people a due process when they were under suspicion of a crime. The rule of law also stipulates that a person is innocent until convicted by a court. Prior to the French Revolution such a procedural rule of law was absent. The powerful could often not only get away with crimes, but also held power over the court's proceedings. When the rule of law is at work fully, procedural law transcends substantive law in relevance and importance.

However, this contains the seeds of its own decline. Modernization entails a radicalization and gradual degeneration of the rule of law. Under the aegis of the rule of law the institution law developed increasingly into an autonomous and highly bureaucratized system in which in the end the law was indeed The Law. An essential component of modernization, we saw before, is professionalization which is tied to rationalization. We can observe this trend in all sectors of society. In medical cure and care, education, politics, sports, arts and sciences volunteers and amateurs have been pushed aside by professionals who are supposed to be qualified for their jobs because they were well trained and educated, and officially licensed to practice their specific profession. Rationality not intuition, magic and charisma is the mental force that drives these professionals. In modern society most professionals will organize themselves in professional associations, which separate professional experts from dabblers, and defend the professional interests in the market and the political arena. Only a few traditional occupations which are more callings than profesions, such university professors and judges, will not organize themselves in professional associations. But truly modern professionals in the sectors mentioned before will as a rule combine their forces and organize themselves in order to acquire power and hold on to it. The professional association promotes and defends the profession's interests.[13] Contemporary society is indeed thoroughly professionalized and ruled, as it were, by professional experts. A Dutch sociologist once dubbed it *expertocracy*.

The problem with professionalism is, of course, that its autonomy and focus on power easily degenerates into isolation from the rest of society. In a witty essay about the avant-garde in the arts in general and architecture in particular Tom Wolfe analyzed and criticized what he called 'the new age of art compound'.[14] Indeed, autonomous professions inhabit compounds. The

law has also followed this modernizing path of rationalization and professionalization. Even the judge who is still a rather traditional authority, has
gone through this evolution. It was a long path from the jurisdiction of the
(magical) prophet, the priest and the wise *khadi* to the contemporary judge
who is an academically trained and formally licensed legal expert. Jurisdictions and codifications have led to many laws and lawbooks, while the formal organization of the administration of justice created the courts with
their scores of clerks and bureaucrats. Indeed, it all led to a 'law compound'.

However, the modernization of law into an autonomous, highly professionalized compound led to an immense problem, because it produced ever
more *legality*, yet lost at the same time more and more *legitimacy*. In fact,
this is the modern variant of the old dictum that too much justice is in the
end injustice. Auden's verselines come to the mind again: 'Others say, others
say, Law is no more, Law has gone away.' Yet, there are ever more laws, and
legal acts and actions. If judges as the experts of conflict solution are called
upon all the time to solve various societal conflicts, that is, if society grows
into a *litigating society*, jurisdictions and laws will eventually become inflatory and thereby lose their legitimacy. Moreover, society loses its ability to
solve its conflicts by means of negotiations and compromises, and declines in
trust. A litigating society is in essence a paranoid society. It cannot, of
course, have been the main objective of the rule of law to cooperate with and
contribute to such a sorry state of affairs.

Meanwhile, one wonders if modernization has not recently gone beyond
this stage of professionalism and its inherent autonomy, societal isolation
and expertocracy. In all the sectors I mentioned before there seems to be a
drift away from professionalism towards the people for whom the professional services are dispensed – citizens, patients, clients and consumers. Not
only in the polity but in the civil society at large there is a general drift towards *empowerment* which gives ordinary men and women a *voice* vis-à-vis
the professionals. This is also happening in the field of law. In 1978 Philippe
Nonet and Philip Selznick published a small treatise on the sociology of law
which testified of a remarkable foresight.[15] Their main idea was that law
went through an evolutionary process of three stages: repressive, autonomous and responsive law. We live more than twenty years later now. It
can be argued that indeed, as in the other sectors of society, the stage of professional autonomy of the law lies behind us. We have entered the third stage
– responsive law. Let us briefly follow Nonet's and Selznick's arguments.

The evolution of law began with *repressive law* which was characteristic
of pre-modern (pre-industrial) society in which the authoritarian rulers had
a profound disregard for the interests of the governed, whose position was
precarious and vulnerable. There was a unity of state and law, the reign of

discretionary powers and a general promotion of class justice in favor of the powerful. Repressive law, the authors claim, carries the seeds of the next stage of legal evolution, namely the general apathy of the subjects, and the discretionary authority of the controlling instances. Both occur more explicitly in the next stage of *autonomous law*. It is a product of modernization. Autonomous law, characteristic of modern (industrial) society, puts a brake on the exercise of power by means of rules, procedures and accountabilities, while the duties of citizens are clearly outlined. It is, in other words, a system of law-and-order based on procedures rather than on substantive notions of justice. Due process is the cornerstone of the rule of law. The ties with the state are severed, and it is the task of the courts to de-politicize conflicts by (re)defining them strictly in legal terms. Finally, autonomous law is driven by a bureaucratic ethos and entails a low-risk vision of the world. Mannheim's New Functionalism, one may add, is very typical of autonomous law. But here also the seeds of the next stage are at work: when power is put under procedural restraint and citizens are bound by clearly defined duties, the spirit of protest vis-à-vis the rule of law will emerge and the call for a more *responsive law* will be heard.

Writing in 1978 Nonet and Selznick realized that the days of autonomous law were not yet over, that responsive law was still something in the future. As a result their discussion of this type of law was less analytical and more normative. More than twenty years later one can conclude that their vision of a responsive law was partly prophetic, as it has begun to surpass the former stage, partly up to date, as the entire drift of society in the Western world since the 1980s has been towards the revitalization of civil society and its institutions. In a responsive law, the authors claim, there is less emphasis on formal rules and procedures and more emphasis on substantive justice. Legal institutions are seen as the appropriate instruments to establish a social order, and in this sense they are political institutions and not 'value-free' as in autonomous law. Yet, this is not a superficial kind of instrumentalism, because responsive law focusses at all times at the establishment of a legitimate order. This order, according to Nonet and Selznick, is not won by subordination but must be negotiated.[16] Citizens, therefore, are not forced to subject themselves to the law, but need to develop civic competence. "Responsive law", the authors note, "contributes to civility because it is informed by an 'ethic of responsibility' rather than an 'ethic of utimate ends'."[17] This is a high-risk vision of the world, based on a post-bureaucratic ethos.

This is not the place to discuss this attractive theorem critically. I only draw attention to the interesting contribution it could possibly make to the neo-institutionalist approach. Autonomous professionalism tends to fossilize into a radical functional rationality in which procedures, means, methods and techniques supersede substantive meanings, values and norms, and aims. In the realm of law this supersedure entails a decline of legitimacy which contributes to a fundamental de-institutionalization of the law. A litigating society with a claims culture based on distrust sticks to the legality of the rule of law, but has in fact been corroded internally since it lacks elemental legitimacy. The institution of law has then become an empty form which can easily be filled with multiple injustices.

In short, the essence of the law is not The Law. Nor is procedural justice, as crucial as it is, the core business of the law. Its essence is substantive justice which is the aim of a post-industrial, post-bureaucratic and maybe also post-modern responsive law. This is not just the responsibility of the legal profession, but also of the world of politics and above all of civil society. It is the responsibility of civil society – individual citizens and collective organizations – to end the drift towards a litigating society and a claims culture. I shall argue at the end of this chapter that permanent discussions and open communications are indispensable the realization of this aim.

Care is the fifth universal institution we must discuss. Human infants need, compared to other species, an extraordinarily long time of care before they can stand on their own feet and manage to survive in the world. Portmann's previously mentioned blunt definition of the first years of an infant as 'the extra-uterine spring' comes to mind. Likewise, infirm older people are generally not left to their own devices or simply disposed of, but cared for by younger generations, often by their own children in the first place. Care is in this sense a biologically inbuilt mechanism which extends easily, of course, in the direction of the sick and indigent, widows and orphans, and other categories of people in need of succor. For that reason, the crypto-Marxist theory that medieval and early-modern state provisions for the poor, as for example instituted in the Elisabethan Poor Law, ought to be seen as a policy of the rich and powerful to ward off unrest and rebellion on the part of the lower classes, is somewhat one-sided, to say the least. These early forms of state succor, the historical origins of the European welfare state, were caused by the care impulse which is part and parcel of the biological constitution of the human species. Sociobiologically, this may all be the working of our 'selfish genes' (Dawkins), but sociologically these genes do aparently have a moral, altruistic bent. Or, the selfish genes are corrected all the time by altruistic memes.

Care as an institution has become specific in Western civilization with such institutes as orphanages, homes for the elderly, and asylums. This differentation was still unknown in the Middle Ages. Hospitals were then undifferentiated and quite chaotic places in which orphans, vagabonds, mental and physical patients, and drunkards were not cured but simply cared for in accordance with Christian neighborly love. In France they were called *hô-tels de Dieu*. Needless to say this type of pre-modern care was not yet professionalized but dispensed by members of religious and semi-religious orders. Only after the seventeenth century did more specialized institutes emerged in which various differentiated categories of people in need of succor and assistance were treated.[18] Gradually care itself was subjected to professionalization. Apart from the poor relief, much of these care institutes were non-governmental. That changed rather radically in this century with the rise of the comprehensive welfare state which attracted many care functions, or rather took upon itself the financial and statutory responsibility thereof. This, of course, enhanced the centralization and bureaucratization and professionalization of the care functions. In fact, if anywhere it was in the care sectors of society that one could witness the close coalition of state and care, the search for professional power and dominance, the claim of expertocracy, and the gradual increase of autonomy and isolation. It all took place under the aegis of a comprehensive welfare state.

But we have already moved beyond this stage. The comprehensive welfare state, I argued elsewhere, is waning. For various reasons the comprehensive welfare states in Europe have been subjected to processes of decentralization, deregulation and privatization since the 1970s.[19] As a result many care institutes have gained greater autonomy vis-à-vis the state and were forced to operate in a market fashion. They were consequently exposed to competitive forces and that, of course, entailed a formidable change in their organizational culture.

Again, should we in view of the developments towards late-modern, rather flexible care functions of various organs and institutes draw the conclusion that the days of the welfare state, as the historical specification of the universal institution of care, are numbered? Or, should we conclude that the comprehensive welfare state as a mega-institute has been subjected to intensive and extensive transformations which shrank its scope and capacity but did not inaugurate the end of the welfare state as such? The question is of course a rhetorical one. There is today a reduced welfare state which entertains scores of network relationships with organizations in the civil society that are independent vis-à-vis the state. There are often public-private partnerships at work which in their turn entertain network relationships with the market and its competitive forces. This very complex and differentiated situation is, for example, observable in the field of health care. It is a field, we all know, that is very hard to manage, to plan and to curb expenditurewise. Many very different players have their own interests at stake: medical and pharmaceutical professionals, patients, insurance companies, state officials, and scores of lawyers when conflict of interests collide.

To sum up, care intitutes constitute these days a typically post-modern world with multiple responsibilities which must be defined, discussed and negotiated. Once again, it is a matter of civic competences and a well-developed 'ethic of responsibility' on the part of the various players and stakeholders to realize the universal institution of care in ways that are in line with the demands of a decentered and debordered world.

Education is the sixth universal institution that I singled out for further discussion in terms of the neo-institutionalist agenda. Like care, education is biologically founded on the need of human infants to be guided by older generations on their road to self-subsistence and autonomy. Parents, siblings, the extended family, teachers, peers and friends educate youngsters in order to be able to acquire character or personality and to function adequately in life. The concrete, historical forms by which education is and, in the past, has been realized are almost countless. But it has been rather specific in Western societies in the *school system* that covers the learning years from roughly six till eighteen years of age, or if college is added twenty two years of age. In some cases, like medical specialists, formal education may even go beyond that age. Primary schools, high schools, colleges, professional schools and universities are educational institutes with relatively long histories, and distinct positions in society.

Ideologies which announce, often in a wishful fashion, the end of the Western school system have been an almost eternal accompaniment of it. Often so-called experiential knowledge was put on a pedestal at te expense of the cognitive knowledge disseminated in the school system. The romantics were good at that. It is still amusing, for instance, to read Henry Brooks Adams's memoirs, called *The Education of Henry Adams* (1907) in which he, at more than seventy years old, recalls his cumbersome journey through various schools and universities in America and Europe. But he did not restrict himself to a formal education, in fact all of life was in his view of things one long educational course. He probably would have applauded Ivan Illich's *deschooling* agenda.

What we see today and will further witness in the coming decades, however, is not the end of formal education in the shape of several educational institutes but an ongoing differentiation in many different types of formal and informal schooling and training. There is and will be a further merging of experiential and cognitive knowledge, and this new type of knowledge is and will be acquired in a junction of formal training and practical internships, and by an increased focus on learning how to learn and how to acquire adequate information. This shift from the 'what' to the 'how' of knowledge has occurred because many cognitive skills, such as adding and subtracting, memorizing facts and data, and so forth, have been taken over by the computer. In addition, due to the greater complexity and flexibility of the late-modern society, acquired knowledge wears out fast. Moreover, late-modern people change jobs and careers regularly. This job rotation recurrently demands new work skills and habits, and new types of knowledge geared to the new working and living conditions. Permanent education and periodic retraining are being institutionalized and organized in most late-modern societies.

But again, it is vital to reflect upon the core business and the core responsibilities of these complex, multiple and flexible educational institutes. How can it be avoided that these flexible educational institutes contribute to the generation and distribution of loose ideas, values and norms, of loose words, sentences and manners which in the end generate a staccato culture which gyrates around and around? It should be avoided, because after all a staccato culture misses the ingredients a society needs in order to be civilized, i.e. durability, stability, and cultural sustainability. Educational institutes have the responsibility of keeping in storage, so to speak, the knowledge and wisdom of the past, to function as the memory banks of past educational experiences and skills. The so-called classics of literature, musics, the arts and sciences are not the dead weight of civilization, nor are they authorities to be taken on face value, to be followed blindly, and to be subjected to endless exegeses. They are instead the pickets in the past which help us to understand how through the succession of the generations we have come to know the things we know today. More often than not these classics will also strike us as visionaries who not yet disturbed by all the complexities and flexibilties we have to take into account today, were able to focus on essences and crucibles. It is what we call in an old-fashioned way *wisdom*.

Indeed, we should not forget that one of the things teachers in all parts of the school system are responsible for is the dissemination of wisdom. In this Age of Information we should heed the distinction between information, knowledge and wisdom. *Information* consists of loose data, as presented in a telephone book, a catalogue, a statistical yearbook, or a computer database. *Knowledge* is structured information, data put together within a coherent, heuristic, i.e. meaningful framework, as in a theory or a handbook for practical skills. Informational data must be collected, knowledge must be taught and learned, *wisdom*, however, is something one can neither collect nor teach and learn. Wisdom – this old-fashioned expression can unfortunately not be avoided – is the fruit of experience, not the result of training and learning. The more experience people have had, that is the older they are, the wiser they potentially become. Early compulsory retirement, as is still customary in Europe, and the unrelenting focus and emphasis upon youth and youthfulness are in almost all sectors, except the world of sports, devastating because they radically exclude wisdom from the mainstreams of society and culture. This waste of wisdom is institutionally irresponsible.

I did not design a complete neo-institutional agenda. The previous discussion of six institutional sectors is only meant as an indication of the sort of debate and policy design deemed necessary in order to enact neo-institutionalism as an alternative to communitarianism and as a parallel to environmentalism. There are in this late-modern day and age two major imperatives: an *environmental imperative* which receives abundant attention in scores of research and policy endeavors, and an *institutional imperative* which, due to a persistent anti-institutional mood fed by progressive flexibility and complexity, has drawn very little attention until now. There is, it must be stressed, no legitimate return to the 'thickly' institutionalized past. Appreciations of traditional institutions by radical conservatives and ultra-right reactionaries are fortunately rather rare these days, but may emerge again when people grow tired of frolicking about in their flexible networks within a staccato culture. It is time to rethink institutions and to design and enact an enlightened brand of neo-institutionalism which avoids these two ideological pitfalls, i.e. ultra-conservatism and post-modernism. They are if put into practice, political and moral pitfalls.

1. Arnold Gehlen, "Ueber die Geburt der Freiheit aus der Entfremdung", 1952, in: Arnold Gehlen, *Studien zur Anthropologie und Soziologie*, ('Studies on Anthropology and Sociology'), (Neuwied-Berlin: Luchterhand Verlag, 1963), pp. 232-246.
2. , This position is best represented by Manuel Castells, *The Rise of the Network Society*, (Oxford: Blackwell Publishers, 1996). This is the first volume of a trilogy, called *The Information Age. Economy, Society and Culture*.
3. Naturally, Friedrich Nietzsche's philosophy which operated 'beyond good and evil', experienced a come-back in post-modernism. See also Alasdair MacIntyre, *After Virtue. A Study in Moral Theory*, 1981, (London: Duckworth, 1987). This comes close to what Gertrude Himmelfarb has called 'the de-moralization of society'. See her *The De-moralization of Society. From Victorian Virtues to modern Values*, (London: IEA Health and Welfare Unit, 1995). Number 22 in the series 'Choice in Welfare', published by The Institute of Economic Affairs (IEA), London.
4. The Economist, "The New Terrorism: Coming soon to a city near you", *The Economist*, August 15, 1998, pp. 15-17.
5. Ibid., p. 16.

6. See Peter Katz (ed.), *The New Urbanism: Toward an Architecture of Community,* (New York: McGraw-Hill, 1994).

7. I discussed this point in more detail in an article published by the Dutch equivalent of the Financial Times: "De bedrijfsvorst: waar Machiavelli de absolute macht vandaag zou waarnemen" (' The corporate prince: where Machiavelli would observe absolute power today'), in: *Het Financieele Dagblad,* Saturday, December 6, 1997, p. 19.

8. Once more, Jean-Marie Guéhenno's essay *La Fin de la Démocratie,* (Paris: Editions Flammarion, 1994) presents a compelling reading.

9. Cf. Gerard Dekker, c.s., *God in Nederland: 1966-1996* ('God in the Netherlands: 1966-1996'), (Amsterdam: Anthos, 1997). The statistics on Dutch atheism are inconclusive. Asked whether one sees oneself as a believing person 20% said 'No, definitely not' in 1996 (20% also in 1979). But the statement 'There is no God or some higher power' is acknowledged by only 10% in 1996 (9% in 1979).

10. Thomas Luckmann, *The Invisible Religion,* (New York: the MacMillan Company, 1967).

11. See Peter L. Berger, *The Sacred Canopy,* (Garden City, NY: Doubleday, 1967), pp. 19-25, passim.

12. W. H. Auden, "Law Like Love", in: W. H. Auden, *Collected Shorter Poems 1927-1957,* (London: Faber & Faber, 1966), p. 155.

13. Cf. Terence J. Johnson, *Professions and Power,* (London: the MacMillan Press, 1972) and E. Freidson, *Professional Dominance. The Social Structure of Medical Care,* (New York: Atherton Press, 1970).

14. Tom Wolfe, *From Bauhaus to Our House,* (New York: Farrar Straus Giroux, 1981), p. 18. As the title indicates Wolfe's focus is on architecture mainly. But his arguments can also be applied to other arts, to music, literature, and the theatre. In professionalism, imbued with what Wolfe called "the spirit of avant-gardism" (*ibid.*), people will see their fellow professionals as the main reference group, not the public, the ordinary citizens. These are with covert or overt contempt labelled as 'the bourgeoisie'. The aim is to baffle and shock bourgeois audiences. But as we saw in chapter 4, bourgeois culture is able to absorb and neutralize this. After a while, avant-gardism is fashionable and often even prestigious. The wealthy bourgeois, not free from snobism, is then prepared to remunerate it lavishly.

15. Philippe Nonet, Philip Selznick, *Law and Society in Transition: Towards Responsive Law,* (New York: Harper Colophon Books; harper & Row Publishers, 1978).

16. Nonet, Selznick, *o.c.,* p. 94.

17. Nonet, Selznick, *o.c.,* p. 90f.

18. I discussed this in my monograph on pre-modern folly *Reality in a Looking-Glass,* (London: Routledge & Kegan Paul, 1982), pp. 33-39.

19. Cf. my *The Waning of the Welfare State: The End of Comprehensive State Succor,* (New Brunswick, NJ: Transaction Publishers, 1999).

Conclusion:
Dilemmas and Maladies of Modernity

Happy but not *glücklich*

Never in the history of mankind have people had so much going for them as we in the Western world of today. Most of us are relatively prosperous, and we live relatively long lives. Since World War II, we in the Western hemisphere have not been plagued by the terrors of warfare. We managed to erect a welfare state which ensures the vulnerable among us a civilized measure of socio-economic security, we also managed to maintain a democratic constitutional state which defends, if necessary, our safety and property, and above all our basic human rights. No wonder numerous refugees and immigrants try to partake of our freedom, our welfare and our prosperity – legally or illegally. Compared to many parts of the world, we in the Western world live in a paradise.

Yet, despite all these advantages many of us are not comfortable in contemporary Western society and its advanced modern culture. The pursuit of happiness has to many not been very successful. It reminds me of the joke about the German-Jewish immigrant, living in Manhattan in the 1970s. He had been successful in the business he had set up and run. His children too were successful and fully assimilated into the American way of life. But the older he got, the more he complained about his life in America which, he felt, did not agree with him. One day his son said to him with an undertone of irritation: 'Listen dad, stop complaining all the time. You must admit, until now you have been quite happy in America!' His old man smiled wryly, and riposteed: 'Yes, happy! *Aber nicht glücklich!*' Certainly in Europe today, many people are happy, but few of these happy people are also *glücklich* in the sense of feeling oneself at home in and an intrinsic part of the surrounding world.

One of the European clichés about America is that it is a naively optimistic country. The thing about clichés is that they are generally rubbish, but some of them contain a kernel of truth. That is definitely so in the case of America's alleged naivety and optimism. Deep down in every American –

black, white, yellow or brown; wealthy or poor; intellectual or illiterate – is this belief in Progress paired to the belief that if things are bad, they can be improved through commitment, hard work and self-help. According to solidly modernized Europeans, most Americans are moralists at heart, and in that sense in their eyes a bit old-fashioned. This naivety and this optimism of Americans are *not* dependent on the state, as is mostly the case in Western Europe where the welfare state was always held accountable for not only the socio-economic security but also the happiness of its citizens. They are instead grounded primarily in civil society, i.e. in many voluntary associations and last but not least in core institutions such as the church and the family. I grant that there are changes taking place in American civil society, but still, each visitor from Europe will be stunned by the faith Americans have in progress and improvement through commitment and self-help. The generally excellent performance of the American economy and the fact that the USA is after the end of the Cold War the only global empire, adds, of course, to this optimism and self-confidence. Europeans in particular are eager to point to the socio-economic and political problems of America – the culture of poverty in many ethnic neighborhoods in the big cities, the amazingly high percentage of illiteracy, the host of poor Americans who are not medically insured, etc. But that is a very partial and often also somewhat prejudicial view of what America and Americans are all about. Moreover, several European countries had to learn in the past decades that these ills are not specifically American. Perhaps the size of the problems is, but then size is in every respect what differentiates the USA from most European nations.

In short, maybe apart from academics and similar intellectuals who are generally plagued by an unhappy consciousness, Americans are generally happy and optimistic. Europeans, on the contrary, may also be happy and optimistic today, but they seem to suffer under the surface from some fundamental maladies that make them *unglücklich*. There is, of course, a simple reason for this. Europe underwent terrible tragedies in the twentieth century through terrible tragedies and numerous changes and transformations. American history in this fateful century has been a series of economic, political and cultural successes. Since the truly tragic Civil War in the 1860s, Americans have not experienced war in their own territories. As terrible as the two world wars have been for individual Americans who often sacrificed their lives for the eventual victories, both global conflicts contributed in the end to the emergence of America as a global super power. In contrast, European history of the twentieth century has been exceedingly complex and at times utterly tragic – not only for individual Europeans but for European nations and nation-states as well. The two world wars made havoc of Europe's economies, societies and cultures. Top talents in the arts and sciences had fled in the 1930s to America, few of whom returned after the war. Until 1989 the continent was partitioned into two hostile parts separated by the Iron Curain and the Berlin Wall. Several Western European nations were prior to the war colonial super powers. But in the late 1940s, the 1950s and the early 1960s European colonialism collapsed which meant a tremendous loss of power and revenues on the part of the colonial homelands. After 1945 most Western European nations rebuilt their infrastructures and economies remarkably quickly and thoroughly, but that was in the first place a material (economic) regeneration. Morally, i.e. as to values and norms, and institutionally, i.e. as far as the family, the church, the university, the trade unions, etc. were concerned, Western Europe went through a prolonged crisis. Europe lost its self-confidence, its determination, its authority. French and German Existentialism (Sartre, Heidegger), Structuralism (Lévi-Strauss, Foucault), Post-modernism (Lyotard, Baudrillard), Deconstructionism (Derrida), *Frankfurter Schule* (Habermas) had in common, despite many differences otherwise, that they testified to a deep-seated pessimism and gloom. These philosophers and their many fans and followers were generally happy. Embraced by the welfare state there was little reason to be unhappy. But few of them were *glücklich*.

Hegel has called this endemic maladie *das unglückliche Bewusstsein* which cannot and should not be translated as 'the unhappy consciousness'.[1] Essentially it is a feeling and awareness of homelessness.[2] Hegel was one of the first to view this homelessness as one of the consequences of modernization. He thought this homelessness had early beginnings, in Judaism and Christianity, but was exacerbated by the French Revolution.[3] In any case, modernity has been a source of grave discontent which particularly in Europe was primarily directed against the institutions. Increasingly, people did not feel at home in them anymore.

This is not the place – and I am not qualified – to enter into a deep philosophical analysis and discussion of these issues. I prefer to stay on the surface of these issues where sociologists are entitled to operate, and may also contribute a few worthwhile observations and reflections. In the conclusion of this book on institutions and neo-institutionalism I shall focus briefly on three dilemmas and two cultural maladies which come into play when a society is fully modernized and still subjected to modernizing transformations. The dilemmas are (a) liberty and constraint, (b) equality and inequality, and (c) solidarity and egocentrism. The two cultural maladies are alienation and anomie.[4] It is not my intention to contribute deep and original thoughts to these well-known issues, but rather to complete the previous analyses and discussions about the institutional imperative and the forces that imperil the institutions.

The dilemmas of modernity

The French Revolution, Tocqueville was one of the first to teach us, was merely the symbolic or even mythological apex of a fundamental *democratization* that had started long before 1789. This 'democratic revolution' (Tocqueville) experienced several backlashes in the nineteenth century, but it accompanied the Industrial Revolution and several political revolutions, and developed almost to the full after World War II. The hard core of this democratization process is the combination of the three values of the French Revolution: *liberty, equality, solidarity*. If the three are politically, socially and economically fully realized, democratization has been successfully accomplished. Yet this rarely happened in the past two centuries which has led to much chagrin and unrest in the Western world, not least in Europe.

In the French Revolution, as is well known, *liberté, égalité et fraternité* were the three basic values which the bourgeoisie wanted to realize against the *ancien régime* of the ruling status groups (*Stände*), i.e. the higher Roman-Catholic clergy and the nobility. What was little realized in the heat of the revolution, was the simple fact that these three values are mutually exclusive, if one wants to realize them radically that is. And radicalization is, of course, what revolutionaries always are after. If liberty is radically advocated, as in libertarianism, inequality will increase in society since the strong and rich will overpower the weal and poor. Solidarity will decline under the impact of individual and collective egoism. (Socialists will always warn of this imbalance of the three values of democracy.) If, however, equality is radically emphasized, as in communism, liberty must be curbed because it creates room for inequalities, while solidarity will degenerate into a dictatorially imposed obedience. (Liberals usually focus their cultural critique on this imbalance.) If, finally, the value of solidarity is radicalized, as in Roman-Catholic corporatism or in ethnic nationalism, liberty will be smothered in communitarian excitements and equality in authoritarian power structures. (Both socialists and liberals are quick to point out this danger.)

That is, the problem of democratization is precisely the fact that these three values are mutually contradictory, yet intrinsically interrelated. Actually, democracy is an impossible dream. Somehow these contradictions must be reconciled. It needs strong, though not necessarily 'thick' institutions to accomplish this task. From the French Revolution on until the contemporary welfare state, industrial societies have struggled with this problem – not just philosophically, but above all politically, socially and economically. Let us elaborate on this.

As to *liberty*, modern society has offered most citizens a personal freedom which is historically unprecedented. We have not only liberated ourselves from most of the constraints of nature, but today's complex, multi-centered and debordered society offers unheard of chances for the development of our individual and collective faculties. However, at the very same time, this enhanced liberty has also created its very opposite. For example, our liberation from the confinements of nature have led to countless environmental problems. Solving them requires drastic constraints in the areas of production and consumption. We are no longer at liberty to manipulate nature as we have done in the first phases of industrialism.

But also morally our enlarged freedom has run into problems. It has led to an immoralist type of ethos in which liberty is often viewed in terms of commitment to private and partial interests, and non-commitment to public and collective interests. Rights supersede duties and responsibilities in this ethos which, as I argued elsewhere, was in Europe strongly stimulated and supported by the comprehensive welfare state.[5] It is, by and large, an ethos of consumption and subjective preferences, not of production and deliberate choices. In addition, the staggering developments of medical technology and genetics have put limits on this supposedly unbridled liberty of ours. If something is possible technologically, it will in all likelihood be executed in practice. But before we know it, we are the slaves of these technological inventions and innovations. In sum, radicalized liberty gives birth to constraints and confinements. As we saw time and again in the former chapters, institutions have among other things the function to limit our freedom, to prevent us from radicalizing our liberty. Freedom without institutions is like paint without a tin, like coffee without a cup, like soup without a bowl. It just pours away and all it leaves is stains.

As to *equality*, we erected the welfare state in order to ban rude injustices from our societies. It was not, as conservatives often believe, an exclusively and typically socialist project. After all, the free-market principle of capitalism remained intact. Moreover, in Europe many Christian-Democratic parties, since the papal bull 'Rerum Novarum'(1891) the Roman-Catholics first and foremost, supported the idea of a state which would bar gross injustices. They were generally in favor of social capitalism.[6] The original idea of a welfare state was indeed noble: the state (national, provincial and local governments) was held responsible for minimal standards of civilized living in the crucial areas of health, housing, education, care of the elderly, and work. However, with the increase of affluence people began to raise their demands and thus the mimum standards of decent living. Politicians obliged which entailed a greater centralization of power in the national government, but also a rather rapid extension and expansion of the various departments of the government. Equality soon changed into a grey uniformity set up and spread over society by ever greater numbers of bureaucrats and associated experts. In addition, the state's financial largesse in the form of countless subsidies entailed an unprecedented growth in the number of laws and regulations because the expenditures of all this public money had to be legalized and controlled. This hampered the freedom of the market and the vitality of the civil society.

Just as libertarianism is a degeneration of true liberty, egalitarianism is a caricature of true equality. Incidentally the irony of all this is that numberless professionals and experts began to contribute unintentionally to a new type of inequality. The often fabulous complexity of social laws, rights and duties, and the labyrinthine bureaucracies of the comprehensive welfare state made it mandatory to possess adequate information and knowledge. Without it one would simply not be able to find one's way to what one is statutorily entitled to. Soon a clear inequality emerged: the haves versus the have-nots of such information and knowledge. The civil servants of the welfare state and the associated experts formed a kind of new elite. They were the managers and brokers of the information and the knowledge concerning the welfare state. Of course, this was a very powerful position. Moreoever, often those most in need of the welfare state's aid failed to receive it, due to a lack of this type of information and knowledge. It is here that one will find welfare state dependence and a dire deficiency of civic competence.

Again, it is not (and cannot be) the task of the state to restore the balance. It is primarily up to the citizens in civil society to fight egalitarianism and the new inequality of knowledge and information. This fight cannot be successful without or outside institutions such as the family, the neighborhood, the church and the voluntary association.

As to *solidarity* (the appropriate contemporary translation of 'fraternité'), it was meant originally as class solidarity. In the French Revolution it was the solidarity of the bourgeois revolutionaries, in the socialist movements of the nineteenth and twentieth centuries it was the social cohesion and collective determination of the working class. Class solidarity was viewed primarily in terms of social and political conflict. There is, however, another type of solidarity in Christian Democracy where it is rather seen in terms of social and political harmony. It is still believed here that the old anithesis between labor and capital can be reconciled in regular, institutionalized consultations which focus on the common and public interest as the common denominator of the fragmented private and particular interests. The system is called *corporatism*. Another type of solidarity still can be found in the so-called one-issue movements. People stick together and engage in common actions for the sake of a single problem, such as the endangered environment, endangered species, endangered languages, political prisoners, etc. Emotions can run high in such movements but experience shows that it is hard to keep the bulk of the rank and file involved and committed for an extended period of time. Indeed, this is more of a 'thin' type of solidarity.

Solidarity can easily routinize and lose its emotional content. It easily transforms next into expediency. This is clearly illustarted by the New Social Democracy, also called the 'Third Way' in Great Britain and the 'Neue Mitte' in Germany. If one reads the pamphlets of the New Socialists, and if one hears Mr. Blair or Mr. Schröder speak, it is hard to recognize even faint traces of the good old socialist solidarity.

The welfare state, it is claimed, depends on the solidarity of the citizens. Through often sharply progressive taxes and payments to the state the well-to-do contribute to the succor of the less fortunate in society, i.e. the people who without personal blame are unable to take care of themselves properly. But as the welfare state routinized, as it demonstrated by its lavish subsidies an unprecedented largesse, and as it grew ever more complex and inscrutable, it became more and more difficult for ordinary citizens to view the many tax and payment deductions on their monthly salary slips as their contributions to the social solidarity upon which the welfare state supposedly rested. Instead, searching the mazes of the fiscal laws, and even bluntly deceiving the tax authorities became more than a sport. It was seen by many as sheer survival. In any case, it was the opposite of solidarity.

Again, it will not make much sense for the state to put up a fight for more solidarity in society, nor will it be helpful to moralize about the possible lack of solidarity and social cohesion in modern society. As we saw before, it makes much more sense to decentralize, deregulate and where possible privatize the central government for the benefit of a vital market and above all a vital civil society. A civil society, however, can only be vital and vibrant if there are mediating structures between the citizens and the state, and between them and the market. The mediating structures in this Democratic Triangle (civil society, state, market) are the institutions as we discussed them in this book.[7]

Two maladies of modernity

Alienation and anomie – these are two related yet different maladies. Anomie – the absence of a meaningful, institutional *nomos* – was the centerpiece of Durkheim's critique of modernity. Alienation – the presence of an overbearing institutional system – was the malady that Marx always emphasized in his critique of capitalism. The two concepts are often used interchangeably, but the phenomena they refer to are essentially different. To reformulate this succinctly, anomie is caused by too little institutional control, alienation is caused by too much institutional control. Both maladies occur in fully modernized societies and reinforce each other.

Anomie is, according to Durkheim, actually a state of social decomposition which sets in when under the pressure of individualism and individual self-interest the consensus and the social cohesion in a society to crumble and disintegrate. Anomie emerges when people revel in what Durkheim called the Cult of the Individual. They then sacrifice the general and public interest to their particular and private interests. Institutions lose grip on these individualists who prefer to live their lives according to the emotional desires of their hearts. Often the aims they set, are oceanic and therefore hard to realize. Merton therefore added the notion that anomie is in essence the practice of designing informal, deviant or even illegal means to realize gains that cannot be reached formally, normally and legally. When one is born in a black ghetto, and as an adolescent hears that being successful and rich is the ultimate goal of the American way of life, one has little chance of realizing this goal formally, normally and legally. One will be tempted to design informal, deviant and illegal means and techniques by which one will take by force the coveted success and wealth. Deviant behavior, drugs trafficking and other criminal acts are such means.[8]

Yet, as we have seen before, anomie is more than normlessness and lawlessness. It is essentially the absence of a meaningful order, a *nomos* in which one can feel at home and in which one can develop one's identity and character, one's capabilities and talents. Anomie is not anarchy, i.e. the absence of an institutional order, but a state of meaninglessness which can occur in the presence of institutions. For example, anomie occurs definitely in a society which is abstract, over-bureaucratized, and strongly controlled. Anomie is what Kafka and Orwell described in their novels. There definitely is institutional control, but this control is abstract, bureaucratic, meaningless. The Soviet Union after the terror of the Stalin regime comes to mind as an example. It did not practice genocide, as Stalin's regime did, but it was totally empty as far as values, norms and meanings were concerned. This state of affairs comes close to the other malady – alienation.

As we saw before, *alienation* is a very old cultural disease. Its origins lie in gnosticism. Gnostics believe that the world was created by a demiurg who threw us into a hostile world which estranges us from our 'true being' which still burns as a spark of fire in the depths of our subjectivity. The world of objectivity – our bodies, others, things and objects, and above all institutions – alienate us by constantly drawing us away from our 'true Selves', our 'pure identity', our 'inalienable consciousness'. A return to this subjectivity is what gnostics see as the cure for alienation. This fateful idea popped up in

Western society all the time – in peasant revolts and in scores of romantic movements – but was elevated into prestigious philosophies by Hegel and Marx, and then in this century reformulated again by Gustav Jung's depth-psychology. Presently, New Age ideas and doctrines bear the marks of gnosticism, although often in intellectually rather poor disguises.

Marx's theory of alienation has been more profound and politically more fateful. Interestingly Marx seems to distance himself from gnostic musings when it comes to the alienation of man's inner and 'true' Self. His arguments are not subjectivistic and psychological, but rather economic and sociological. As is well known, he saw alienation as the ultimate disease of capitalism. In this system the means of production are not owned by the actual producers, i.e. the workers, but by the providers of capital, i.e. the owners of the productive system. All the workers own is their manpower, their physical ability to produce. This is sold in the labor market which is also in the hands of the owners of capital. Workers then work as slave laborers in factories where they produce commodities which are being sold for prices that are higher than the costs of production. This difference, the profit, goes to the owners of the means of production, i.e. the capitalists. This exploitation of the workers is exacerbated by the fact that they as the producers of commodities are themselves treated and viewed as commodities which can be bought and sold in the labor market. In other words, capitalism produces a pervasive commodification. Through commodification workers are reduced to things. They are coerced to function as machines which operate machines and produce profitable commodities. That is, workers are subjected to a pervasive *reification*, 'thingification'. Both reification and commodification alienate workers from their 'true' human nature. Incidentally, reification and commodification are pervasive processes, because in the end capitalists themselves also fall victim to them. After all, they too are slaves of the system. Their relentless pursuit of profit estranges them from their fellow human beings and from their own human nature.

Alienation is to Marx the result of a perverse economic system. There are few adherents to this idea left today. Marxism was already an empty and powerless ideology prior to the demise of the Soviet Union, as it is today a rather meaningless and abstract philosophy in Castro's Cuba and the Chinese People's Republic, not to mention the lunatic fringe of Marxism in North Korea. In these nations communism is an empty ideological shell which, incidentally, precisely for that reason can be very repressive if it comes to basic human rights. In Western societies communist parties have disappeared, while in socialist or social-democratic parties Marxist ideas and notions have lost their lustre and appeal. The 'Third Way' and the 'Neue Mitte' will not lament about capitalist alienation. They are far to neo-liberal for that.

Yet, alienation is not an exclusively Marxist or gnostic malady. If anomie is ultimately a lack of institutional control and a surplus of individuality, alienation is essentially a surplus of institutional control and a lack of individuality. The institutions are, so to speak, overbearing, as in traditionalism, leaving little or no room for individual freedom and creativity. In religion, for example, individuals have often been coerced to adjust blindly to traditional values and norms, and to negate their own ideas and sentiments. The individual is put in an institutional straightjacket and instilled with a deep-seated fear of deviation from what has been presented as 'the right path'. Indeed, 'thick' institutions have the tendency to alienate people – not just from their alleged 'true, inner being' or 'true subjectivity', but from their individual integrity, from their individual capabilities and talents.

Alienation comes close to anomie, if the institutions are not only 'thick' but also abstract, over-bureaucratized, rationalized and formalized as is often the case in modernity. When, for example, an institution like the university modernizes to the extent that functional rationality supersedes substantial rationality, so that efficiency and effectiveness, not intellectual integrity and truth are its ultimate values, that attracting funds and research contracts and not the painstaking 'search for truth' becomes its ultimate end, a pervasive sense of alienation will gradually affect the faculty, the students and the administration. Alienation is therefore in a sense de-institutionalization. However, this is, also anomie, because the university is no longer a *nomos* which provides teachers, students and administrators with a sense of meaningful belonging.

This leads to a general conclusion. Anomie and alienation are the twin maladies of modernity. These maladies cannot be cured by gnostic subjectivism or Marxist activism. The heart of these maladies is a disturbed relationship between modern men and women on the one hand and their institutional environment on the other. There is, for hard biological reasons, an institutional imperative which cannot be violated without grave consequences for human individuals and the society they are living in. It is not the state, i.e. the welfare state, but civil society resting upon a cultural infrastructure of institutions and networks which will minimize, or maybe even cure these twin maladies of modernity.

Permanent discussions

More than forty years ago the German sociologist Helmuth Schelsky (1912-1984) discussed in one of his sociological essays a very important question. Starting with Gehlen's analysis of modern man's anti-institutional subjectivism which would endanger the survival of the human species as it would fatally impair man's capacity to act and produce, Schelsky wondered, if subjectivism itself could not be institutionalized. The essence of modern subjectivism, Schelsky argued pursuing Gehlen's theory of institutions, is an ongoing and endless reflection – *Dauerreflexion*. Is it possible to curb its negative effects by institutionalizing it?[9] The question was, of course, rhetorical. Schelsky believed that our typically modern propensity of incessant reflexion – i.e. to answer questions with questions, to relativize traditional truths, and to throw always doubt on the certainties our parents and grandparents still possessed – can indeed be curbed and channeled by institutional arrangements. He discusses a few such institutions but that was forty years ago. Things have changed since then.

The institutionalization of our ongoing discussions and reflections has occurred in the past in universities, academies, and debating clubs. It is being done in modernity in the same institutions, but also in new institutional, para-institutional and network-like arrangements. Universitites, for instance, organize numerous seminars and conferences as extra-curricular courses for civil servants in the public sector and managers in the private sector. Many professional associations organize such seminars for their own members and corporations often organize in-house seminars for their personnel. The primary aim of these activities is not the transmission of cognitive knowledge or technical skills. In many cases such seminars and conferences rather intend to stimulate beyond cognitive knowledge and technical skills substantial reflections and debates. This takes place in an institutional setting which lies outside the customary world of daily work routines, and outside the hierarchy of power of the corporation. These reflections and debates must stimulate mental flexibility and help to develop people's orientation in the complex world of modernity. This is a neo-institutionalist stance, because if successfully performed such reflections and debates would counteract the typically modern supersedure of substantial rationality by functional rationality. That is, if permanent reflections and debates are practiced in institutional settings they will begin to counteract the anomie and alienation that is endemic to modernization without, however, relapsing into an old-fashioned or maybe even reactionary type of conservatism.

Finally, it stands to reason that these institutionalized debates and reflections in seminars, conferences, extra-curricular courses, and network-like discussion groups cannot be conducted in an authoritarian and undemocratic manner. These are Socratic discussions in which teachers and students, speaker and audience engage in meaningful interactions. In this respect we could endorse Jürgen Habermas's theory of communicative action in which he emphasized the need for 'unconstrained discussions'. In such discussions all force is eliminated except that of the better argument.[10]

Arnold Gehlen, the intellectual *daimon* of this book, would not be impressed. He would remark, probably with a sarcastic smile, that these debates and reflections within democratic, unconstrained settings would but produce an endless tosh that would not lead to anything, except that it would impair action and production. What we moderns need, after all is said and not done, is solid institutions under the aegis of a strong state which is not afraid to apply its power and coercive strength when the institutional order is disrupted and has to be restored. Institutions can only function properly, if people are prepared and willing to let themselves be consumed by them. People who complain about anomie and alienation are weaklings who demonstrate once more the need for 'thick' institutions whose prime function is to enforce and maintain discipline, if necessary with the assistance of the powerful state. Force and constraint are essential, if the institutional order is to be defended or restored.

Gehlen's theory of action and institutions was in combination with Plessner's theory of social roles constitutive for the present theory of the institutional imperative, but its ultimate course in the direction of an old-fashioned and reactionary type of conservatism was rejected. We added to the philosophical anthropology of Gehlen and Plessner the evolutionary ideas of sociobiology (Wilson) and genetics (Dawkins), and confronted the ensuing theory of institutions with the idea that in modern society flexible networks and permanent flows rather than traditional institutions and fixed structures constitute the world in which we live, work and recreate today. An attempt was made to avoid the easy solutions of post-modernism as in the theory of the supposedly post-institutional network society. In modernity there is a remarkable confluence of institutions which are 'thin' and networks which must be 'thick' in order to function adequately. It is in this peculiar constellation that permanent reflections and debates within ongoing communicative actions (or symbolic interactions) are of crucial importance, because they enable us to avoid the two maladies of modernity, i.e. anomie as the absence of meaningfully directive institutions and alienation as the presence of overbearing and abstract institutions.

If one follows the generally positive developments of civil society in Western democracies, one can be optimistic as to the future evolution of modernity. One only hopes that similar developments will occur in Eastern Europe and in the developing nations of the world. In these regions there is more at stake than just economic development. Institutions operating in a vital civil society will at least be of equal importance. After all, institutions caught in traditionalism and ceremonialism will arrest changes and stifle development. But if they are flexible and open, they will function as formidable stimulants of transformation and progress.

1. Charles Taylor, *Hegel*, (Cambridge: Cambridge University Press, 1975), translates 'unglückliches Bewusstsein' as 'unhappy consciousness', and misses the strongly gnostic content of it. See *o.c.*, pp. 57-59, 159-161, 206-208, 497f.

2. Cf. Peter L. Berger, Brigitte Berger, Hansfried Kellner, *The Homeless Mind. Modernization and Consciousness*, (New York: Random House, 1973).

3. I relied on Hans Schmidt, *Verheissung und Schrecken der Freiheit*, (Promise and Terror of Freedom), (Stuttgart-Berlin: Kreuz Verlag, 1964) which is a thorough study of Hegel's view of history. See also my *The Abstract Society*, (Garden City, NY: Doubleday, 1970), pp. 137f.

4. In what follows I use portions of an earlier Dutch publication: *Sociologie als cultuurwetenschap. Een beknopte methodologie van de cultuursociologie*, ('Sociology as a humanity. A brief methodology of cultural sociology.'), 1983, (Culemborg: Lemma, 1988), pp. 98-101.

5. Anton C. Zijderveld, *The Waning of the Welfare State. The End of Comprehensive State Succor*, (New Brunswick, NJ: Transaction Publishers, 1999), chapter 3: 'The Ethos of the Welfare State', pp. 69-92.

6. Cf. Kees van Kersbergen, *Social Capitalism. A Study of Christian Democracy and the Welfare State*, (London: Routledge, 1995).

7. On the Democratic Triangle see my *The Waning of the Welfare State*, *o.c.*, pp. 127-160. On mediating structures see once more Peter L. Berger, Richard J. Neuhaus, *To Empower People. From State to Civil Society*, edited by Michael Novak, (Washington, DC: The AEI Press, Publisher for the American Enterprise Institute, 1996), in particular pp. 157-214.

8. Robert K. Merton, *Social Theory and Social Structure*, 1949, revised and enlarged edition, (New York: The Free Press of Glencoe, 1964, 9th printing), pp. 131-194.

9. Helmuth Schelsky, 'Ist die Dauerreflexion institutionalisierbar?', 1956, ('Can permanent Reflection be institutionlized?'), in: Helmuth Schelsky, *Auf der Suche nach Wirklichkeit. Gesammelte Aufsätze*, ('In Search of Reality. Collected Essays'), (Düsseldorf-Köln: Eugen Diederichs Verlag, 1965), pp. 250-275.

10. Jürgen Habermas, *Toward a Rational Society. Student Protest, Science, and Politics*, 1968, translated by J. J. Shapiro, (London: Heinemann, 1971), p 7f.

Index

Names

Farias, Victor, 74
Ferraro, Thomas J., 42
Fichte, Johann G., 44
Fiore, Joachim of, 86, 101
Fitzgerald, Scott, 99
Flaubert, Gustave, 138
Foqué, René, 11
Foucault, Michel, 43, 194
Francesco, Grete de, 130
Freidson, E., 191
Freud, Sigmund, 13, 90f., 120
Fukuyama, Francis, 100
Fustel de Coulanges, N. D., 101

Gay, Peter, 101
Galilei, Galileo, 157
Gaulle, Charles de, 49, 150
Gehlen, Arnold, 49-60, *passim*
  action theory (*Handlungslehre*), 44,
  51-63,202; Anglo-Saxon pragmatism
  and behaviorism, 63; authenticity, 61;
  behavioral circle (*Handlungskreis*)
  54; beneficent security (*bienfaisante
  certitude*), 60; class and status, 60;
  Confessing Church (*Bekennende
  Kirche*), 62; conservatism, reactionary, 56f., 60, 72, 94; consumption,
  58f;, cultural thresholds, 57f., 62f.,
  89; culture as second nature, 52f.; decline, cultural/insitutional, 56f.;
  democracy, liberal, 56f.; de-institutionalization, 58f.; desacralization,
  disenchantment and secularization,
  58; division of labore, 55; empirical
  philosophy, 44; ethic of responsibility,
  59-61; ethic of ulotimate ends, 60;
  familistic humanitarianism, 60f.; feedback mechanism, 54; feminization,
  59; German Christians (*Deutsche
  Christen*), 62; gestures, 54;
  hiatus,53f.; hyper morality, 59-63;
  Idealism, German, 53; Industrial Revolution, 57-62; instinctive residues,
  52,65; institutional autonomy
  (*Eigengesetzlichkeit*), 32, 70; institutional decline (*Institutionsabbau, institutionsverlust*) 57f., 63, 98, 123,,

125f., 180; institutional theory (*Institutionslehre*), 44, 48-63; institutionalism, 94; intellectualization, conceptualization (*Verbegrifflichung*), 59; intellectuals, 56f., 59f.; Kantian categories, 63; libertarianism and egalitarianism, 60; man as insufficient being
(*Mängelwesen*), 52; man as world-
open (*weltoffen*) being, 52f.; meaningful interaction, 54f.; modern art, 59;
moral philosophy, 59-63; Nazi's and
Nazi party, 51, 62f.; permanent reflections, 58; *post-histoire*, 57; primitivization, 59; Protestant theology, 62;
racism, 602f.; rationalization, 58f.; relief functions of institutions, 53; reification of institutions, 56, 63; reactionary resentment, 51, 56f.; *Selbstwert* of institutions, 32; senso-motorial unity of action, 53; separation of
motive and goals, 55f; Social Darwinism, 62; *Spätkultur*, 57f.; state, 56f.,
61, 164, 203; stereotypical patterns of
behavior, 56; stereotyping, 55; stimuli
and impulses, 53f.; subjectivism, 57-
60; taken-for-granted autonomy of institutions, 55; *Third Reich*, 62; tosh,
endless, 57,203; tradition, 55; warrior
morality, 60; Western civilization, 57;
wit, 51.
Gennep, Arnold van, 136f., 161
Gianturco, E., 102
Giddens, Anthony, 102
Gide, André, 100
Goethe, Johann W., 48
Goffman, Erving, 130f.
Gorbatchev, Michael, 151
Gouldner, Alvin, 41, 129
Graña, César, 23, 99, 161
Grene, Marjorie, 73
Groethuysen, Bernard, 161
Gründgens, Gustaf, 48
Guardini, Romano, 84, 100
Guéhenno, Jean-Marie, 100, 130, 191

Habermas, Jürgen, 25, 63, 194, 202,
  204

Subjects

e-mail, 97, 154f.
emancipation, 148, 184
Empire of the Rising Sun, 39
empiricism, Anglo-Saxon, 26, 101
empowerment, 184
emulation, 22
enculturation, 32, 34, 37
Enlightenment, 15, 80f., 87f., 101f.,
  115, 123, 137, 177
entelechy (Aristotle), 92
Entfremdung (alienation;Hegel, Marx),
  88
entrepreneurs, 150, 160
environment, 172
environmentalism, cultural, 173-175;
  natural -, 173f.
ETA, 168
État providente (welfare state), 117
ethic of responsibility (*Verantwortungsethik*; Weber), 29, 11, 111f., 126,
  174, 177, 185, 188; - of ultimate ends
  (*Gesinnungsethik*; Weber), 29, 111f.,
  177
ethnic cleansing, 112, 171f.
ethnicity, 111f.
ethos, economic, 81; Calvinist -, 87; immoralist -, 196
euro, 115
euregions, 178
eurocities, 178
European Commission, 115
evolution, biological, 45f.; institutional -, 30f.
evolutionism, 45
exclusiveness, 171f.
existentialism, 10, 16, 26, 43, 47, 50f.,
  62
Existenzerhellung (making existence
  understandable), 16
Ex Oriente Lux, 13
expertocracy, 183
expressionism, 48, 80

fads and fashions, 51
family, 13, 15-17, 30, 35, 37f., 40, 73,
  24, 116, 123, 125, 143f., 159, 174-
  177, 197

fax, 154f.
fertilization, *in vitro*, 119, 128
Festival of Fools, 137
feudalism, the shackles of, 157
feuds, rancorous, 156f.
flexibility, network, 50, 143, 165; aimless -, 160
flows, 9, 50, 98, 122, 165, 203
folly, traditional, 137, 161, 191
'Fordism' (Reich), 114f.
formal rationality (Weber), 149
Founding Fathers, American, 149
fragmentation, 35, 167f.
Frankfurter Schule, 26, 105. 194
French Revolution, 194-199
Freudianism, 10, 43
functionalism, 18, 33f., 84, 104f.,
  140f., 148f.
fundamentalism, 79, 94, 158
funerals, 141f.

Gemeinschaft, 29, 62f., 106, 109-113,
  119, 128, 171f.; crypto-fascist -, 112
gender, 143f.
generalization, cultural, 92f.
genetics, 9, 38, 64-69, 203
gentil'homme, 140
gestures, theory of, 53f.
Gesellschaft, 29, 106, 109-113
Gestalt, 36
ghettos, 146, 199
globalization, 113, 115. 165-170
gnosticism, 50, 82f., 100, 165, 199
gossip, 154f.
Götterdämmerung, 39, 170, 177
governance, corporate, 109
gravity, cultural, 124f.
Grünen, 173
gurus, 13f.

Hegelians, 25, 88
Herrenmoral (Nietzsche), 62, 151, 164
history, 10, 76-103; definition of -, 77f.,
  the end of -, 76f., interests and -, 77-
  79; subjectivism versus -, 80-83;
  tyrants and -, 76
hisoricism (Popper), 83f., 99

help, 193; - preservation, 17

séparation (van Gennep), 136f.

Sermon on the Mount, 61, 182

shem Jahwe, 86

shul, 69

socialization, 32, 34, 37

sociobiology (Wilson), 9, 44, 64-69, 186, 203

Socratic discussions, 202f.

solidarity, 229, 90f., 195-199; class -, 197; social -, 91, 198; 'thin' -, 198

Sophists, 85

Southern German School, neo-Kantian, 25f.

sovereignty in one's own circle, Calvinist, 115

Soviet imperium, 39; - Union, 84, 92, 151, 177, 199f.

speech, ordinary, 16; loose -, 152-156

Spirit of Protest, 15

spleen, 133

staccato, social and cultural, 99, 135-138, 160, 189f.

status and contract (Maine), 29

state, 13-15, 17-19, 30, 35, 37f., 55, 72f., 94, 123; constitutional -, 157, 168, 178f.; core business of the -, 108f., 159, 164, 174, 177-180, 193; - and its monopoly on the use of violence, 178-180; Stalinist -, 168

structuralism, 10, 38f., 43, 194

subjectivism, 13-17, 39, 48, 50, 80-83, 158, 165f., 170, 176, 201f.; gnostic -, 152, 199-201; Heidegger's -, 50f; institutionalization of -, 202f.

Summa Theologiae (Aquinas), 85

Symbolic Interactionism, 25

Swiss Guard, 32f., 70f.

taboo, 23, 71, 156f., 162

Taliban, 158

Talmud, 152f.

telos (destiny), 83, 92

Ten Commandments, 182

terrorism, 167-170, 179; New -, 168-170, 190

therapists and therapy sessions, 13f.

'thick' and 'thin' institutions and networks, 17, 20, 23, 50, 98, 122-127, 152-156, 167-170, 201, 202

Third Reich, 62, 76

Third Way, 92, 103, 149, 198, 200

time awareness, 140-142

tolerance, 147f.; 'repressive -' (Marcuse), 138

top-down method (katascopie), 112, 171, 178

'Toyotism' (Reich), 114

tradition, 10, 17, 34, 149, 153, 159

traditionalism, 23, 32, 79f., 125, 156f., 201

tragedy, 14, 168, 193

transformation of institutes, 9, 63, 89-92, 98, 113, 123, 125, 142f., 180

transitions, ritual, 135-138

transsexuality, 119, 144f.

trust, 35, 97-99, 122, 126

ultra-conservatism, 190

understanding of reality (*Verstehen*; Weber) 27, 29; - strange cultures, 72

unemployment, 179

uniformity, 113-116

union, 13, 17, 35; European -, 166, 178; trade -, 148

university, 15f., 20, 35f., 55, 78, 80, 94, 159, 188-190, 202

utility values, 55

utopias, 27f., 77f.

values, meanings and norms, *passim*

value judgements, 26, 106, 148; - free sociology, 26, 41; - rationality, 36; - relatedness, 26, 29, 99

values, morally 'thick' and 'thin', 35f.

violence, unscrupulous, 167

virtual reality, 9, 26f., 29

virtues, conservative, 159-161, 174-190; - and values (Himmelfarb), 162f., 190

visions of the world, high-risk and low-risk, 185

Vitalism (Bergson), 79